A Complete Chess Course

Antonio Gude

Translated by Phil Adams

First published in the UK by Gambit Publications Ltd 2015

ISBN-13: 978-1-910093-64-1
ISBN-10: 1-910093-64-5

DISTRIBUTION:
Worldwide (except USA): Central Books Ltd, 99 Wallis Rd, London E9 5LN, England.
Tel +44 (0)20 8986 4854 Fax +44 (0)20 8533 5821. E-mail: orders@Centralbooks.com

Gambit Publications Ltd, 99 Wallis Rd, London E9 5LN, England.
E-mail: info@gambitbooks.com
Website (regularly updated): www.gambitbooks.com

Edited by Graham Burgess
Typeset by John Nunn
Cover image by Wolf Morrow
Printed in the USA by Bang Printing, Brainerd, Minnesota

10 9 8 7 6 5 4 3 2 1

Gambit Publications Ltd
Directors: Dr John Nunn GM, Murray Chandler GM, and Graham Burgess FM
German Editor: Petra Nunn WFM

Contents

Introduction

What a shame that such a beautiful day should be wasted without playing chess!
The Chess Players
SATYAJIT RAY

Chess is an age-old war game. There are many theories about its origin, but the most reliable ones state that it was invented in India, spreading out in a number of directions throughout the world and reaching its height in Europe. Over time it has become a sporting activity played by millions of people, a sport with more than 130 countries affiliated to its international federation (a number inferior only to the number of those who belong to athletics and football federations). But what interests you and me is how to play chess well, how to master the techniques of the game, how to defeat our friends and family and how to get into the top places in tournaments.

This book is directed to that end.

Before we begin, we must get one thing clear: are you one of those who think that chess pieces are little wooden or plastic figures, that they are lifeless toys? If you think that, you are very much mistaken: chess pieces are full of life, they have a job to do on the chessboard and they are prepared to carry it out to the end. You must be completely aware of this, because you will be a general who has to lead his army to victory, and to accomplish that you depend on beings full of energy, capable of invading enemy territory and of achieving the final objective of chess: capturing the enemy king.

A game of war, but also of intelligence, chess presents a mental challenge that few can ignore. Be very aware of that, for if you cross the threshold of this page, chess will become for you a passion that will not leave you for the rest of your life.

How to Study this Book

The author is well aware that the reader will study this book in the way that suits him best, in line with his initial interest and the time he has available, and also depending on the stimuli that he comes across as he progresses in that study. However, the writer would like to point out a few things about its content and the methodology used.

This book is written in clear and direct language, organized so that independent learners will not find any unusual difficulties when they begin to play a game as complex as chess. We cannot promise, as they do in sensationalist advertising, to teach you **everything** about chess in four days. Chess takes time, it demands that you master its basics and come up again and again against opponents who, just like the reader, **always** want to win.

This is an introductory work, yes, but not one that claims to leave you ready to go out and compete in the big world of chess just as you are. The first six chapters cover, step-by-step, the basic aspects of chess. Once you have absorbed those six chapters, then if you have accompanied your study with playing some games, you will already have become a chess-player, a modest one but still a chess-player.

Chapter 7, which studies all types of combinations quite thoroughly, and Chapter 8, which deals with direct attacks on the king, together with the final two (opening repertoire and preparation for tournaments), assist you in reaching new levels in the royal game.

Special emphasis has been placed on the properties of the pieces, as well as on their ability to work together (in teams or 'tandems'), and many examples of checkmate have been included, to help you memorize the patterns almost photographically; this will prove really useful at the chessboard.

The chapters are quite long and the first eight all include 15 questions and 20 exercises. The questions are theoretical and conceptual, to check that you have fully understood the explanations in the text, while the exercises are of a practical nature. If you are studying independently, then you can keep track of your rate of progress. To do this, when you check your answers to the questions, you should award yourself a point for each correct answer. As for the exercises, you should award yourself one point for the first fifteen and two each for the last five in each set. In order to feel that you have made good progress, you should achieve 80% of the total possible points (separately, in other words, a minimum of 12 points for the questions and 20 points for the exercises). If you have not achieved this, you should try again, revising the chapters and topics which you know (or suspect) you have not fully understood.

Finally, the book has also been planned with the idea that it can be a useful aid to the chess teacher or instructor, who often has to invent his own specific teaching programmes and does not always find texts with the right kind of methodology. That is why there are lots of questions and exercises, as well as a few dozen complete illustrative games and many hundreds of carefully chosen part-games, each with its corresponding instructions, commentary and analysis. I believe this material is a good teaching aid, because anyone who has had occasion to instruct and train groups of players knows how difficult it can sometimes be to find an appropriate example position. The recommendations included at the end of each chapter might turn out to be doubly useful to instructors who are using this book as a basic text or as a teaching aid for their courses: firstly because nobody will know better than they do how to put those recommendations across to their group and secondly because their experience will allow them to decide, *à la carte* as it were, which is or are the most suitable for each particular student.

In the end, if you have absorbed the content of the book, followed its recommendations and played a certain number of games, you will be armed and ready to go out into combat, to face the hard struggle of competitive chess. You will still be alone, but with a level of knowledge and training that on a theoretical plane will make you the equal of a mid-level club player. After this leap, you must not neglect your training, studying strategy and openings and, above all, taking part in as many tournaments as you can find!

1 The Basic Rules of Chess

* **The Chessboard** * **The Forces in Play** * **Initial Position** * **Camps, Flanks and Edges**
* **How the Pieces Move** * **Capturing** * **Check** * **Checkmate** * **Winning the Game**
* **Notation** * **Questions** * **Exercises** * **Further Tips** *

Chess is a game for two players (or two sides) who make their moves in turn, and it takes place on a chequered board of 64 squares. One of the players will have the white pieces and the other the black pieces. The first move of the game is always made by White.

The Chessboard

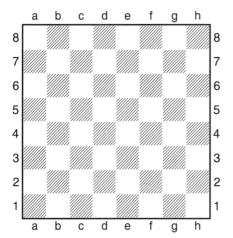

The chessboard is the battlefield on which the game is played. It is flat and square, with eight horizontal rows and eight vertical ones. The board is divided into 64 squares, alternately light and dark in colour.

The horizontal rows are called **ranks**, and the vertical ones **files**.

The chessboard should be placed in such a way that the bottom right-hand corner square, on the first rank, is always a light square. Memorize: 'Always light in bottom right'.

The Forces in Play

Each player has the following 16 pieces:
1   King
1   Queen
2   Rooks
2   Bishops
2   Knights
8   Pawns

The king, the queen, rooks, bishops and knights are called **pieces**. The pawns are not considered pieces, although sometimes they are included to simplify things, for instance: **white pieces** and **black pieces**, to name all the elements of a given side.

Initial Position

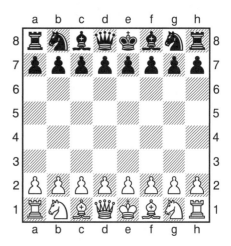

The pieces and pawns are placed on the two ranks closest to each player, i.e. white pieces on the first and second ranks, and black on the seventh and eighth ranks. The pieces are placed on the first and eighth ranks, and the pawns on the second and seventh.

Let's imagine that we take the kings and queens off the chessboard. Then, all the forces can be divided into four sets, each of them composed of one rook, one bishop, one knight and four pawns.

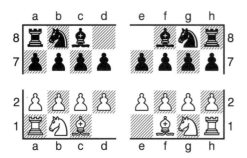

Understanding and playing with these four **equal** sets, composed of the same pieces and pawns, isn't as difficult as most people think. Playing chess is easy. Playing **well** is another matter altogether. This book will help you to master the game in its essential aspects, but, logical as it is, everything depends on you: on your natural abilities, the time you devote to the study of chess and... you need to play chess for at least twice as much time as you study the game!

Camps, Flanks and Edges

Camps

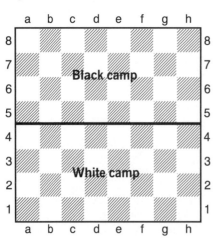

If we divide the board horizontally at the mid-point, one half, composed of the first four ranks, is called the **white camp**, and the other half, composed of the last four ranks, is called the **black camp**.

Flanks

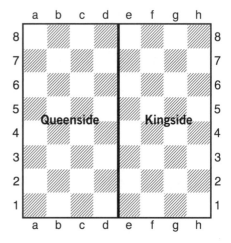

If we divide the board vertically down the middle, the half to the right, made up of four files (including the one on which the kings are situated) is called the **kingside**.

The other half of the board, consisting of the four files to the left and starting from the squares on which the queens are situated, is called the **queenside**.

Edges

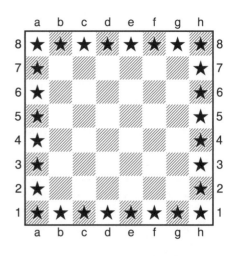

The four rows round the rim of the board are called the **edges**, i.e. the first and eighth ranks and the outermost two files.

It is necessary to know all these terms, as they form part of the universal chess language, and we meet them every time we open a chess book or magazine, as well as in the comments of the players.

How the Pieces Move

Every piece has a characteristic way of moving, although some movements are common to several pieces. Now I'll describe the moves of the different pieces, which are very easy to learn. Normally you will need no more than 15 minutes to assimilate them.

The Pawn

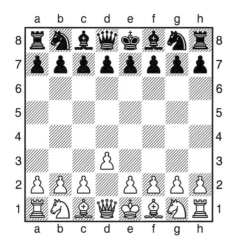

The pawn moves in a straight line, vertically, advancing one square in its own file. It cannot go backwards. From its initial position, a pawn can advance two squares in a single move. This is a privilege, not an obligation. Consequently, it may also be advanced only one square (as in the diagram).

The Rook

The rook is a powerful piece that moves in a straight line, as many squares as the player wishes. However, the rook cannot jump over other pieces (either its own pieces or opposing ones), but it may capture any enemy piece that occupies a square that the rook could move to.

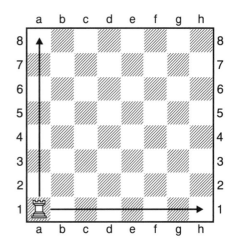

From any point of the board (and assuming that there is no other piece in the way) the rook can move to 14 different squares, not counting the one on which it is situated.

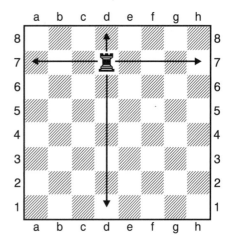

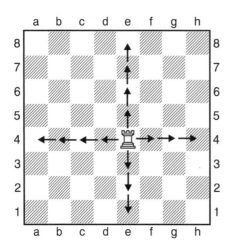

The Bishop

The bishop is another piece that also moves in a straight line, but only along the diagonals on which it is situated. This means that if it is placed initially on a dark square, it can only move to dark squares for the duration of the game, while conversely, if it starts the game on a light square, it will only be able to move to light squares. As with the rook, the bishop can move as many squares as the player wishes, but cannot jump over other pieces, either its own or opposing ones. But it can capture an enemy piece that is in its way.

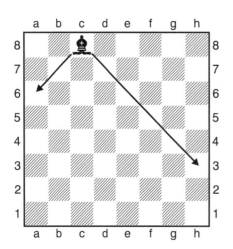

From its initial position the bishop can move to 7 different squares, which is also its minimum number of squares, wherever it is situated. Its maximum activity comes when it is on

any central square, from where it can move to 13 different squares, as in the following diagram.

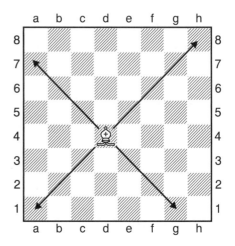

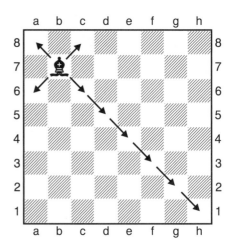

The Queen

The queen is the most powerful chess piece. It moves in a straight line, in any direction, i.e. it can move along the rank or file on which it stands, as well as along the diagonals.

We can see that the queen therefore combines the moves of the rook and the bishop, and as with these pieces, it cannot jump over another piece.

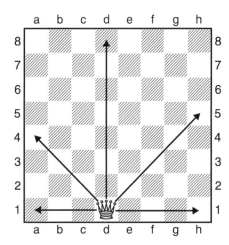

From its initial position the queen can move to 21 squares, and the same from any edge square, whereas from the centre it develops its maximum activity, as it can reach up to 27 different squares.

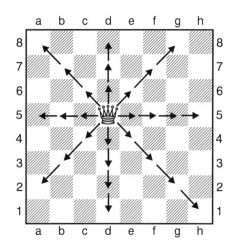

As a curiosity, we may say that five queens can control all the squares on the chessboard. Why don't you try to place them so that they do that?

The King

The king is not as powerful a piece as the queen, but it is the most valuable one, since if one of the kings disappears, the game is over.

The king moves like the queen, except that it only has the right to move one square at a time i.e. it can only move to any of the squares it is in contact with.

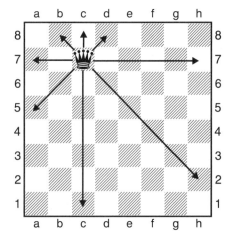

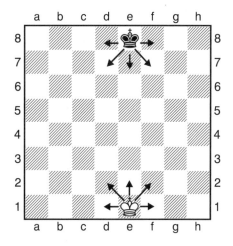

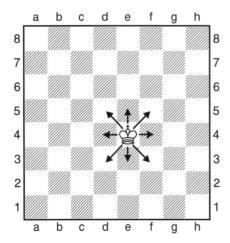

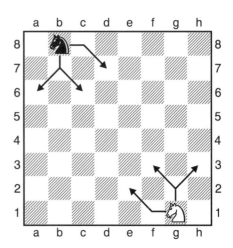

From its initial position the king can move to five different squares, the same number as from any other edge square, except for the corners, from where it can only move to three squares, which is its minimum activity, its maximum activity being from any square away from the edge.

The Knight

The knight moves in a strange way, and it is the only one that can jump over other pieces.

Let's move the knight one square in a straight line (to any of the four squares, in any direction: to the left, to the right, forward or backwards); and then one square diagonally (to either of the two possible squares). This move can be imagined the other way round, i.e. one square diagonally and then one in a straight line. In the next two diagrams this can be seen graphically. In the first of these diagrams the arrows execute the move described in the first way; in the second, the arrows show the move done in the second way, which reaches the same result.

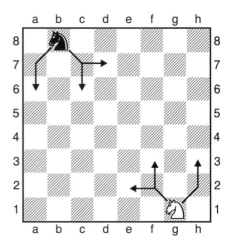

In the next diagram you can see the eight squares to which a knight can move, when placed in the centre of the chessboard, which is where it develops its maximum activity. If we compare this position with the ones in the last two diagrams (where both knights are situated in their initial positions), you will see that there the knights can only reach three squares. And a knight placed in one of the four corners can only move to two squares.

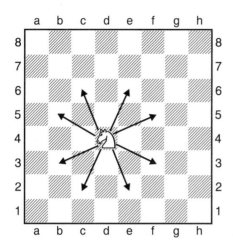

Capturing

All the pieces (king, queen, rook, bishop and knight) capture in the same way as they move. So if an enemy piece is located on a square attacked by one of your pieces, the enemy piece can be captured, by removing it from the board and replacing it with your piece.

The pawn is different. Whereas it moves only directly forwards, it captures only *diagonally*, one square to its left or its right (but not backwards). Consequently, the enemy pieces that may be taken by the pawn will always be situated on squares of the same colour as the one where the pawn stands.

In the next diagram, the white pawn attacks the black rook.

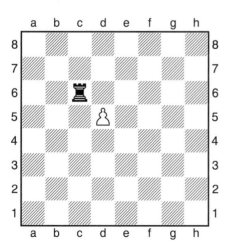

Taking *En Passant*

Taking *en passant* is a special way of taking, a privilege of pawns situated on their fifth rank. If, in such cases, one of the opposing pawns advances two squares, it may be taken as if it had only advanced one square. In the next two diagrams we have an example. In the first, we can see a position in which the black pawn moves two squares forward, as indicated by the arrow.

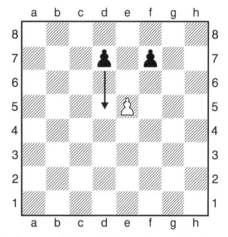

The next diagram shows the resulting position after the capture, as if the black pawn had only advanced one square.

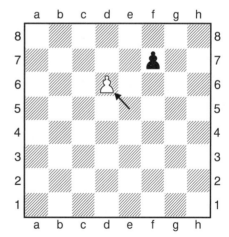

It is important to know that the pawns **only** have this privilege at the very moment that the opposing pawn advances, and they lose that possibility if the pawn is not captured immediately.

Check

When one of the kings is attacked by an enemy piece, it is said to be **in check**. In the next five diagrams you can see some examples of check from all kind of pieces.

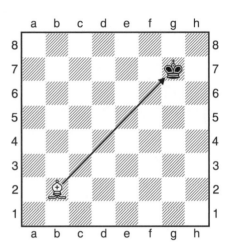

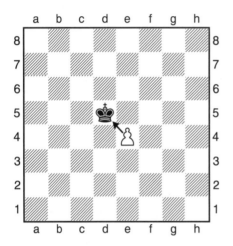

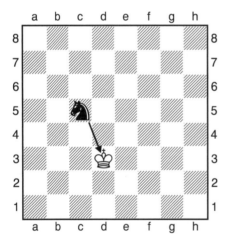

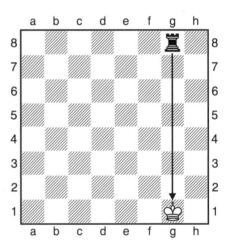

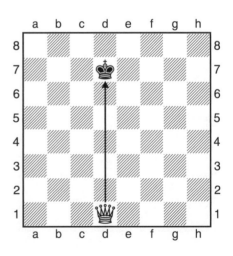

Since the loss of the king would also mean the immediate loss of the game, the attacked king must escape from the check, which can only be done in three ways:
- Taking the checking piece
- Blocking the check by interposing one of one's own pieces between the attacking piece and the king
- Moving the king to a safe square, one that is not attacked

The next five diagrams show positions in which the checking piece can be taken. Do you see how?

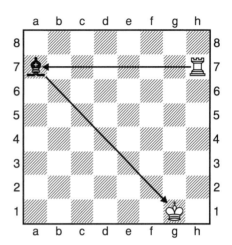

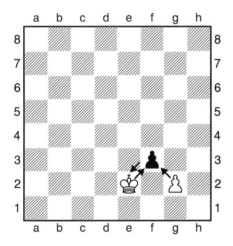

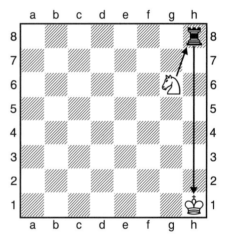

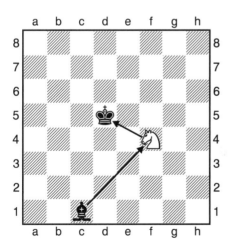

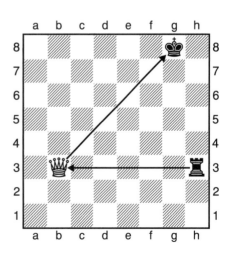

Taking will generally be the best defence against a check, since besides getting out of check you will have captured an enemy piece.

In the next three diagrams, we see three cases in which, in answer to the checks, pieces are interposed.

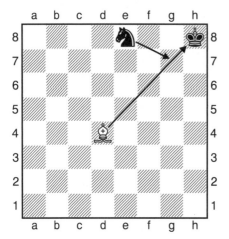

The white bishop is checking the black king, but the black knight may be interposed on the dark square diagonally next to the king.

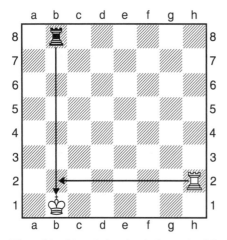

The white king is in check from the black rook, but the white rook can be interposed, on the dark square in front of the king.

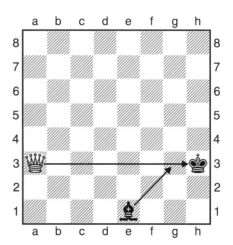

The white queen is checking the black king, but the black bishop may be placed on the square indicated by an arrow, thus protecting the king.

When a pawn or a knight gives check, it's not possible to interpose a piece. In the case of the pawn, it's because there is no square between the pawn and the opponent's king. In the case of the knight, it's because its move, as we know, is a jump which always reaches the precise square attacked.

Concerning the third possibility, moving the king, it is suggested that the reader practises by himself, escaping with his king from the checks he may suffer from the opponent's pieces.

Checkmate

When none of these solutions is available, we say that the king is **checkmated**, which means that it cannot avoid being taken on the following move. The game is over as soon as checkmate is delivered; the king is never actually captured.

Checkmate is often shortened to **mate**.

The following diagrams show different positions of simple mates, just using pieces, without the participation of the king. From now on we shall often be using part-diagrams, i.e. sections that represent one half or one quarter of the board.

The highlighted piece is the one that is delivering checkmate.

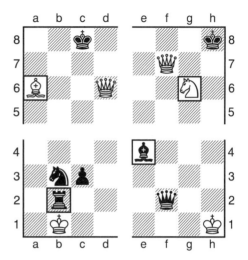

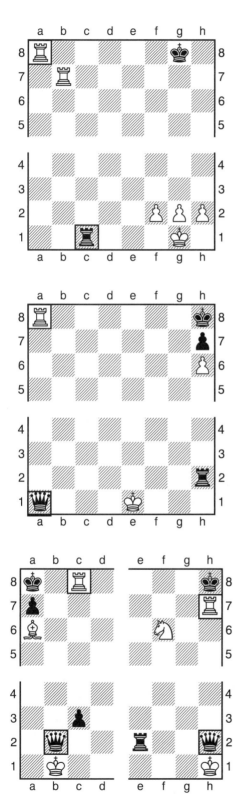

Winning the Game

You win the game when:

- you put the opponent's king in checkmate; or
- your opponent 'resigns', which means that he gives up, perhaps considering that he has too great a material disadvantage, or for some other reason, such as he sees that he cannot avoid being checkmated; or
- in tournament chess, when your opponent has exceeded the stipulated time-limit.

Notation

The signs used to describe the moves constitute the language of chess. Algebraic notation is now the universal system for recording chess moves and is the one we shall use in this book.

In algebraic notation, the ranks are numbered from 1 to 8, although when referring to them we say first, second, third rank, etc. The files are named from a to h. In the following diagram the ranks and files are indicated.

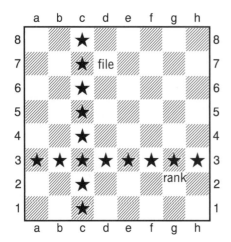

Now you know to which rank or file we refer when mentioning one of them. But the most important thing is knowing which square we are talking about, when referring to a particular move.

In algebraic notation, every square has a unique name, resulting from the intersection of one rank and one file. It is just like coordinates on a map. The next diagram features two examples. The point where the c-file intersects with the sixth rank is the c6-square, and the point at which the fourth rank and the e-file intersect is the e4-square.

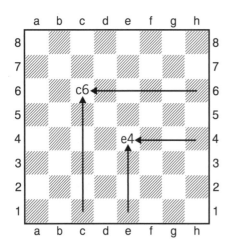

In the next diagram you can see a board with the names of all 64 squares.

Now you also know the names of all the squares of the algebraic board (and soon you will know them by heart), but you still don't know how a move is written down.

One method is as follows: first we write the initial letter of the piece to move, using capitals (K, Q, R, B or N). Then we write the name of the square where the piece is now, and finally the square it's moving to, with a dash between.

Let's imagine, for instance, that we want to move White's kingside knight to the f3-square. First we should note that (as so often) the knight is an exception; since we need the letter K for the king, to denote the knight we use its second letter, N. So, the complete move should be written as follows:

Capital letter for the piece: **N**
Original square: **g1**
Destination square: **f3**
Thus, correctly written, the move is: **Ng1-f3**

When it's a pawn move, the initial letter is not necessary. If we advance, for instance, the pawn situated in front of the white queen two squares, the correct description of the move is: **d2-d4**.

This method of annotating moves is known as **'long algebraic' notation**. However, the method generally used (in books and magazines and in tournaments) is **'short algebraic' notation**, in which only the initial of the piece and the destination square are recorded, omitting the square of origin. In the case of the moves mentioned above, the result would be: **Nf3** and **d4**, respectively.

Taking (or capturing) is indicated with an **x**, and a check with the sign **+**. One other convention is that when we refer to a move by Black on its own, we put three dots before it.

In printed books, it is usual to use **figurines** for the pieces (♔, ♕, ♖, ♗, ♘) – small versions of the symbols you have seen in the diagrams for each piece. We shall use these from now on in this book, though of course when writing moves down by hand, you should use letters.

Questions

1) What is the colour of the square in the bottom right corner of both players?

2) What is the colour of the squares on which the kings are situated in the initial position?

3) What is the ultimate aim of the game of chess?

4) How many pieces (including pawns) does each player have at the beginning of the game?

5) What is a rank?

6) What is a file?

7) What is meant by the black camp?

8) What files make up the kingside?

9) How many different squares may a king move to, if it is in the middle of an otherwise empty chessboard?

10) Free of any obstructions, what is the maximum number of squares available to a bishop?

11) Free of any obstructions, what is the minimum number of squares to which a rook can move? And the maximum?

12) How many squares can a knight move to when it's in a corner? and from a central position?

13) How would you describe, in algebraic notation, the two possible advances of the pawn situated in front of the black queen in the initial position?

14) Can a piece interpose to block a knight check?

15) What do we call the situation where a king is in check, but there is no piece available

to interpose, nor has the king any safe square to move to, and the checking piece can't be taken?

Exercises

When board segments (i.e. halves or quarters of the board) are used in the exercises, the diagram will contain all the elements necessary to solve the position.

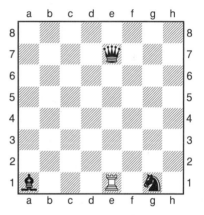

1) Which pieces are attacked by the white rook in this position?

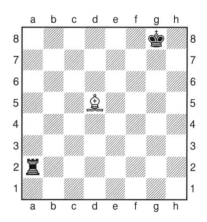

2) Which pieces are attacked by the bishop?

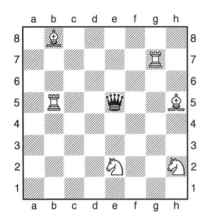

3) Which pieces are attacked by the black queen? And are any of the white pieces attacking the black queen?

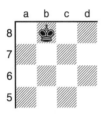

4) Place a rook and a bishop so that they both attack (i.e. check) the black king.

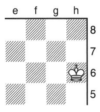

5) Indicate all the squares from which a knight can put the white king in check.

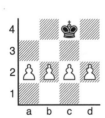

6) Indicate which pawn(s) can put the black king in check on the next move.

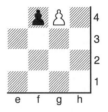

7) The white pawn has just advanced two squares on its first move. Can the black pawn capture it?

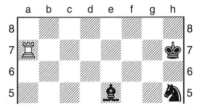

8) What piece(s) can be interposed to block the check by the rook?

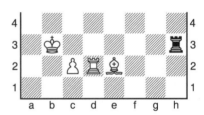

9) What piece(s) can interpose, protecting the white king from the check by the black rook?

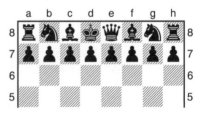

10) Is this initial position of the black pieces correct? Why not?

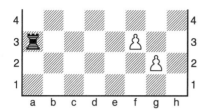

11) Can the black rook capture the pawn on f3 and, if so, could the second pawn capture the rook in turn?

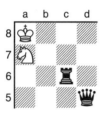

12) Can Black mate in only one move? If so, with which move? (Indicate it in algebraic notation).

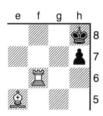

13) Can White mate in only one move? If so, which move? (in algebraic notation).

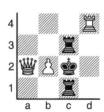

14) Can White mate in only one move? Indicate it in algebraic notation.

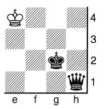

15) Can the black king play ...♔f3, putting the white king in check?

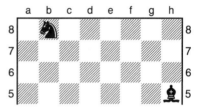

16) Can the knight reach f6 in two moves? And the bishop, also in two moves, to b5?

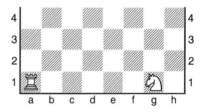

17) How can the rook reach the h4-square in two moves? And how can the knight, also in two moves, move to d4?

18) Without looking at the board, can you name all the squares that a bishop can reach from a1?

19) Can you say, from memory, the names of the squares where the four knights are situated in the initial position?

20) Can you say, from memory, which is the shortest way to move a rook from a8 to f5?

Further Tips

Knowledge and visualization of the chessboard should be absolute, so I suggest all kinds of exercises that may contribute to this end, such as ensuring that you know the dimensions of the board, the exact colour of the squares in the initial position of the pieces, and all the related geometrical aspects.

I suggest practising with 'mini-games', such as:

• The **pawn game**, in which only the pawns of both sides take part, without any pieces. The game is played using the natural moves of normal chess (advance and capture). The winner will be the first player to eliminate all the opponent's pawns, or reach the eighth square with a pawn of his own.

• The **pawns and knights game**, in which, as in the previous one, pawns and knights are situated in their original positions, the winner of the game being the player who achieves one of the same goals as in the previous game.

• The **pawns and bishops game**, which is exactly the same as the previous one, but with bishops instead of knights.

This practice will be a wonderful exercise, as you will get used to a board full of pawns, and become familiar with the moves of knights and bishops. There seems to be no need for similar games using rooks and queens, because the straight-line moves of these powerful pieces seem to be easy to learn.

If you are an instructor, ask the players to place the pieces on squares of maximum and minimum activity, and give the students various positions in which they need to protect the king from checks, by capturing or interposing pieces.

Using the demonstration board, ask for the precise description of moves in both long and short algebraic notation. It is essential that the students know perfectly the geometric characteristics and details of the chessboard, as well as the 'language of chess', which will help them to reduce the number of mistakes when recording their own games.

2 Your First Chess Games

• **Castling** • **Material Values of the Pieces** • **Pawn Promotion** • **Stalemate**
• **Perpetual Check** • **How Games are Drawn** • **Symbols** • **Early Checkmates**
• **Questions** • **Exercises** • **Further Tips** •

Castling

Castling is a special move whose purpose is to increase the safety of the king and bring a rook quickly into play. It consists of moving the king two squares towards either the king's rook (known as **castling kingside**), or towards the queen's rook (**castling queenside**), and immediately afterwards moving that rook to the adjacent square on the other side of the king. This manoeuvre counts as a single move, and it can only be done once in each game. While there is no rule saying that you have to castle, it is very useful, and something you will want to do in most games.

In the next three diagrams these manoeuvres can be clearly seen.

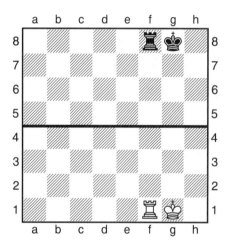

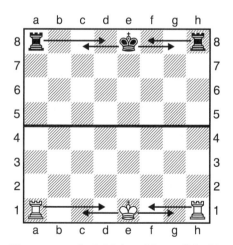

Here we see the initial positions of the kings and rooks. In the next two diagrams, both kings are now castled (kingside and queenside, respectively).

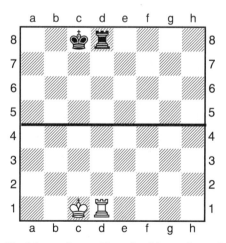

Besides safeguarding the king, since the struggle normally starts on the central files, another purpose of castling is to activate the rook, i.e. bring it to a central file, where it is usually more useful than on one of the edge files.

In chess notation, castling is recorded with two zeros separated by a dash (0-0) in the case of castling kingside, and with three zeros, separated by dashes (0-0-0), for queenside castling. The number of zeroes is the same as the number of squares moved by the rook.

Rules for Castling

The legal conditions to be able to castle are these:
- The king and the rook must not have moved previously
- There must not be any pieces on the squares through which king and rook must pass
- The king must not be in check or, in other words, castling **cannot be a response** to a check
- The squares through which the king will pass must not be attacked by an enemy piece

Material Values of the Pieces

Just as in life, where our parents give us our basic values, in chess some rules of thumb are necessary. Besides, chess is a complex game, so any standards or values to guide us are welcome!

Thus, knowing the rules of the game and the moves of the pieces is not enough, since the student would then be at his opponent's mercy when playing a game.

The first material standard for a beginner to consider is the scale of **material values** of the pieces. Although they cannot be taken as absolutes, they are useful as a first point of reference. If we give the pawn the value of 1 point, then the values for each piece are as follows:

Pawn	1
Knight	3
Bishop	3
Rook	5
Queen	9
King	3½ or infinite

The value of the king deserves special consideration. Since the game depends on the king's survival, its value can be considered to be infinite. The above value of 3½ should be

understood to represent the king's comparative worth as a fighting piece, in positions (generally in the endgame) where it can be used as a fighting piece.

From the above scale we can establish simple relations between different pieces. For instance: three pawns are equivalent to a knight or a bishop. One rook and one pawn are equal to two knights. The queen is somewhat weaker than two rooks, etc.

It is important to appreciate that these values are relative, since everything will always depend on the concrete position in which the different forces operate on the board. However, you should always bear in mind this table of values, especially when considering sequences of moves in which pieces are taken or exchanged.

Let's now look at some examples, so that you can practise calculating the worth of the material captured or exchanged.

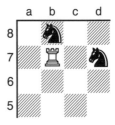

The white rook can capture either of the opponent's knights, but if so, the remaining knight could in turn take the rook. The result of the operation: White has eliminated a piece valued at 3 points, but Black would eliminate a piece valued at 5 points. Balance sheet: -2 points. Consequently, the exchange is unfavourable to White.

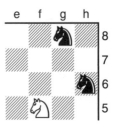

The white knight can take the black knight on h6 and, in turn, would be taken by the one on g8. This exchanging operation is equal, since a piece is exchanged for another of the same value. Theoretically speaking, it is neither profitable nor harmful.

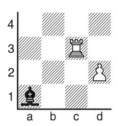

The black bishop can take the rook on c3, but will then be taken by the d2-pawn. However, this transaction is interesting, since Black would have taken material valued at 5 points, whereas he will only have lost material valued at 3 points. Balance sheet: 2 points. A good deal.

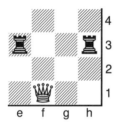

The white queen can take the black rook on h3, but since the rook is protected by its colleague on e3, and since the queen (9 points) is much more valuable than a rook (5 points), in that case taking would be a bad deal.

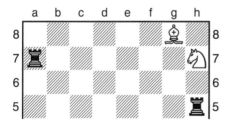

Either rook can take the white knight, then the bishop can take the rook and finally the remaining rook can then take the bishop. For instance: 1...♖axh7 2 ♗xh7 ♖xh7. Balance-sheet of the operation: three pieces have disappeared from the board, and only a black rook has survived. Calculation: 6 (3+3) − 5 = 1. A small profit.

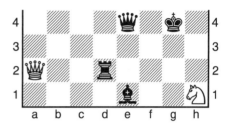

Here the white queen is attacked by the rook on d2, but the best solution for White is to play 1 ♕xd2, since after 1...♗xd2 he can play 2 ♘f2+ ♚f4 3 ♘xe4 ♚xe4, and the balance-sheet is a positive one for White, as he has won a queen and a rook, whereas Black has only won a queen and a knight. Consequently we have a 14 (9+5) − 12 (9+3) = 2 points advantage.

As was previously mentioned, this type of calculation is always necessary when considering any manoeuvre in which captures or exchange of pieces take place.

Pawn Promotion

The pawn is a foot-soldier and its main purpose should be to survive in any conflict, including chess. But in our harmless war the pawn may have ambitions. He can even be transformed into a powerful queen, a right that any pawn has if it reaches its eighth rank. In fact, the pawn can be converted into any piece of its own colour (queen, rook, bishop or knight), except the king (a sacred and irreplaceable piece). As a small price for its exploit, it will lose its nature as a pawn, something that, by the way, would not be of any use, since on the last file a pawn does not attack anything and would be a kind of zombie or living-dead piece. Note that you can't delay the choice of piece; the move is not completed until you have replaced the pawn with queen, rook, bishop or knight.

We should add that the conversion of a pawn that reaches the last rank does not depend on whether the chosen piece is present on the board. If a pawn reaches the last rank and his side still has a queen, the player can still convert his pawn into a new queen. Many tournament chess sets come with a spare queen of each colour for this purpose, though this is just for convenience. In theory each side could have nine queens on the board at the same time! (the initial one, plus another eight resulting from the eight pawn promotions).

Thus the pawn, despite initially being the most modest chess piece, is in fact one of the most dynamic elements in chess, precisely for its ability to convert itself into a powerful piece, which can often prove to be a decisive factor.

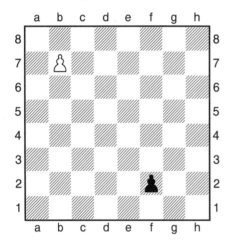

Here we have two cases of pawn promotion. The white b7-pawn can advance to b8 and be transformed into any piece the player chooses. The black f2-pawn can reach the first rank, and thus the promotion square, f1, also converting itself into any other piece.

Assuming that the players would each convert the promoted pawn into a queen, these moves would be written in algebraic notation as follows: b8♕ and ...f1♕, respectively.

If the pawn is promoted into another piece, the symbol of that piece should be written, i.e. b8♖, b8♗, or b8♘.

A more curious case of promotion (and also more attractive for the player who achieves it) is when a pawn reaches the promotion square moving off his normal track, in other words by taking an enemy piece.

In the following diagram, the white pawn can promote on three different squares: e8, d8 and f8. If promoted on d8 it will, at the same time, take the bishop. If on f8, it will take the

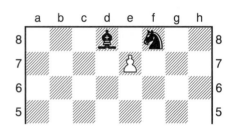

knight. Assuming that White decides to promote to a queen, these two moves should be written exd8♕ and exf8♕.

So far we haven't yet seen the best deal that we can make with the pawn promotion. See the next diagram.

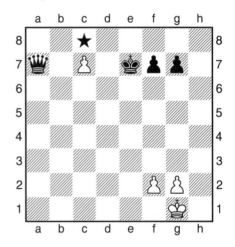

If White promotes his c7-pawn to a queen, then the position will be balanced, since both sides will have a queen and two pawns. But if White sees the possibility of promoting to a knight, then he will discover buried treasure: 1 c8♘+, since in so doing the knight is attacking both the king and queen (which is known as a fork), and after the black king moves, it will take the queen, 2 ♘xa7, with a winning endgame for White, thanks to a material advantage of 3 points (the value of the knight).

Stalemate

When the king of the side to move, although not in check, cannot legally move to any square, and nor can any piece on his side make a move, we have a **stalemate**. In that case, the game is immediately drawn.

In the four positions that follow you can see examples of stalemate.

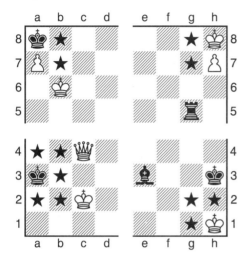

As you can see, the kings on a8, h8, a3 and h1, it being their turn to move and **without being in check**, cannot make any legal move, since all the squares to which they could move (marked with stars) are attacked by enemy pieces. Consequently, the four positions are drawn.

Perpetual Check

In chess we give the name **perpetual check** to a series of checks that cannot be avoided and that force a draw. In the following diagrams, perpetual check is clearly illustrated.

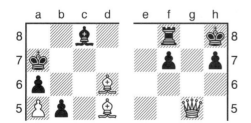

On the left, White delivers perpetual check by using his dark-squared bishop: 1 ♗c5+ ♔b8 2 ♗d6+ ♔a7 3 ♗c5+, etc. In this position it is important that the b7- and a8-squares are controlled by the other bishop on the long diagonal.

On the right, White can force perpetual check by 1 ♕f6+ ♔g8 2 ♕g5+ ♔h8 3 ♕f6+, etc.

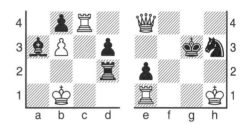

On the left, the white king cannot escape from the perpetual attack by the black rook: 1...♖d1+ 2 ♔a2 ♖d2+ 3 ♔b1 (or 3 ♔a1) 3...♖d1+, etc.

On the right, the white king cannot avoid perpetual check by the black knight: 1...♘f2+ 2 ♔g1 ♘h3+ 3 ♔h1, etc. Here the black e2-pawn that controls the escape-square on f1 is important.

In all these cases the game should logically end in a draw, since the continuous repetition of checks creates a sort of cul-de-sac, and the players must conclude a peace agreement.

How Games are Drawn

The aim of a chess game is to win, conquering the opponent's king. However, not all games are won or lost. On many occasions both opponents have played with the same accuracy or have committed equally bad mistakes, so that the fight leads to positions which are very difficult to decide in favour of either side. In those cases, the games usually end in a draw.

The game is a draw in the following cases:
- When both kings are left alone on the board
- In the endgame ♔+♗ vs ♔, without any other material
- In the endgame ♔+♘ vs ♔, without any other material
- In an endgame in which each side has a bishop of the same colour (i.e. moving along squares of the same colour), without any other material
- When the position is stalemate

- By repetition (when, for the third time, the same position on the board is reproduced, either player can claim a draw); technically, this is how perpetual check leads to a draw
- If fifty moves by both sides have been made without a capture or a pawn move, then either player can claim a draw
- By agreement between the two players

The last case has been one of the most debated ones from the point of view of the chess rules, but none of the measures taken have had the desired effect, because nobody can prevent the two players from agreeing a draw in a given game. It is not the duty of the author to decide whether this constitutes *fair play*. What I can say is that all competitions and all games are reliant on sporting behaviour, i.e. fair play, and that it is very useful to know all the possible tricks and traps, not to make use of them, but to avoid falling victim to them.

A king and two knights, in spite of their great material advantage, cannot force checkmate against a lone king. However, this *isn't a* draw by insufficient material, since checkmate *is* possible, but it can only happen if the defender makes a one-move blunder allowing instant mate. So this endgame would normally be agreed drawn (but failing that, the fifty-move rule would apply). Let's study the position of the following diagram.

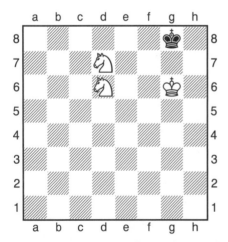

Here we have the most favourable position for the attacker, i.e. a position in which the

defender might go astray. Checkmate is possible with 1 ♘f6+ ♚h8?? 2 ♘f7#. But if Black plays 1...♚f8 there is no mate and all White's attempts run into a brick wall.

However, suppose Black had a pawn in the diagram position, let's say on b5. Then White *could* force a win, as he could leave the black king with no moves, and this wouldn't be stalemate because the pawn could move. Thus he could play 1 ♘f5 b4 2 ♘h6+ ♚h8 3 ♘e5 b3 4 ♘ef7#.

Symbols

Now we are going to complete our study of algebraic notation, and here we shall also become familiar with the graphical representation of the pieces, as you will see them in this book.

King	K	♚
Queen	Q	♛
Rook	R	♜
Bishop	B	♝
Knight	N	♞

The symbols normally used to write the chess moves are the following:

x	capture
+	check
++	double check
#	checkmate
0-0	castles kingside
0-0-0	castles queenside
!	good move
!!	brilliant move
?	bad move
??	blunder
!?	interesting move
?!	dubious move
1-0	The game ends in a win for White
1/2-1/2	The game ends in a draw
0-1	The game ends in a win for Black

Early Checkmates

Scholar's Mate

The popular *Scholar's Mate* will allow us to practise algebraic notation. It features a couple of standard moves followed by a cheeky mating threat that brings the game to an abrupt end if Black fails to parry it. Let's see the game in long algebraic notation:

1 e2-e4 e7-e5 2 ♗f1-c4 ♘b8-c6 3 ♕d1-h5 ♘g8-f6 4 ♕h5xf7# *(D)*

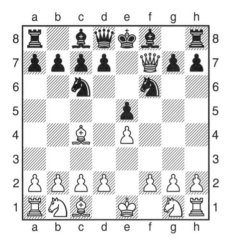

Now we will see this mate in short algebraic, the notation that, as previously said, will be used throughout this book. At the same time we shall annotate some moves with symbols.

1 e4 e5 2 ♗c4 ♘c6 3 ♕h5? ♘f6?? 4 ♕xf7#

The move 3 ♕h5? is bad since White prematurely exposes the queen (we shall come back to this topic), and Black could answer with, for instance, 3...g6, repelling the white queen. Naturally, 3...♘f6?? is a blunder, as it does not prevent the mate on f7.

Scholar's Mate is one of the quickest possible checkmates, and is an eternal temptation for beginners. But it is not the absolute quickest, which can take place in only two moves! We have to say that our opponent would have to give us a little help.

Fool's Mate

1 f3?

A bad move, very weakening. Later on we will study the concept of weakness.

1...e5

Black plays a good move: the advance of one of his central pawns, opening the queen's diagonal.

2 g4??

Weakening the white king's position still more (now dramatically). The punishment is not long in coming.

2...♕h4# *(D)*

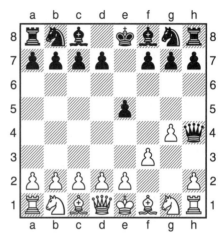

It's quite clear that the management of the white army was not exactly faultless.

Questions

16) Can you put the opponent's king in check, while yours is in check?

17) Can a king check the opponent's king?

18) On which square does the b-file intersect with the sixth rank?

19) On which square is the black queen situated in the initial position?

20) From memory, can you say whether a white pawn, placed on e5, may capture *en passant* a black pawn that plays to d5 on its first move?

21) Can Black castle kingside if a white bishop on d5 is controlling the g8-square?

22) Can White castle queenside if a black rook on b8 attacks the b1-square?

23) What are the differences between checkmate and stalemate?

24) Suppose that you capture two knights and a pawn, but in exchange you lose a rook and a bishop. According to the scale of material values, which side benefits more? Explain your calculation.

25) If you could choose between an endgame with two bishops and one with two knights,

without any other material, which one would you prefer? Why?

26) When promoting a pawn, is it always appropriate to promote to a queen? Explain.

27) You still have your original queen. Is it permissible for you promote a pawn into a second queen?

28) The opponent has just a king, whereas you have a king plus one or more pieces, but no pawns. However, it is not possible to force mate. Which combination of pieces do you have?

29) How should you record, in algebraic notation, kingside castling and queenside castling?

30) After castling kingside, can the same player, and in the same game, castle queenside? Explain.

Exercises

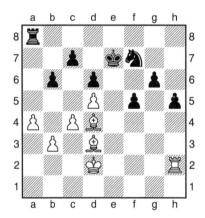

21) Which side has a material advantage? Explain your calculation.

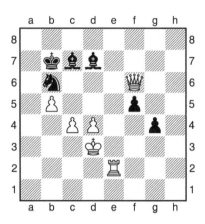

22) Which side has a material advantage? Explain your calculation.

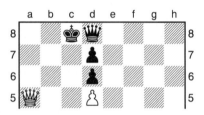

23) How can the white queen give perpetual check?

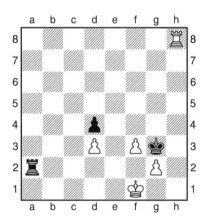

24) Can the black rook give perpetual check?

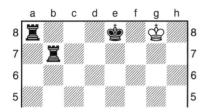

25) Can Black mate in one move? How? (Note: this could be considered a trick question.)

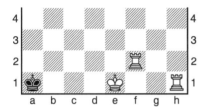

26) Can White mate in one move? How?

27) Imagine a position of perpetual check with two bishops and set it up on a board.

28) Imagine a position of perpetual check with one or two knights and set it up on a board.

29) Imagine three different stalemate positions and set them up on a board.

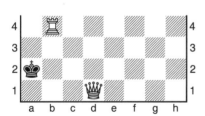

30) Can White mate in one move?

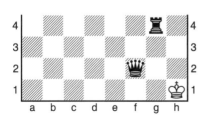

31) Can Black mate in one move?

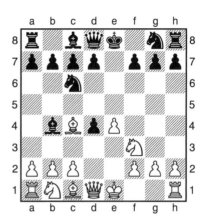

32) Black has just played ...♝b4+. Can the white king castle?

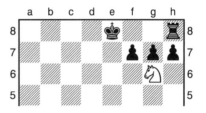

33) Can Black castle? Explain.

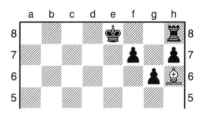

34) Can Black castle? Explain.

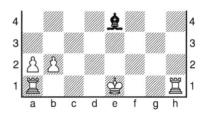

35) Can White castle queenside? Why?

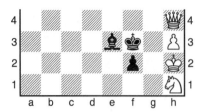

36) Which piece should the pawn be promoted to after ...f1?

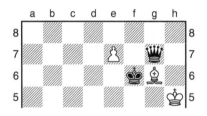

37) Which pieces should the white pawn be promoted to after c8?

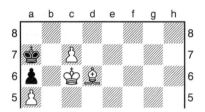

38) Which is the best way to promote for the e-pawn here?

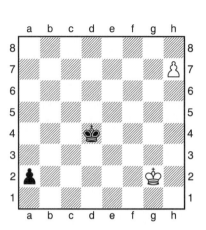

39) In this position it's Black to move. Who wins?

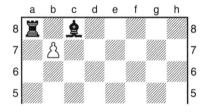

40) How many different moves can the b7-pawn make?

Further Tips

Knowledge and understanding of the geometry of the chessboard continue to be of great practical importance. I recommend further practice with exercises regarding ranks, files and squares.

It is vital to know the relative value of the pieces, and to be able to calculate the total value of a group of pieces.

You need to learn how to distinguish clearly between checkmate and stalemate.

It is useful to memorize and practise the theoretically drawn endgames covered in this chapter.

The castling rules should be learnt thoroughly and practised on a board.

The various possible pawn promotions should be practised.

3 Openings and Basic Principles

• The Laws of Chess • The Centre • The Opening: Time, Development and Space •
Classical Openings • Gambits • Classification of the Openings • Blunders and Traps in the
Open Games • Basic Mates • Questions • Exercises • Further Tips •

The Laws of Chess

Don't be afraid. I am not going to make you wade through a lot of dusty old law books. For the moment, there is only one rule to remember, but it's a golden one: **if you touch a piece, you must move it**, otherwise known as the **touch-move** rule. Engrave this on your memory, as otherwise you may have problems with your opponents, the arbiters and in fact with everybody.

By now you should already know how the pieces move, you are acquainted with the board, and you also know when and how games are won or drawn. You also know the rules for castling and pawn promotion. Nevertheless, knowing how the pieces move and a few other basics is still not enough to play a chess game.

My task is to equip you with weapons that will enable you to play effectively and confidently.

We are now going to study each phase of the game: opening, middlegame and endgame.

We shall also study the basic mates, so that, should they occur in your games, you won't have to rack your brain to work out whether such and such a position is winning. When you are faced with such a position, **you'll just know it**.

From now on, you will have to get stuck into the **real** mobilization of the pieces, into the strategy and tactics of chess.

We shall start, logically enough, at the beginning, and, without rushing, we shall cover all the elements you need to be equipped with to enable you to compete on the chess battlefield with chances of success.

In the meantime, you are expected to have been playing lots of games of chess with your friends or fellow chess students. In those games it's possible at times that you felt lost in the chess jungle. Don't worry. There is a solution for that, but you will need to make the effort to assimilate the technique and the knowledge we are going to pass on to you.

The Centre

Just as in every military campaign or war game, and every team sport, control of the **centre** is essential. In chess everything revolves around the centre. The development of the pieces during the opening or the middlegame is absolutely conditioned by their relationship with the centre.

By centre we mean the four central squares e4, d4, d5 and e5.

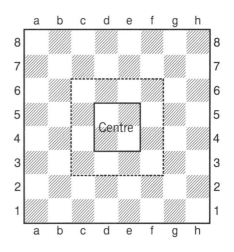

Some authors refer to the section of the board made up of the square **c3-c6-f6-f3** as the **extended centre**. In this book, we shall just refer to the centre as e4+d4+d5+e5, but you should understand that in the concept of 'the centre' the neighbouring squares are also of great significance.

The importance of the centre is not merely theoretical and you will understand this better as you play more and more games of chess. For the moment it's sufficient to learn that the struggle for the centre is essential.

The fight for the centre can be conducted by means of **occupation** (by pieces and especially pawns) and/or **control** (attacking the central squares with pieces and pawns, even at a distance).

The Opening: Time, Development and Space

The opening is, naturally, the first phase of the game, during which a player tries to:
• control the centre
• develop his pieces to active squares
• make his king safe

Time

Since chess is a game in which each player takes turns to move, it is obvious that we should try to derive maximum benefit from every move, on the assumption that our opponent will do likewise. Each move counts as a unit of time to be used to further our plans. In chess this unit of time is called a **tempo** (plural: tempi), and sometimes you will hear or read expressions such as 'Black has two tempi less', 'White lacks one tempo to promote his pawn', 'Black loses by one tempo', etc. If we spend a move on something that turns out to have no value (or spend two moves doing something that could have been accomplished in one move), then we have 'wasted a tempo'.

In the opening you have to play with great concentration, since if you make any indifferent moves, the risk is high that you will fall behind and your opponent will threaten you with

an attack. Thus, you need to look for purposeful moves which, if possible, also pose concrete threats.

Development

In the first few moves it is useful to **advance central pawns** and **develop pieces**. The first of these ideas doesn't require any explanation: most games start with the advance of the e-pawn or the d-pawn. But the second idea introduces us to a key concept in chess: the mobilization or bringing into play of the pieces is known as **development**.

Let's summarize then: the goals are: occupation of the centre by pawns, development of minor pieces and security for the king.

But let's put aside the words and let's go to the action. We shall see some examples of classical play.

1 e4 e5

Both players have placed a pawn in the centre. With his advance, White has opened the d1-h5 diagonal for the queen and the f1-a6 diagonal for the king's bishop, so that these pieces already have possible developing moves. The knights can also move, of course, and at the start they had two moves each, but now, after the pawn's advance, the knight on g1 can also move to e2.

We have to make the first decision in the game. What to play? Let's proceed by elimination. Developing the queen early in the opening is generally a poor idea. The reason is that the queen might be attacked by other pieces and since it is the piece of greatest worth, **all** the opponent's pieces and pawns may attack it and every time the queen would have to retreat, as otherwise it could be trapped in a minefield. There are also concrete reasons. On e2 or f3 it does not attack anything and would occupy a square useful for other pieces. On g4 Black could answer 2...♘f6, forcing the queen to move again and developing a piece with a **gain of time** (remember the importance of making good use of your turn to move). On h5 the queen looks more **active**, inside the black camp, and also attacks the e5-pawn. However, after protecting this pawn, Black will again be able to drive the queen away with a developing move that he gets 'for free', i.e. gaining *tempi*. Thus it's best for White to forget about bringing his queen out so early.

The white bishop can move to e2, d3, c4, b5 and a6. Once this last possibility is eliminated (since it would be taken by the b7-pawn), there remain four options. The development to e2 is safe but very passive, and also obstructs other pieces (queen, g1-knight). 2 ♗d3 is not good either, as it blocks the advance of the d-pawn, which will be needed in the fight for the centre. 2 ♗c4 is a natural move: the bishop is placed on an open diagonal, attacking the f7-square, the most vulnerable point close to the black king. It only has one disadvantage: it does not threaten anything specific at this point, which gives Black more freedom. On b5 the bishop enters the black camp, but only to be attacked by the opponent's pawns, presenting Black with a free tempo with 2...a6 or 2...c6.

Let's now consider the prospects of the b1-knight. The development to a3 may be discarded on principle, as it would be a move to the edge of the board and from there the knight could only move to two squares (c4 and b5); in addition, on a3 the knight does not contribute to the fight for the centre. More useful is 2 ♘c3, as from this square the knight attacks two central squares: e4 and d5. But it has the same disadvantage as 2 ♗c4, i.e. it does not immediately threaten anything.

Let's look now at the moves of the king's knight. The development to e2 should be discarded (as it would be a hindrance for other pieces, and contributes little to the fight for the centre), and 2 ♘h3 is bad for the same reasons as 2 ♘a3. More interesting seems 2 ♘f3. Let's consider this move. From f3 the knight attacks the central squares d4 and e5 (where there is a black pawn), it does not interfere with other friendly pieces and, as with the bishop, by moving off the back rank it clears the way for the king to castle in the near future. This is the best move!

2 ♘f3 *(D)*

What is Black's best response? Black has a problem: the defence of the e5-pawn, and he also needs to develop his pieces, as otherwise he will fall behind, and in chess, as in war, the

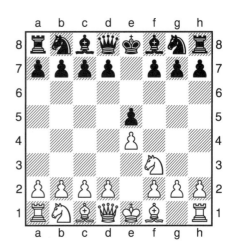

army whose forces are better and faster mobilized is the one with the greater chances of victory.

The defences which use the queen (2...♕f6, 2...♕e7) are artificial and do not develop a minor piece.

2...♗d6 is unsatisfactory for the same reasons as 2 ♗d3.

The defence using pawns restricts his own pieces and delays his piece development. Nevertheless, 2...d6 is a solid defence, known as the **Philidor Defence**. But 2...f6? (Damiano's Defence) is incorrect. 3 ♘xe5! could follow and the knight cannot be taken: 3...fxe5 4 ♕h5+ g6 5 ♕xe5+, and White wins the rook on h8. After 4 ♕h5+, 4...♔e7 is no better, as White would then have a decisive attack by 5 ♕xe5+ ♔f7 6 ♗c4+ d5 (or 6...♔g6 7 ♕f5+ ♔h6 8 d4+, winning more simply) 7 ♗xd5+ ♔g6 8 h4! h5 9 ♗xb7! (a strong *sacrifice*; we shall see many more of them later in the book) 9...♗xb7 10 ♕f5+ ♔h6 11 d4+, winning.

There is also a possible **counterattack**, i.e. Black can make a developing move which attacks the white pawn on e4, with 2...♘f6, but in a sense it is a somewhat risky strategy to copy White's moves. Let's do an exercise in very simple technical philosophy to keep things clear. If Black keeps copying White's moves, then what will happen when White mates? Will Black also be able to mate? No, since the game will be over. The king is dead, long live the king! (but in another game). That said, 2...♘f6 is very far from being a bad move (indeed, it is quite popular among top-class grandmasters), but at some point Black will need to stop copying White's moves, and that may involve a concession of some sort.

Thus we arrive by elimination at...

2...♘c6

...a piece is developed, defending the e5-pawn at the same time, and putting **pressure** on the d4-square in the white camp.

How to proceed now? White wants to keep up the pressure in order to control the game, so that Black would be left trailing. What is this called in chess? Seizing the **initiative**.

Now White gets an idea: if the c6-knight could be eliminated, the e5-pawn could be taken for free. This immediately suggests the move...

3 ♗b5 *(D)*

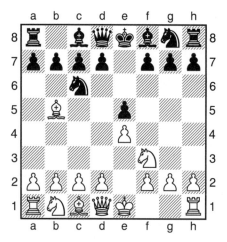

The remaining minor piece on the kingside sallies forth with no loss of time, apparently threatening the planned manoeuvre: 4 ♗xc6 dxc6 5 ♘xe5. White's threat, however, is not yet a real one as after that Black could answer 5...♕d4! (attacking both the white knight and the e4-pawn), thus recovering the pawn with good play.

Does this mean that 3 ♗b5 is a bad move? No! It's possibly the best move in this position, but we should evaluate it differently: even if it doesn't create an immediate threat, it creates problems, **pressure**, and it's a consistent and **flexible** developing move that also creates the immediate possibility of kingside castling.

With these moves we have on the board the **Ruy Lopez**, invented by Ruy Lopez de Segura, considered the best player of his time, the second half of 16th century.

Space

It is not unusual that the side with the better-developed pieces also gains a space advantage, based on his superior control of the centre. This advantage can be important, as long as the extra space can be kept under control and especially if it helps to cramp the movements of the enemy pieces. Remember the importance of controlling the conquered space with your own forces, as otherwise such an advantage might be fruitless.

Classical Openings

We have annotated above the opening moves of the Ruy Lopez, which is possibly White's best option after 1 e4 e5. But in the opening the best moves are generally not the only playable ones. If an opening consists of logical developing moves which do not interfere with other 'friendly' pieces and are directed to the centre, they are usually good enough. We have an example in the **Giuoco Piano**:

1 e4 e5 2 ♘f3 ♘c6 3 ♗c4 ♗c5 *(D)*

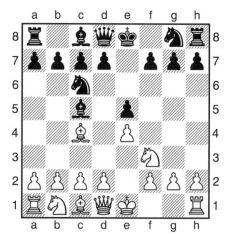

Compared with the Ruy Lopez, only the bishop has developed to another square, c4, from where it aims at f7 and occupies a good central position. Black has answered with a symmetrical development and both sides are now ready to castle kingside, and also to contest the centre – often quite ferociously.

Now we shall summarize the characteristic moves of the main classic openings.

Defence

The names of many openings contain the word **defence**. Why? The reason is that in those openings the move(s) characteristic of the system is (are) black ones. For instance, 2...d6 is the move that denotes the **Philidor Defence**, while 2...♘f6 is the characteristic move of the **Petroff Defence**.

Gambits

A **gambit** is a sacrifice of a pawn or pawns, generally in the opening, to gain time for development. It's a risky operation in which the side offering the gambit gives up material in exchange for active play or even attacking prospects. But we should not forget that sometimes one pawn is enough to win a game!

Let's look at an example, the **Scotch Gambit**, after 1 e4 e5 2 ♘f3 ♘c6 3 d4 exd4 4 ♗c4 *(D)*.

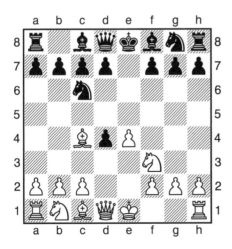

White has moved the bishop to speed up his development, deferring the eventual capture of the d4-pawn, or maybe considering offering another pawn with c3, planning to recapture with the knight (♘xc3), which would be in line with his **plan** of mobilizing his pieces as quickly as possible.

This kind of approach is a search for the **initiative** at all costs, which might be transformed into an attack.

In other gambits the immediate control of the centre is the main target. Thus, for instance, the **King's Gambit**, where after 1 e4 e5 2 f4 exf4 3 ♘f3, White is planning to follow up with d4, ♗c4, etc., in a combined action of central control and fast development of the pieces. In so doing, however, White is weakening his kingside.

In the **Queen's Gambit**, the immediate aggression to the d5-pawn, 1 d4 d5 2 c4, also has the purpose of gaining central superiority.

Classification of the Openings

The Queen's Gambit is part of a group of openings known as **Closed Games**. This is the moment for talking about sorting the openings into families.

The games starting with the moves 1 e4 e5 are grouped under the generic name of **Open Games**, since generally (though not always!) they lead to sharp fights and open lines, the consequence of early exchanges of pawns and pieces. So far, all the openings mentioned are Open Games, except for the Queen's Gambit.

When Black answers to 1 e4 with a move other than 1...e5, then these openings are called **Semi-Open Games**, as in general the resulting positions are less open than in the above-mentioned ones. In other chapters I will mention the main openings of this group, with their characteristic moves.

All the remaining first moves by White belong to a large group of openings known as **Closed Games**, in which usually (though, once again, not always!) the play is slower, with a lot of manoeuvring, characteristic of present-day chess.

Naturally, all these concepts are rather simplistic and you should not take them too literally.

They serve as a guide and it's convenient to know about them in order to be on familiar ground.

In the following chapters we shall return to the main Semi-Open and Closed Games.

Blunders and Traps in the Open Games

Opening Blunders

In the opening itself and when practically all the pieces are still on the board, the fight takes place as if in a jungle or a minefield and you must be very smart to survive there. We shall now look at some examples of games containing blunders in the opening.

King's Gambit
1 e4 e5 2 f4 ♗c5

A crafty move. While probably playable, 2...♕h4+ is not very strong yet, since after 3 g3 the queen has to retreat.

3 fxe5?? ♕h4+ 4 ♔e2

4 g3 avoids instant loss, but after 4...♕xe4+ Black wins the h1-rook.

The king's move allows a curious mate that you should try to remember, just in case you have the opportunity of delivering it in your own games.

4...♕xe4# (D)

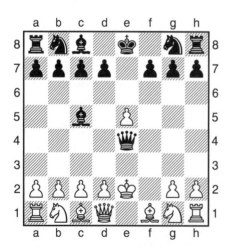

The following example illustrates the dangers of an early queen expedition in the opening.

Bishop's Opening
1 e4 e5 2 ♗c4 ♕f6?

An artificial mode of development. As previously mentioned, it's useful to give priority to developing the minor pieces. Besides, what does this move threaten?

3 ♘f3 ♕g6?

Now the black queen threatens two pawns (e4 and g2), but the target is too trivial to justify two queen moves in the opening, rather like using a sledgehammer to crack a nut.

4 0-0 ♕xe4? (D)

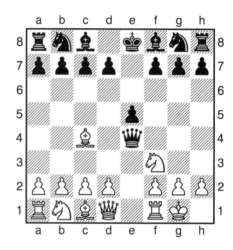

This capture will cost Black dear, as we shall see.

5 ♗xf7+! ♔d8

If 5...♔xf7, 6 ♘g5+ is a **fork** that will win the queen.

6 ♘xe5! ♕xe5

The black queen accepts all the booty, but it's the only black piece in play and that will have dramatic consequences.

7 ♖e1 ♕f6?

After having played five moves, the queen returns to its first developing square.

8 ♖e8#

In the following example Black makes a mistake in the opening, which allows White to create a succession of threats.

Giuoco Piano

1 e4 e5 2 ♘f3 ♘c6 3 ♗c4 ♗c5 4 d3 ♘ge7?

Passive. Better is 4...♘f6, which would avoid the attack that follows.

5 ♘g5 0-0?

5...d5 is better, although after 6 exd5 ♘xd5 7 ♘c3, the black position is very bad.

6 ♕h5!

Threatening mate on h7, as well as attacking for a third time (queen, knight and bishop) the f7-square, which is protected only twice (king and rook).

6...h6 7 ♘xf7 ♖xf7

Forced, since the knight attacked the queen as well as threatening dangerous **discovered checks**. For instance, if 7...♕e8, 8 ♘xh6++ ♔h8 9 ♘f7++ ♔g8 10 ♕h8#.

8 ♗xf7+ ♔f8 9 ♗b3 ♕e8 (D)

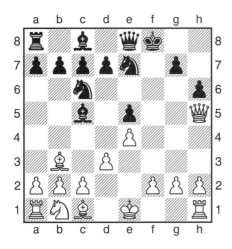

Now comes an unexpected finish:

10 ♕xh6!?

Threatening to win straight away by 11 ♕h8+.

10...gxh6 11 ♗xh6#

Philidor Defence

1 e4 e5 2 ♘f3 d6 3 d4 ♘d7 4 ♗c4 ♗e7? (D)

With this imperceptible mistake Black loses a pawn. 4...♘gf6? is also bad in view of 5 dxe5 ♘xe5 (not 5...dxe5? 6 ♘g5) 6 ♘xe5 dxe5 7 ♗xf7+!, winning a pawn. 4...c6 is the main move; with continued careful play, Black can avoid material loss and obtain a viable middlegame.

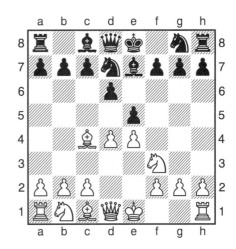

5 dxe5 ♘xe5

5...dxe5? is even worse, on account of 6 ♕d5.

6 ♘xe5 dxe5 7 ♕h5!

With a double attack on f7 and e5, winning the e5-pawn.

Here's another mistake in the same opening.

Philidor Defence

1 e4 e5 2 ♘f3 d6 3 ♗c4 ♗e7 4 d4 exd4 5 ♘xd4 ♘d7?

5...♘f6 is a more precise move.

6 ♗xf7+! ♔xf7 (D)

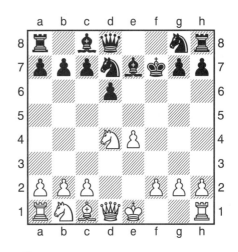

7 ♘e6! (D)

Drawing the king into a mating-net. If now 7...♕e8, 8 ♘xc7 ♕d8 9 ♕d5+ ♔f8 10 ♘e6+ wins the queen.

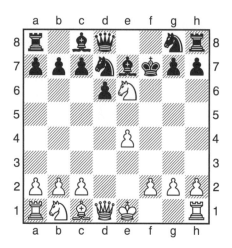

7...♔xe6 8 ♕d5+ ♔f6 9 ♕f5# (D)

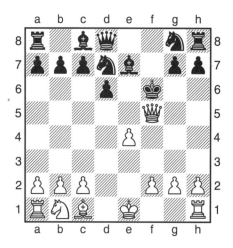

Tricks and Traps

A **trick** is a self-explanatory manoeuvre, which may have a dramatic outcome for the intended victim, but which may also have disadvantages for the side setting the trap, if the opponent knows how to avoid it! If the trick is not discovered, then the victim may fall naïvely for it. But if the supposed victim can discover it in time, then he will sometimes be able not only to avoid it, but also to profit from its weak points.

A trap may be well-founded and sound, but a trick is an artificial sort of trap which shouldn't work, and is not 'good chess'. Let's look at an example.

Ruy Lopez
1 e4 e5 2 ♘f3 ♘c6 3 ♗b5 ♘d4 4 ♗c4

One of the purposes of this retreat is to provoke the advance ...b5. This is the trap. The standard method is 4 ♘xd4 exd4 5 0-0.

4...b5? 5 ♗xf7+! ♔xf7 6 ♘xd4 exd4 7 ♕h5+ (D)

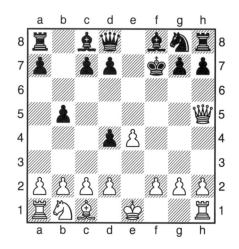

White now wins the a8-rook.
7...♔e7

If 7...g6, then 8 ♕d5+ wins the rook immediately.

8 ♕e5+ ♔f7 9 ♕d5+ (D)

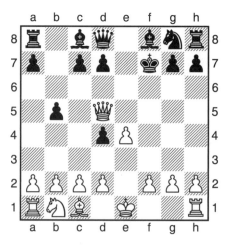

Winning the rook. Naturally, Black is not obliged to play 4...b5?, and can develop normally instead.

Another curious trap is the following one.

Italian Game

1 e4 e5 2 ♘f3 ♘c6 3 ♗c4 ♘d4?! *(D)*

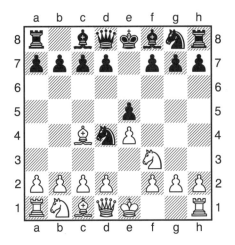

This last move sets a trap, but is not good. With 4 ♘xd4 exd4 5 0-0, White would have an excellent game, essentially refuting the move 3...♘d4?!. But the temptation of winning a pawn and attacking the f7-square is too strong to resist, so countless beginners have fallen into this trap.

4 ♘xe5? ♕g5! 5 ♘xf7?

5 ♗xf7+ is better, but even in that case White still has problems.

5...♕xg2 6 ♖f1

If 6 ♘xh8 then 6...♕xh1+ 7 ♗f1 ♕xe4+ 8 ♗e2 ♘xc2+, when 9 ♕xc2 ♕xc2 costs White his queen, while 9 ♔f1 allows 9...♕h1#.

6...♕xe4+ 7 ♗e2 ♘f3# *(D)*

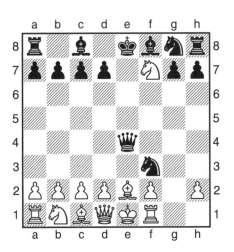

Legall's Mate

Legall de Kermeur was one of the best players who frequented the famous Café de la Régence in Paris in the days before the French Revolution. The following game introduced a typical checkmate which bears his name.

Legall – Saint Brie

Paris 1750
Philidor Defence

We should note that White gave odds of his queen's rook; that is, he started the game without the rook on a1 as a form of handicap.

1 e4 e5 2 ♘f3 d6 3 ♗c4 ♘c6 4 ♘c3 ♗g4

It is said that at this moment Legall touched his knight on f3 and his opponent insisted that he move it, in accordance with the 'touchmove' rule. Maybe this wasn't true and, even if it was, nobody knows whether it was a trick on the part of the master to mislead his opponent. In any case, Legall, forced or not, picked up the knight and played...

5 ♘xe5?? *(D)*

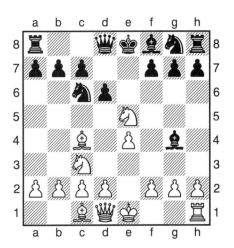

Now, if the knight is taken with the d6-pawn, 5...dxe5??, White answers 6 ♕xg4, winning a pawn (of course, in this odds game, Black still has his extra rook...). But if the knight is taken with the c6-knight, Black wins a piece for a pawn. That was the flaw in the trap. But the temptation to eliminate the white queen from the board was too strong for an amateur who could not dream of defeating a champion such as Legall. So he promptly grabbed the white queen...

5...♗xd1??

...only to receive a big surprise:

6 ♗xf7+ ♔e7 7 ♘d5# (1-0) *(D)*

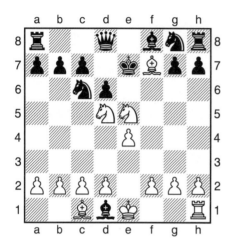

An impressive mate!

Basic Mates

Mate with Queen and Rook

Queens and rooks are called **major pieces**, to differentiate them from the **minor pieces** (bishops and knights). And they are so called because their mobility is much greater than that of the minor pieces. Remember that the number of squares to which a well-placed queen can move on an open board is 27, while for a rook the total is 14 squares. In contrast, the bishop can only move to 13 squares even in optimal positions (far fewer in most cases), while the knight can only reach 8 in the best case.

The major pieces are also known as **heavy pieces**, which explains their strength, since they are pieces with a long range, like heavy artillery.

We are now going to explain the procedure to mate with queen and rook, without the help of the king. It's a very simple procedure. (Naturally, you would have your own king somewhere on the board, but it isn't involved in the mating process, so I have omitted it from the following diagrams.)

With the defender's king in the centre, where the mate may take longer, the method consists of restricting the space available to the king along ranks or files, until it is pushed to the edge. One of the pieces cuts off the king's retreat, while the other attacks it.

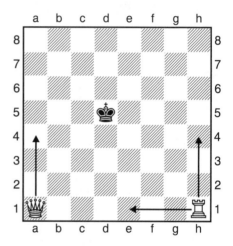

The arrows show three possible restricting moves that are equivalent. Let's start with one of them.

1 ♕a4 ♔e5

1...♔c5 would be answered with the same move. 1...♔d6 or 1...♔e6 would make things easier. In both cases 2 ♕a5 or 2 ♕b5 would follow.

2 ♖h5+ ♔f6 3 ♕a6+ ♔g7 4 ♖b5 *(D)*

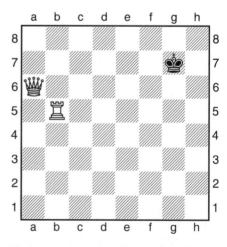

Given the closeness of the black king, the rook cannot safely check, so it simply retreats to a safe distance. This illustrates why the major pieces work more effectively from a distance.

4...♔f7 5 ♖b7+ ♔f8 6 ♕a8# *(D)*

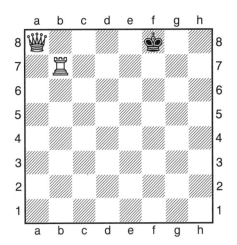

You have seen how easy it was. All you need to do is restrict the king, using the great strength of the major pieces.

To reinforce this simple technique, let's go back to our starting position. Now we shall use another move to reach the same target (all roads lead to Rome). In this way, the reader may check how easy it is to deliver this mate.

1 ♖e1 ♔c4 2 ♖d1 ♔c5 3 ♕c3+ ♔b5 4 ♖b1+ ♔a6 5 ♕a1# *(D)*

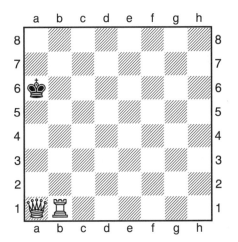

This time it was even easier! Only five moves.

Queen and rook together are too strong a team to have any difficulties whatsoever in mating. However, I suggest you practise this mate until you can do it blindfold. Wherever the defender's king is situated, it shouldn't take more than six or seven moves to mate.

Mate with Two Rooks

The mate with two rooks (without the help of the king) is a bit more difficult than the one with queen and rook, but the procedure is similar. The rooks must gradually restrict the space available to the defender's king, until it is confined on the edge of the board, where it will be mated.

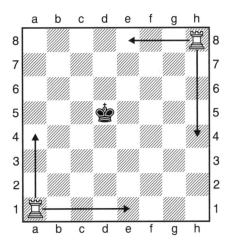

The defender's king is situated on one of the central squares, and there are four equally good moves that confine the king to one half of the board: ♖h4, ♖e8, ♖a4 and ♖e1. Let's try the first of these.

1 ♖h4 ♔c5 2 ♖a5+ ♔b6 3 ♖g5 *(D)*

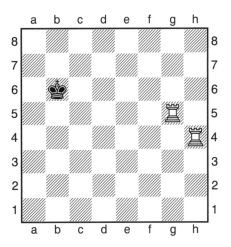

The attacked rook should be shifted as far away as possible, but not on to the same file as the other rook, so that they do not interfere with one another.

3...♔c6 4 ♖h6+ ♔d7 5 ♖g7+ ♔e8 6 ♖h8# *(D)*

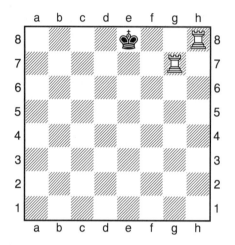

Let's see another example.

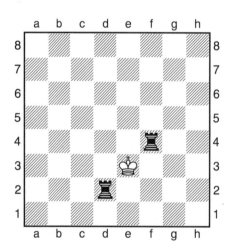

The king is attacking both rooks. We have to connect them, so that they protect each other, and this can be done in several ways; for example, by moving the d2-rook to f2. This will also allow us to explain a detail of algebraic notation. When more than one piece of the same kind (as in this case) can go to the same square, we need to make clear which one we are moving. Accordingly, after the piece's initial (or

figurine) you should add the letter of the file on which it is situated.

1...♖df2 2 ♔d3 ♖2f3+

Another peculiarity of algebraic notation. When two pieces of the same kind are placed on the same file and can both move to the same square, to make clear which of them is the one we are moving, we should indicate the rank number. In this case, if the other rook had moved, we would write 2...♖4f3+.

3 ♔d2 ♖h4

On the same file, the rooks get in each other's way and prevent the method of systematic restriction, so one of them moves away.

4 ♔e2

When the f3-rook is attacked, it should move as far away as possible. Once more the reader should reflect upon the usefulness of deploying the major pieces at long range.

4...♖a3 5 ♔f2 ♖h2+ 6 ♔g1

The king is now on the edge, but has gained a tempo attacking the h2-rook.

6...♖b2 7 ♔f1 ♖a1# *(D)*

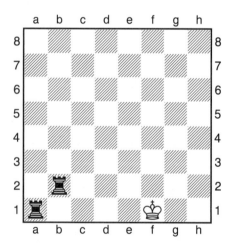

As you can see, mate with two rooks is also very easy, pure geometry, using straight lines. However, I recommend practising from different starting positions. Even if you make a few mistakes, eight or nine moves should be enough.

Mate with King and Queen

Checkmate by the queen, supported by the king, does not present any difficulties either. You have to exploit the strength of the queen, restricting the scope of the enemy king, and bringing the attacking king close to collaborate in the pursuit of the defender's king. Once the defender's king is on the edge, the mate is very easy. You just need to be careful to avoid stalemate. The next four positions illustrate the possible mating patterns.

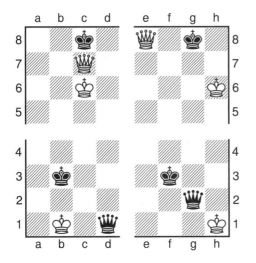

You should try to learn these mating patterns, since familiarity with these positions makes an immediate mental visualization easier in practice, but above all in order to be very clear about the final aim of our previous manoeuvres.

Let's move on to the action. We have to mate the white king in the next diagram.

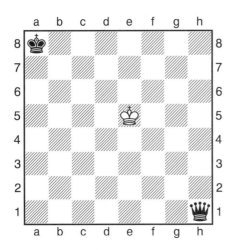

1...♕h4

The first step is to confine the king in one half of the board, similar to the procedure with queen and rook, or two rooks.

2 ♔d5 ♕f4

Now the white king is practically caged in one quarter of the board.

3 ♔c5 ♔b7

The black king has to approach, to restrict still more his black counterpart.

4 ♔d5 ♔b6 *(D)*

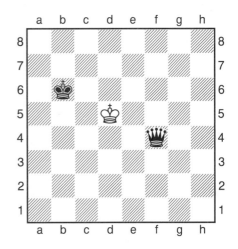

5 ♔e6 ♔c6 6 ♔e7 ♕f5

After this move, the white king must move to the edge.

7 ♔e8 ♕h7 8 ♔f8 ♔d6

The ideal position: mate is now unavoidable.

9 ♔e8 ♕e7# *(D)*

There was also another mate: 9...♕g8#.

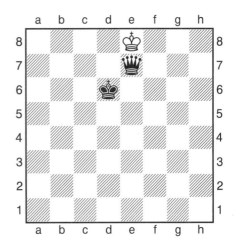

Here's another example, in which we shall try a different method, this time using some checks.

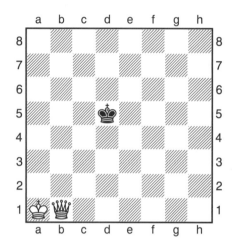

I will make no comments. The reader, once again, is invited to question every move and consider alternative moves.

1 ♕e1 ♚d4 2 ♚b2 ♚d5 3 ♚c3 ♚c5 4 ♕e5+ ♚c6 5 ♚c4 ♚b6 6 ♕c5+ ♚b7 7 ♚b5 ♚b8 8 ♕e7 ♚c8 9 ♚b6 ♚b8 *(D)*

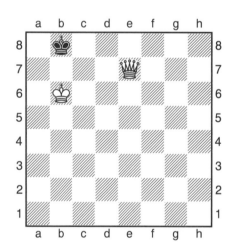

We have reached the position of one of our mating patterns: the defender's king is on the edge and the kings are facing each other. White can now deliver four different mates: 10 ♕d8#, 10 ♕e8#, 10 ♕f8# and 10 ♕b7#.

A future champion must practise these mates until he can deliver them almost automatically. Fifteen moves should be (more than) enough from any position.

Mate with King and Rook

The mate with a single rook and the help of its king takes a bit longer, but is not at all difficult. The procedure consists of driving the defender's king to one of the edges of the board (something that you already know!), the only place where mate can be delivered. For that purpose we shall use the method of domination, i.e. gaining space little by little, first confining the king in one half of the board, in a similar way to the previous mates. Then, to a quarter of the board and, finally, we shall further limit his range, always with the help of the attacking king. The general technique of all these mates is very similar.

The defence of the defender's king is based on trying to stay in the centre and keep as far as possible from the attacker's king.

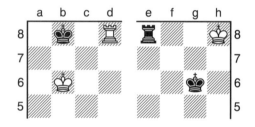

These two positions show the patterns for this mate.

We will now study a concrete position, with the defender's king in the centre of the board (where he can offer most resistance) and rook and king of the attacking side far away.

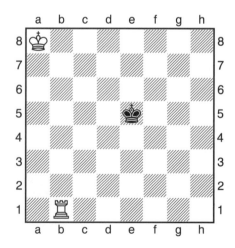

In this position there are two equally good moves: 1 ♖d1 and 1 ♖b4.

1 ♖d1

The black king is now imprisoned on the kingside, i.e. the e- to h-files.

1...♚e4 2 ♔b7 ♚e5

The weak king must try to remain in the centre.

3 ♔c6 ♚e4 4 ♖d5

Now the black king is confined to a quarter of board.

4...♚f4 5 ♔d6 ♚e4 6 ♔e6 ♚f4

If 6...♚e3, 7 ♔e5.

7 ♖d4+ ♚e3 8 ♔e5

The black king now has only 12 squares.

8...♚f3 9 ♖e4 *(D)*

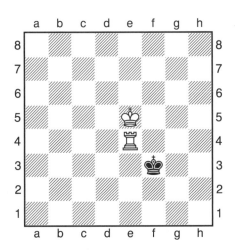

And now only 9!

9...♚f2 10 ♔f4 ♚g2 11 ♖e2+

The defender's king now has four possibilities, but all of them require retreating to the edge of the board. After 11...♚f1 White would answer 12 ♔f3, while after 11...♚g1 or 11...♚h1 he would play 12 ♔g3.

11...♚h3 12 ♔f3

One of the key positions in this endgame. Both kings are facing each other, with the defender's king on the edge. The mate is near.

12...♚h4

The only move.

13 ♖e5

A typical procedure. The rook moves to a rank ahead of the opponent's king, to cut off his escape-squares, forcing him to retreat to a square facing the attacker's king, and so reaching a mating pattern.

13...♚h3 14 ♖h5# *(D)*

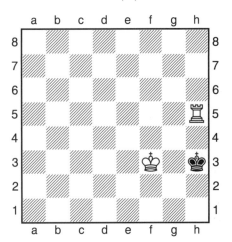

Questions

31) Why is the bishop better than the knight in an open position?

32) What squares define the centre?

33) What is a gambit?

34) What does a *tempo* mean?

35) What is meant by development?

36) Which moves are characteristic of an Open Game?

37) When is an opening called a defence?

38) Besides the fight for the centre and development, what else is a primary objective of opening play?

39) Where on the board can a king and a rook force checkmate, without any other material?

40) What is the generic term for queens and rooks?

41) At the beginning of this chapter, we mentioned the most important rule of chess from a practical viewpoint. What is this?

42) Which pawns should be advanced at the start of the game?

43) Why is not useful to develop the knights on the edge of the board?

44) When two rooks, on the same file, can both move to the same square, how should the move be recorded in algebraic notation?

45) Where on the board can a king and a queen force checkmate, without any other material?

Exercises

41) The white king is on e6 and the white queen on h1. The black king is on e8. Can White mate in one move? (Try to solve this without looking at the board).

42) The black king is on c3 and the black queen on a2. The white king is on d1. Can Black mate in one move? (Try to solve this without looking at the board).

43) The white king is on g6 and there is a white rook on a1. The black king is on g8. Can White mate in one move? (Try to solve this without looking at the board).

44) The white king is on c6 and the white queen is on g7. The black king is on c8. How many ways can White mate in one move? (Try to solve this without looking at the board).

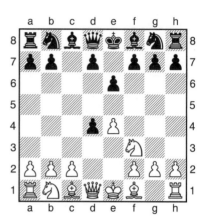

46) Which move is better for White, from the point of view of development: 4 ♘xd4 or 4 ♕xd4?

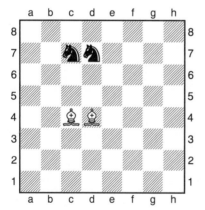

45) In this imaginary position (as there are no kings), which pair of pieces is stronger: the two bishops or the two knights? Why?

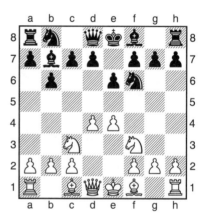

47) Black has just played 4...♗b7. Does this move contribute to the struggle for the centre? Why?

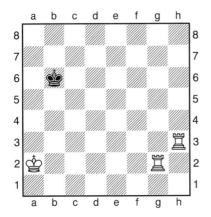

48) How can White mate in three moves?

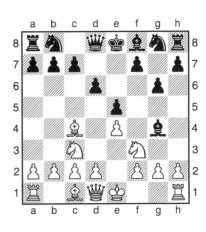

51) What is the best move for White?

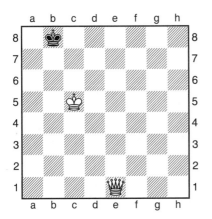

49) How can White mate in two moves?

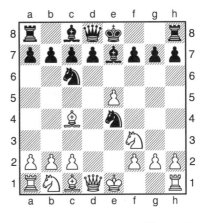

52) Which move is stronger: ♕d5 or ♗xf7+?

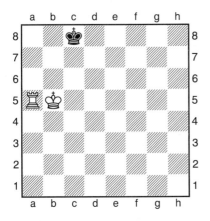

50) How can White mate in three moves?

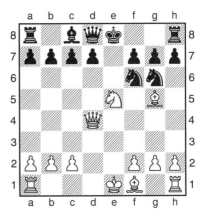

53) Find the best move for White.

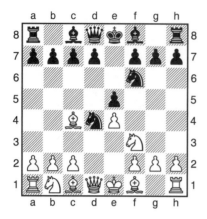

54) After 1 e4 e5 2 ♘f3 ♘c6 3 ♗c4 ♘f6 4 d4, Black has just taken the d4-pawn by 4...♘xd4. Was it a good idea? How should White answer?

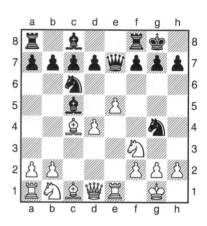

56) With 1 e4 e5 2 ♘f3 ♘c6 3 ♗c4 ♗c5 4 0-0 ♘f6 5 ♖e1 0-0 6 c3?! ♕e7?! 7 d4 exd4?! 8 e5?! ♘g4 9 cxd4??, White has fallen into a trap, already known by Greco in the 17th century. How can Black win?

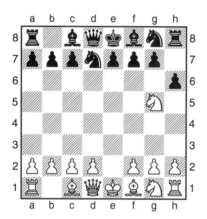

55) How could a mate similar to Fool's Mate be produced?

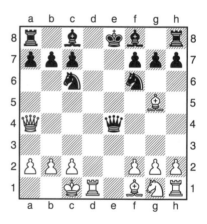

57) A simple (but not obvious) move wins the game on the spot. Can you find it?

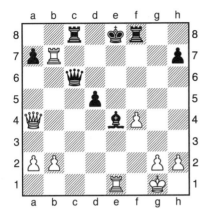

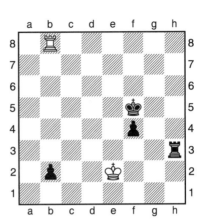

58) Despite being a piece down, White can win quickly here. How?

60) This position arose in an important game. Black has just advanced his pawn to b2. Can White capture it? Explain.

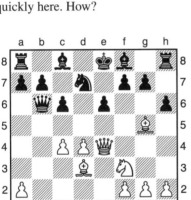

59) How can White win here in two moves?

Further Tips

Never forget the most important chess rule: 'touch-move'. Remember that, although you don't have all the time in the world to think about your move, you should take your time, since nothing forces you to rush.

Play Open Games, such as the King's Gambit, the Ruy Lopez, the Giuoco Piano and the Two Knights Defence. Refer to an openings book to view the various lines of play.

For practice, try offering gambits. For instance, I suggest that you play games using the Scotch Gambit (1 e4 e5 2 ♘f3 ♘c6 3 d4 exd4 4 ♗c4) and the Göring Gambit (1 e4 e5 2 ♘f3 ♘c6 3 d4 exd4 4 c3).

Practise the basic mates with ♔+♕ and ♔+♖. Imagine what a pity it would be to waste time chasing the enemy king all around the board, when what you really want to do is finish quickly.

Study the possibilities for opening lines for an attack on the king. How can this be evaluated in each case, in terms of material? A pawn, two pawns, a piece? How many threats will you be able to create, in exchange for the sacrificed material?

4 Putting Your Pieces to Work

• Open Games • Contacts between Pieces • Pawn Endgames • Mate with Two Bishops • The Powers of the Pieces • Questions • Exercises • Further Tips •

Open Games

We will now continue by looking at some examples of the Open Games, which in fact constitute models of how to exploit the opponent's mistakes to attain victory.

The first game was played by Gioacchino Greco, an Italian master from the 17th century, who was considered one of the best players of his day.

Greco – NN
1619
Giuoco Piano

1 e4 e5 2 ♘f3 ♘c6 3 ♗c4 ♗c5

Following a scheme of development that we are already familiar with. White now has an immediate plan, based on castling and fighting for the centre.

4 c3 ♕e7 5 0-0 d6 6 d4 ♗b6 7 ♗g5 f6 8 ♗h4 g5? (D)

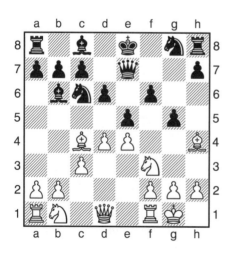

A big mistake, as *Il Calabrese* (Greco's nickname), will show. It was better to develop the c8-bishop, or even play 8...♘h6 or 8...h5!?.

9 ♘xg5! fxg5 10 ♕h5+ ♔d7 (D)

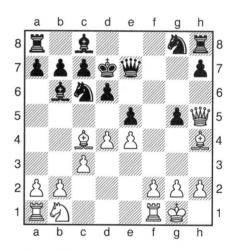

11 ♗xg5 ♕g7?! (D)

Now follows a brilliant **combination** (this topic will be studied in another chapter).

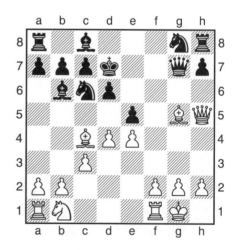

12 ♗e6+! ♔xe6 13 ♕e8+ ♕e7

If Black blocks with any other piece, the outcome would be just the same.

14 d5# (D)

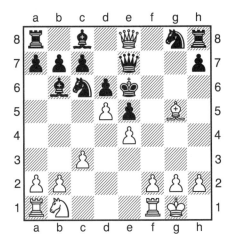

Bravo!

The following game is related to Legall's mate.

Berger – Frölich
Graz 1888
Ruy Lopez

1 e4 e5 2 ♘f3 ♘c6 3 ♗b5 a6 4 ♗a4 d6 5 ♘c3 ♗g4

It would be better for Black to develop his kingside.

6 ♘d5 ♘e7 7 c3 b5 8 ♗b3 ♘a5? (D)

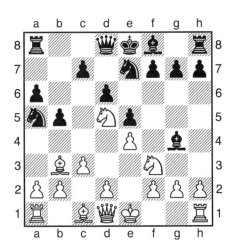

This knight move is very optimistic. Black has two unprotected pieces and this factor, in connection with the b3-bishop (on the a2-g8 diagonal) reminds us of Legall's famous mate. We already have a knight on d5!

9 ♘xe5! ♗xd1?

It was better to accept the loss of a pawn with 9...dxe5 10 ♕xg4, but not 9...♘xd5? 10 ♘xg4 or 9...♘xb3? 10 ♘xg4 ♘xa1? 11 ♘gf6+ gxf6 12 ♘xf6#.

10 ♘f6+! gxf6 11 ♗xf7# (1-0)

In the following game we shall see a surprising outcome in only seven moves.

Imbusch – Hering
Munich 1899
Vienna Game

1 e4 e5 2 ♘c3 ♘f6 3 ♗c4 ♘xe4 (D)

To simplify in the centre. The move is sound, since after 4 ♘xe4 d5 Black recovers the piece with a good position.

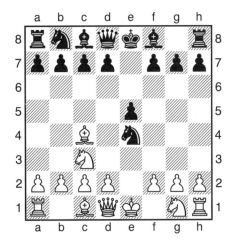

4 ♗xf7+

This is not the best. White gives up his bishop to prevent the black king from castling. But the move is a bad one from a strategic viewpoint.

4...♔xf7 5 ♘xe4

Black could now achieve a good position with 5...d5!, in spite of the apparently exposed situation of his king. His development is better and in addition he dominates the centre with his pawns and can rely on having the two bishops.

5...♘c6?! 6 ♕f3+ ♔g8??

The king should retreat to its original square: 6...♔e8! keeps a good position.

7 ♘g5! *(D)*

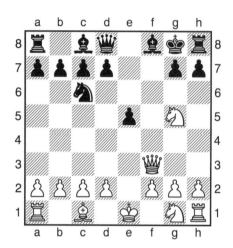

1-0

The knight cannot be taken (7...♕xg5 8 ♕d5#), and the problem for Black is that the white queen now threatens two mates: on f7 and d5, and there is no possible defence.

Taylor – NN
London 1862
Petroff Defence

1 e4 e5 2 ♘f3 ♘f6 3 ♗c4 ♘xe4 4 ♘c3

Played in gambit style. White prefers to speed up his development, rather than routinely recovering the pawn.

4...♘c5?!

If 4...♘xc3 5 dxc3, White would have a clear advantage in development, although current theory considers that after 5...f6 6 0-0 d6 the black centre is very strong and compensates for the lag in development. Please note that the knight has made three out of the four black moves so far. 4...♘c6 is a good safe option, based on 5 ♘xe4 d5, winning back the piece.

5 ♘xe5

In answer to this move, Black only has 5...♘e6, which would mean Black's fourth knight move (of the total of five moves so far). However...

5...f6? *(D)*

...he commits a serious mistake, which allows White to end the game easily.

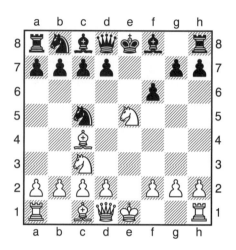

Taylor announced mate in eight when playing his next move.

6 ♕h5+ g6

Or 6...♔e7 7 ♕f7+ ♔d6 8 ♘b5+ ♔xe5 9 ♕d5+ ♔f4 10 g3+ ♔g4 11 h3#. All of Black's remaining moves are forced.

7 ♗f7+ ♔e7 8 ♘d5+ ♔d6 9 ♘c4+ ♔c6 10 ♘b4+ ♔b5 11 a4+ ♔xb4 12 c3+ ♔b3 13 ♕d1# (1-0)

The black king made a long and unpleasant journey, which allowed the white queen to mate, back on its original square.

Blake – Hooke
London 1888?
Philidor Defence

1 e4 e5 2 ♘f3 d6 3 ♗c4 f5?!

The most aggressive and risky variation in the Philidor Defence.

4 d4 ♘f6 5 ♘c3 exd4 6 ♕xd4

Now White already has a clear advantage in development. On the other hand, Black has neglected the centre, which goes against the spirit of this opening, which is based on reinforcing the e5-square.

6...♗d7?

With the idea of playing ...♘c6, without having to worry about ♗b5. But Black has a horrible weakness on the a2-g8 diagonal, dominated by the opponent's bishop.

7 ♘g5 ♞c6? 8 ♗f7+ ♚e7 *(D)*

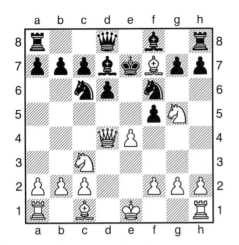

Now White had at his disposal a devastating move:

9 ♕xf6+!!

In the game, White played 9 ♕d5??, and went on to win in any case.

9...♗xf6

Or 9...gxf6 10 ♘d5#.

10 ♘d5+ ♚e5 11 ♘f3+ ♚xe4 12 ♘c3# *(D)*

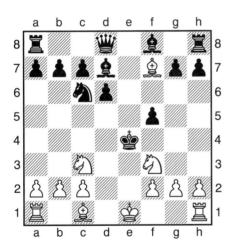

Both white knights have returned to their original squares to deliver this beautiful mate, with the supplementary help of the c1-bishop (which covers f4 and e3) and the c2-pawn (covering the d3-square).

The following game has gone all round the world in chess books and magazines. The great

Paul Morphy (1837-84) gives a real demonstration of how to exploit the inadequate play of his opponents (in consultation) and get the most out of the active position of his own pieces.

Morphy – Duke of Brunswick & Count Isouard
Paris 1858
Philidor Defence

1 e4 e5 2 ♘f3 d6 3 d4 ♗g4?

A mistake. Sounder are 3...exd4, 3...♘d7 and 3...♘f6.

4 dxe5 ♗xf3

4...dxe5 5 ♕xd8+ ♚xd8 6 ♘xe5 leaves Black a pawn down for nothing.

5 ♕xf3 dxe5 6 ♗c4

Immediately threatening 7 ♕xf7#.

6...♘f6 7 ♕b3

This strong move creates serious problems for Black. White's threats are 8 ♗xf7+ ♚e7 (8...♚d7) 9 ♕e6#, and also 8 ♕xb7.

7...♕e7

The players in consultation assume that they will lose their b7-pawn, but they are hoping to exchange the queens after 8 ♕xb7 ♕b4+ 9 ♕xb4 ♗xb4+ and then put up tough resistance in the endgame. Morphy, however, ignores the pawn and opts for completing the development of his pieces.

8 ♘c3! c6 9 ♗g5 b5? *(D)*

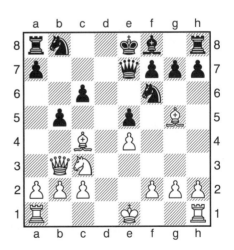

Too optimistic. White has practically finished his development and can castle on either

side. Nevertheless, he now has to deal with this attack on his bishop.

10 ♘xb5! cxb5 11 ♗xb5+ ♘bd7 12 0-0-0 ♖d8

White was threatening 13 ♗xd7+.

13 ♖xd7!

Morphy sacrifices the rook to eliminate an important defensive piece, banking on the **pin** (a theme that we shall encounter when we come to study combinations; in brief: a piece is *pinned* if it cannot move, because doing so would expose a more important one behind it to attack) that the b5-bishop exerts along the a4-e8 diagonal.

13...♖xd7 14 ♖d1 ♕e6

There is no alternative. 14...♕b4 is met by 15 ♗xf6 and 16 ♗xd7+, recovering the piece with a strong attack.

15 ♗xd7+ ♘xd7 *(D)*

Now comes a spectacular finish:

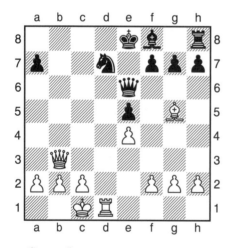

16 ♕b8+! ♘xb8 17 ♖d8# (1-0)
Fantastic!

Now we are going to see a miniature game in which the triple Spanish champion, Francisco Jose Perez, defeats the then world champion, Alekhine. It's a 'blitz' game, with five minutes per player.

F.J. Perez – Alekhine
Madrid (blitz) 1941
Vienna Gambit

1 e4 e5 2 ♘c3 ♘c6 3 f4

This is the characteristic move of the Vienna Gambit. It's an opening similar to the King's Gambit (1 e4 e5 2 f4).

3...exf4 4 ♘f3 g5

Black decides to keep the pawn at all costs, while also retaining the possibility of advancing the g-pawn (...g4).

5 d4 g4 6 ♗xf4

The move then recommended by theory was 6 ♗c4, and after 6...gxf3, 7 0-0 with attacking chances. The text-move was F.J. Perez's idea.

6...gxf3

No indecision. This is why the World Champion advanced his g-pawn.

7 ♗c4 fxg2? *(D)*

It was imperative for Black to develop his pieces (e.g., 7...♗g7 or 7...f2+, disturbing the white king first). After 7...fxg2? Black is lost. This pawn has moved four times out of Black's seven moves so far, and this is the main cause of his defeat.

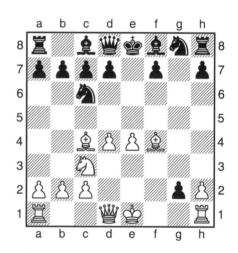

8 ♗xf7+!

A brilliant and crushing sacrifice by the Spanish master.

8...♔xf7 9 ♕h5+ ♔g7

9...♔e7? allows 10 ♘d5+ ♔e6 11 ♕f5#.

10 ♖g1 ♘ge7 11 ♗h6+ ♔g8 12 ♖xg2+ 1-0

Black resigned as 12...♘g6 would allow mate by 13 ♖xg6+ hxg6 14 ♕xg6+ ♗g7 15 ♕xg7#.

In the following game White's advantage in development and the weakness of Black's back rank allowed a spectacular finish.

Bonch-Osmolovsky – Baranov
Moscow 1953
Petroff Defence

1 e4 e5 2 ♘f3 ♘f6 3 d4 exd4 4 e5 ♘e4 5
♕xd4 d5 6 exd6 ♘xd6 7 ♗d3 ♕e7+ 8 ♗e3
♘f5

An ambitious idea, but also a little risky since this knight has moved four times already. 8...♗f5 is safer.

9 ♗xf5 ♗xf5 10 ♘c3 *(D)*

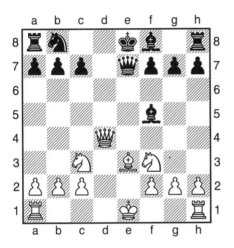

10...♕b4?

On the 7th move the black queen obstructed the f8-bishop and now tries drastically to solve this problem, but White will prove that the move is a mistake. 10...♘c6 is necessary.

11 ♕e5+ ♗e6 12 0-0-0 ♘c6 13 ♕xc7 ♖c8
14 ♕f4

White has no objection to a queen exchange as he has an extra pawn.

14...♕a5

The black pieces (the queen, rook, knight and e6-bishop) are in threatening positions against White's castled position.

15 ♕g5

A fresh exchange proposal.

15...♕a6 16 ♖he1

White's development has been completed. In contrast, Black still has to develop his f8-bishop and his king remains in the centre.

16...♘b4

Creating some threats against the white king.

17 ♘d4! ♖xc3? *(D)*

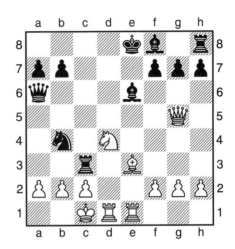

At first sight this seems very dangerous, as it destroys the protection of the white king. Calculating a little, the sacrifice seems good enough for a draw, i.e. 18 bxc3? ♘xa2+ 19 ♔d2 ♘xc3! 20 ♔xc3 ♕c4+ with perpetual check. The problem is that the white position is already too strong and Black's rook move has weakened his back rank. In fact, there is now a winning combination for White.

18 ♕d8+!!

A **decoy** sacrifice to enable a decisive **double check** (combinative motifs that we shall study in Chapter 7).

18...♔xd8 19 ♘xe6++ ♔e7

The other possibilities were no better for Black: 19...♔c8 20 ♖d8# or 19...♔e8 20 ♘xg7+! ♗xg7 21 ♗g5+ and 22 ♖d8#.

20 ♗g5+ f6 21 ♘d8+! 1-0

The check on the e-file can only be blocked by rook and queen, which would be captured in succession. Mate cannot be prevented.

Contacts Between Pieces

We already know that when a piece is placed on a square attacked by an enemy piece, the latter can capture the former. If both pieces are of the same kind, they attack each other. The everyday task of the chess-player is made up of the relationships and contacts between pieces and, similar to what happens in everyday life, some are attracted and some repelled. The pieces of one side are all in the same boat. They have a common destination; they are a team. To survive, they have to destroy the hostile forces. It's not quite *Mad Max*-style warfare on the highway, but there is no doubt that a war has been declared.

We have already talked about the mobilization of the pieces and how useful it is to place them in good locations. We have also studied how to execute the basic mates, i.e. you know how to mate if ever you have an extra rook on a board from which all the other pieces have disappeared. It's not usual, however, for the advantages in a game to be quite so big, unless you or your opponent fall into an opening trap or commit blunders at an important moment.

The game is traditionally divided into three stages: **opening**, **middlegame** and **endgame**.

We have to give credit to Capablanca (World Champion 1921-7 and one of the great legends of our game), when he said that the endgame is the stage that most deserves to be studied. But Capablanca was most probably referring to, as he perceived it, the excessive study of opening theory by some of his contemporaries. On the other hand, and as a very sensible friend once said to me: "What use would it be to become an artist of the endgame if I lose in the opening or the middlegame?"

The problems that you will meet continually in the opening and the middlegame should be solved by means of a thorough examination of the relationships between the pieces: Should I attack this or that enemy piece? How should I protect my attacked piece? Should I exchange my piece for the opponent's, or not? Who comes off best in the position resulting from this series of exchanges?, etc.

These problems are of two kinds: **strategic** and **tactical**. The immediate contacts between pieces are tactical. We shall leave the first strategic ideas to the next chapter. In this one we shall concentrate on the immediate or tactical contacts between pieces.

When one piece is attacked, there are five ways of responding to the attack:
- Move the piece away from the attack
- Defend the piece with another
- When the attack is linear (i.e. not from a knight), interpose or block the line of attack

- Counterattack against another piece of the same or greater worth
- Create a more important threat, e.g. a threat of mate

We now shall consider some concrete positions.

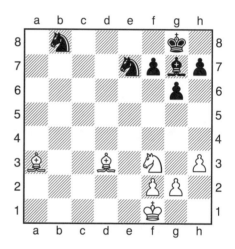

Both sides have equal material (three minor pieces and three pawns each). The a3-bishop is attacking the e7-knight. The knight can avoid the attack by moving, for instance, to c6 or d5. But it can also be defended by the other knight (...♘bc6), or by the bishop (...♗f6, ...♗f8), or even by the king (...♔f8), although this last move is not advisable. However, Black cannot counter this attack with an equivalent one, as there is nothing that he can attack in the white camp, nor can he create a more significant threat.

In the following diagram, White is attacking the b7-knight. This threat can be answered in several ways:

1) moving the knight (for example, by ...♘c5 or ...♘d6);

2) defending the knight with the rook (...♖b8 or ...♖h7);

3) with ...♘e5, which creates a superior threat. Let's imagine that the game goes this way:

1...♘e5 2 ♗xb7??

White doesn't see the check on c4.

2...♘c4+ 3 ♔f4 ♘xa3

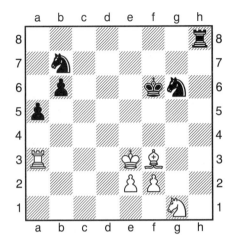

White has captured a knight and Black a rook, which means a material difference of two points in favour of Black.

Exchanges

We have mentioned the word **exchange**, as used in everyday chess parlance. An exchange, self-explanatory as the term is, is the capture of a piece of equal value (knight for knight, knight for bishop, rook for rook, queen for queen, etc.)

Nevertheless, the exchange operation is extremely delicate and should be considered carefully. When talking about the material values of the pieces, we said earlier that they are **relative**, and that their real value depends on the position. The position always dictates the real or effective values of the pieces.

In the following two diagrams you can see clearly how the value of a knight and bishop can vary.

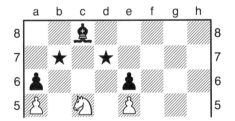

The bishop is blocked by its own pawns and cannot move, since the white knight controls the b7- and d7-squares. In this case, the knight is far superior to the bishop.

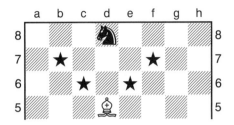

Here, however, it's completely the other way round: the black knight is paralysed by the white bishop, which controls all the squares the knight could theoretically move to (b7, c6, e6 and f7). On the other hand, here the bishop controls thirteen squares and is greatly superior to the knight.

In the four positions that follow, we can see examples of pieces that have an optimal value, given their respective positions on the board.

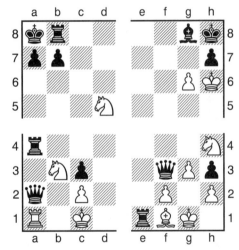

In the top left, it is obvious that if, in order to get the move in this position, White had to sacrifice his queen, then that sacrifice was fully justified, as now White can mate with 1 ♘c7#.

In the top right, White might have sacrificed any amount of material here as well, since his next move is 1 g7#.

In the bottom left the black queen can be given up in exchange for rook and knight to force mate: 1...♕xa1+! 2 ♘xa1 ♖xa1#.

In the bottom right, a **decoy** sacrifice (a theme we shall study in Chapter 7) grants maximum value to the rook: 1...♕h1+! 2 ♔xh1 ♖xf1#.

Pawn Endgames

Since the pawn is one of the elements that create the greatest imbalances in the game, given its ability to transform itself into a piece, the study of basic pawn endgames is essential, in order to know how to exploit a favourable position or how to defend in an unfavourable one.

As we know, a pawn that reaches the far side of the board must be converted into any piece of its own colour, whether such a piece is still on the board or not. Thus, in theory one side may acquire nine queens (the initial one, plus eight pawn promotions), although in practice that is almost impossible. Nevertheless, it is not unknown for four or even five queens to participate in the fight.

King + Pawn vs King

This is, naturally, the simplest endgame, as it contains the minimal possible forces in play: a pawn, just one point on the material scale, and of course the unavoidable presence of kings.

Let's study some typical positions. Assuming that both kings are close by, the main question is whether the attacker's king is placed in front of or behind the pawn.

The next position is drawn, irrespective of whether it is White or Black to move:

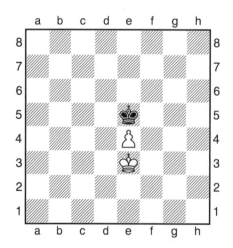

White to move: 1 ♔f3 (if 1 ♔d3, then still 1...♔e6) 1...♔e6! 2 ♔f4 ♔f6! 3 e5+ ♔e6 4 ♔e4

♔e7! 5 ♔f5 ♔f7! 6 e6+ ♔e7 7 ♔e5 ♔e8! 8 ♔f6 ♔f8! 9 e7+ ♔e8 10 ♔e6 with a draw by stalemate.

Black to move: 1...♔e6! 2 ♔d4 (2 ♔f4 ♔f6! reaches the same position as in the White-to-move analysis) 2...♔d6! 3 e5+ ♔e6 4 ♔e4 and we have transposed to the previous variation. Draw.

Black's defensive mechanism is based on a geometric motif known as **opposition**. This arises when both kings face each other in a straight line (on a file, rank or diagonal), with an odd number of squares between them. In that situation, we say that the king whose turn it is **not** to move has the opposition.

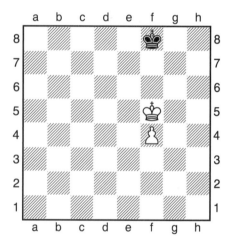

Here the result depends on which side is to move. If it's White to move, then he wins by gaining the opposition: 1 ♔f6! ♔e8 (or 1...♔g8 2 ♔e7 and the pawn advances) 2 ♔g7, and Black cannot prevent the pawn's triumphal march, as the white king controls the key squares f6, f7 and f8.

If it's Black to move, the result, on the contrary, is a draw. The defensive key is again seizing the opposition: 1...♔f7! 2 ♔e5 (if 2 ♔g5, then 2...♔g7, always staying in opposition) 2...♔e7! 3 f5 ♔f7! (but not 3...♔e8? due to 4 ♔e6, nor 3...♔f8? 4 ♔f6, when White wins) 4 f6 ♔f8! (now the black king can move to f8, as the f6-square is occupied by the pawn) 5 ♔e6 ♔e8! 6 f7+ ♔f8, and the pawn cannot promote.

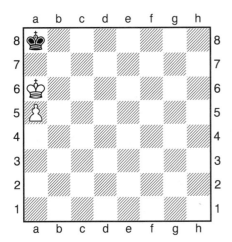

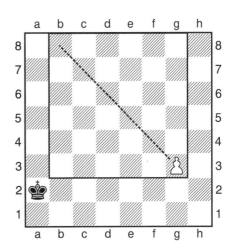

This position is drawn, since the white king cannot gain control of the promotion square (a8), because of stalemate. The logical course of the play should be (with White to move): 1 ♔b6 ♔b8 2 a6 ♔a8 3 a7 stalemate. If it's Black to move: 1...♔b8 2 ♔b6 (in this case, the opposition is not useful, as the decisive factor is the stalemate motif) 2...♔a8 3 a6 ♔b8 4 a7+ and, on the next move, it's stalemate.

This means that when the pawn is situated on one of the edge files (a- or h-), the game is drawn if the defender's king can control the promotion square.

The Rule of the Square

We are now going to study a rule that is very simple, but it is the most important guideline in endgames where a king has to fight against a passed pawn.

It is called the **rule of the square** and it allows us to know at a glance whether a king can catch an enemy pawn that is racing towards the promotion square. To make use of this rule we need to draw an imaginary square. Mentally draw a diagonal from the pawn to the eighth rank. Now imagine a square that encloses the pawn, the queening square and the diagonal. Let's look at it graphically, since it is far easier to see it than to describe it.

In the following diagram, when Black is to move it's a draw, since with 1...♔b3 his king enters the square b3-b8-g8-g3. For instance: 2 g4 ♔c4 3 g5 ♔d5 4 g6 ♔e6 5 g7 ♔f7. Draw.

The king, as you can see, made its way diagonally, avoiding losing any time.

However, if it is White to move, he wins as after 1 g4 the black king cannot enter in the new square c4-c8-g8-g4.

For the rule to apply, the king mustn't be obstructed (e.g., by the white king); the rule of the square assumes that the king will be able to take the shortest route to intercept the pawn. This brings us to a difficulty in this kind of endgame.

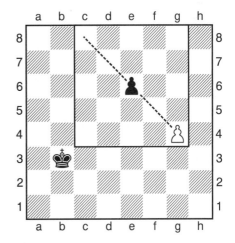

In positions like the above diagram, the problem is that, whereas the king can enter the square of the g-pawn, it is not in time to stop the white pawn. The reason is that there is an obstacle in the way: the e6-pawn forces the king to go round it, losing a tempo, which means that to get to f7 Black needs five tempi, instead of four and, consequently he cannot prevent the white pawn from queening.

Thus after 1...♔c4 (entering the square c4-c8-g8-g4) 2 g5 ♔d5 3 g6 ♔d6 4 g7, the pawn is unstoppable, because of the e6-pawn.

Another feature to take into account is when the pawn is on its original square and can advance two squares in one move, as in the next diagram.

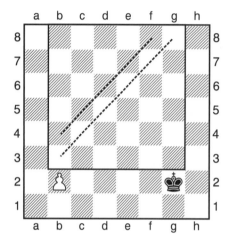

In this case the square must be drawn from the square in front of the pawn (b3 instead of b2). Black's king can force a draw if it is him to move, as he is able to enter the square b3-b8-g8-g3, but he loses if it is White to move, as he is not in time to enter the square b4-b8-f8-f4.

This rule may seem unnecessary when the king and the pawn are close to each other, since in such a case the calculation of precise moves is easy ('I go there, he goes there...'). But when they are widely separated it is very useful, since it allows you to tell at a glance whether the king will be in time to stop the pawn. (It's equally useful, in fact, to the defender and to the attacker.)

Tactical Promotion Manoeuvre

There is a characteristic position, with three united pawns per side facing each other, separated by one rank. The 'attacking' pawns are situated on their fifth rank and the defending pawns on their second rank. The pawns on the fifth rank, to move, can force an immediate promotion, by an almost magical procedure.

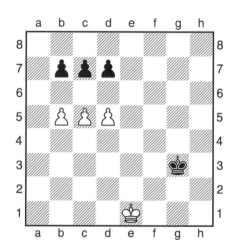

In this position White wins playing 1 c6! (this advance seems harmless, as the normal sequence would be 1...bxc6 2 dxc6 or 1...dxc6 2 bxc6 bxc6 3 dxc6, with the two survivors blocked) 1...bxc6 2 d6! cxd6 3 b6, and nothing can prevent this pawn from reaching the queening square. In the event of 1...dxc6, the answer is the symmetrical manoeuvre 2 b6! cxb6 3 d6. Naturally, this manoeuvre only works if neither king can intervene in the fight.

If it is Black's turn to move, he can neutralize the threat by playing 1...c6! (only this one; as an exercise you may try to work out why 1...b6? and 1...d6? lose).

Mate with Two Bishops

The mate with two bishops, plus the help of the king, is quite easy. The method consists of the bishops, moving on adjacent diagonals, progressively restricting the space of the defender's king, and at the same time, the attacker's king approaches, to collaborate in the pursuit of the defender's king. The stages of this endgame are: first, confinement of the defender's king to one quarter of the board, followed by driving him to the rim, where he will finally be mated in one of the corners.

The following position, with the defender's king centralized and the attacker's in a corner, is one of the least favourable for the attacker. We shall start the winning process by approaching the king:

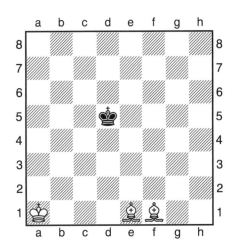

1 ♔b2 ♚e4 2 ♔c3 ♚d5 3 ♗g2+ ♚e5 4 ♗g3+ ♚f5 5 ♔d4 ♚e6

Now the black king is practically confined to one quarter of the board.

6 ♗h3+ ♚e7 7 ♗c7 (D)

Creating a barrier to stop the black king reaching d8. This is a cycle of domination which we shall see again in this endgame.

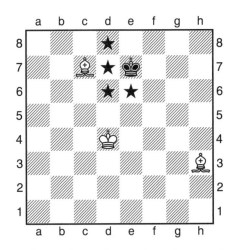

7...♚f6 8 ♗d8+ ♚f7 9 ♗d7 ♚g6 10 ♚e5 ♚h5 11 ♚f5 ♚h6 12 ♚f6 ♚h5 13 ♚f7

Thus reaching the ideal position for the attacking king. In this mate, the attacker's king needs to reach the squares f7 or g6, if the corner is h8; b6 or c7 if it's a8; b3 or c2 if it's a1, and f2 or g3 if it's h1.

13...♚h6 14 ♗g4

Again the domination method. Now the black king is cut off from h5.

14...♚h7 15 ♗g5 ♚h8

The king is now in the corner. Now White must lose a tempo (by making a waiting move), but be careful: not 16 ♗f5??, with a draw by stalemate.

16 ♗h3 ♚h7 17 ♗f5+ ♚h8 18 ♗f6# (D)

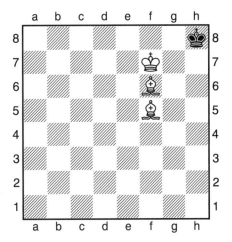

The Powers of the Pieces

Although in the first chapter we described the moves of the different pieces, now we'll consider the optimal power of each of them, including the pawn.

The Pawn

The pawn is one of the most magical pieces in chess. Philidor, considered the first theorist, said "pawns are the soul of chess". Why the soul? In a battle (and I beg your pardon for referring so much to the art of war) when one of the sides is lost, it can only have two hopes: that a miracle occurs or that reinforcements arrive. Miracles are rare and the reinforcements almost never arrive. In chess, however, when a pawn reaches its final destination, it gets promoted and its side will have a new queen or any other piece.

The pawn is not only essential for its ability to transform itself into a piece. It is also important in the protection of the king, since the protective barrier of pawns is the key to its security.

And finally, the pawn is also vital in the opening itself, when it is the first piece to establish contact with the opponent's forces in the fight for the centre.

The pawn contains, therefore, the key to success in many cases and, as the struggle approaches the endgame, the pawn grows in strength, precisely because its possibilities of promotion are greater. Let's look at some cases in which its strength comes to light.

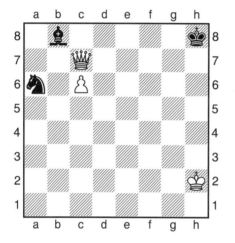

Appearances can be deceptive, as the position is winning for White thanks to his pawn: 1 ♕xb8+! ♞xb8 2 c7, and the pawn becomes a new queen.

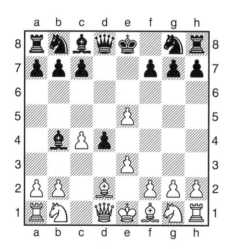

This position is a variation of the Albin Counter-Gambit (after 1 d4 d5 2 c4 e5 3 dxe5

d4 4 e3? ♗b4+ 5 ♗d2). White made a mistake on his 4th move, as now Black plays 5...dxe3, which forces the answer 6 fxe3, with a damaged pawn-structure. In the event of 6 ♗xb4? Black would play 6...exf2+ 7 ♔e2 (7 ♔xf2 ♕xd1) 7...fxg1♞+!. The pawn has done a tremendous job! It has reached the far side of the board on only the 7th move! If it were to become a queen (7...fxg1♕?), White could exchange with 8 ♕xd8+ and afterwards take the new queen. But after the promotion to a knight, White is lost, since if the knight is captured (8 ♖xg1), 8...♗g4+ follows, winning the queen (a tactical motif known as a **skewer**), while if 8 ♔e1, Black plays 8...♕h4+, with a decisive advantage.

The next game features an opening trap that illustrates well the dynamism of an 'uncontrolled' pawn.

Schuster – Carls
Bremen 1914
Caro-Kann Defence

1 e4 c6 2 d4 d5 3 ♞c3 dxe4 4 ♞xe4 ♞f6 5 ♞g3?! (D)

A dubious move. It's not losing, but it's not the best option for White, who should play 5 ♞xf6+.

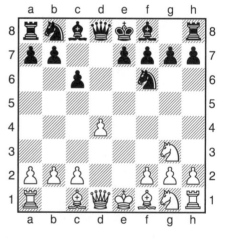

5...h5 6 ♗g5?! h4 7 ♗xf6?? hxg3!

The key to the idea: the h-pawn becomes a monster.

8 ♗e5

With this move White hopes to deal with the threats on the h2-square.

8...♖xh2! 9 ♖xh2

Expecting, naturally, 9...gxh2 10 ♗xh2, but...

9...♕a5+! 10 c3 *(D)*

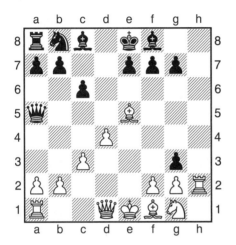

10...♕xe5+!! 11 dxe5 gxh2

Now the clumsiness of the knight in the fight with the pawn is decisive, since White cannot prevent the promotion of the pawn and thus the loss of the game.

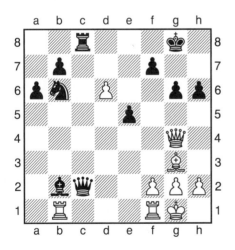

Engels – Maroczy
Dresden 1936

White took advantage of strength of his **passed pawn**:

1 ♖xb2! ♕xb2 2 ♕xc8+! ♘xc8 3 d7 1-0

We saw this theme in the first diagram of this section.

Some authors have called mate by the pawn the **disgraceful mate**, and mate by the pawn in the opening the 'most disgraceful mate'. Let's see an example of this kind of mate, as a kind of joke, since Black, of course, cooperated too much. It happened in a simultaneous display.

Pytel – NN
Romans (simul.) 1982
Two Knights Defence

1 e4 e5 2 ♘f3 ♘c6 3 ♗c4 ♘f6 4 d4 exd4

So far, the play is quite standard.

5 e5 ♕e7?

Artificial and compromising. The best move is 5...d5, counterattacking against the white bishop.

6 0-0 *(D)*

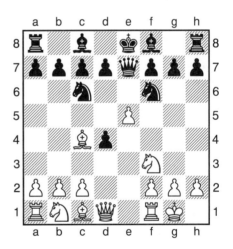

6...♘g8?

6...♘xe5 is strongly met by 7 ♘xe5 ♕xe5 8 ♖e1 ♘e4 9 f4! ♕e7 10 ♘d2 f5 11 ♘xe4 fxe4 12 ♕xd4, but Black should have risked 6...♘g4. Now White holds all the trump-cards.

7 ♗g5 f6? 8 exf6 ♕c5

White threatened the black queen not only by a direct attack, but also with 9 ♖e1, but which is the more valuable in chess: the queen or the king? The game, in any case, was already lost.

9 f7# (1-0) *(D)*

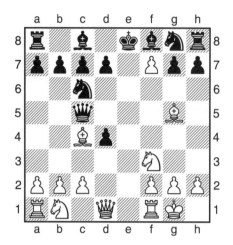

The 'Disgraceful Mate'!

In the following four positions you can see various patterns of pawn mates, in which the pawn is supported by the king or another pawn. This mate is only possible with the cooperation of the opponent's pieces, blocking escape-squares for the king.

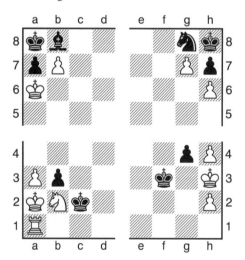

The Knight

We have seen that the knight can only attack eight squares at best and its way of moving prevents it from travelling quickly from one area of the board to another. On the other hand, its peculiar move, jumping over pieces, allows it to create threats on two or more squares which

have no apparent connection, thus converting the knight into a dangerous piece and a real nightmare for beginners.

One of its trump cards is its ability to attack two (or more) pieces at the same time (known as a **fork**), which gives rise to a number of combinations, a theme which we shall study in Chapter 7.

In the positions that follow, we have four mating patterns involving the knight, alone or with the help of the king. In all cases we can see that in order to mate, the knight needs the unwilling cooperation of the opponent's forces, blocking the escape of their own king.

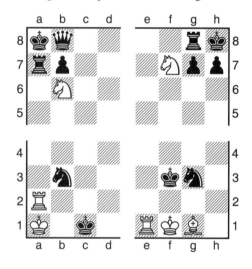

In the following game, the Peruvian master Esteban Canal exploits the power of a knight, although in order to execute its mortal leap the collaboration of the bishop was needed.

NN – Canal
Barcelona (simul.) 1935
Alapin Opening

1 e4 e5 2 ♘e2 d5 3 exd5 ♕xd5 4 ♘bc3 ♕a5 5 d4 ♘c6 6 d5 ♘b4 7 ♗d2?

White should have played 7 ♘g3.

7...♗f5!

Attacking the poorly-defended pawn on c2.

8 ♖c1? ♗xc2!

Destroying the defence of d3.

9 ♖xc2 ♘d3# (0-1) *(D)*

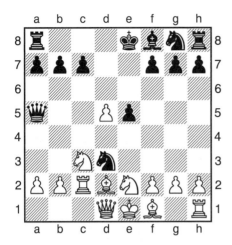

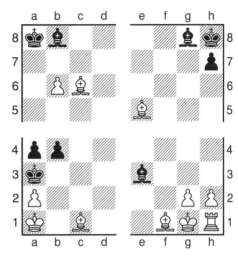

In no other position is the knight's strength so obvious as in **Lucena's Mate**, a manoeuvre also known as **Philidor's Legacy**, and ending (like the previous example) with *smothered mate*.

These four positions show typical mating patterns with the bishop. As you see, in all cases the opponent's pieces are blocking the escape of the defender's king.

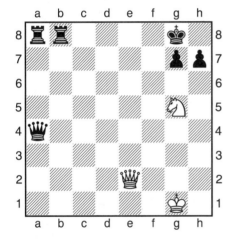

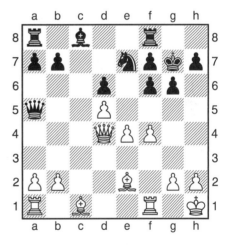

White mates with **1 ♕e6+ ♔h8** (if 1...♔f8, 2 ♕f7#) **2 ♘f7+ ♔g8 3 ♘h6++** (double check) **3...♔h8 4 ♕g8+!** (forcing the occupation by the rook of the g8-square) **4...♖xg8 5 ♘f7#**. Spectacular!

The Bishop

The bishop can display its full powers on open diagonals and, with the help of the king or the 'self-blockade' of enemy pieces it can achieve some outstanding checkmates.

Vanka – Skala
Prague 1960

White won with:
1 b4! ♕d8

If the black queen retreats to any other safe square the same thing will happen.

2 ♕xf6+! ♔xf6

If Black declines the queen sacrifice and retreats with 2...♔g8 or 2...♔h6, then 3 ♗b2 would follow, with unavoidable mate threats.

3 ♗b2# (1-0)

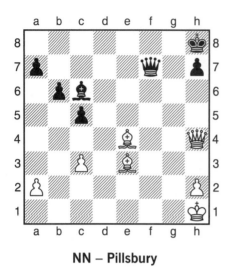

NN – Pillsbury
USA (simul.) 1899?

White must have been happy with an extra piece, but the great Pillsbury knew how to exploit the strength of his bishop. The continuation was:

1...♕f1+ 2 ♗g1

The check on f1 was necessary to force this self-blocking move.

2...♕f3+! 3 ♗xf3 ♗xf3#

This is sometimes known as an **X-ray mate**, a motif which will be studied in the chapter on combinations.

The Rook

With its powerful play in straight lines, the rook can control ranks and files. It's like a cannon, with great fire-power. In the endgame it is especially fearsome, as it can create a number of mating threats, in collaboration with other pieces, or even pawns.

In the next eight positions you can see different mating patterns involving the rook. In the first four, the rook alone delivers mate, although with the help of some self-blocking on the part of the opponent's pieces. In the remaining four the rook uses the help of a friendly pawn.

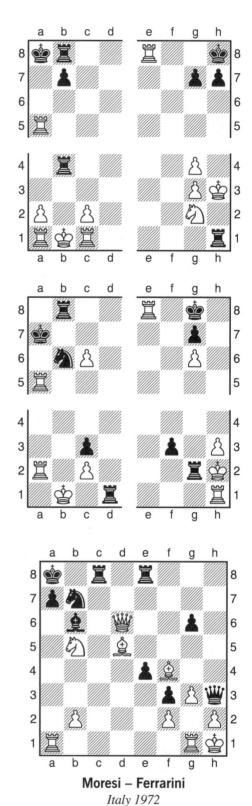

Moresi – Ferrarini
Italy 1972

Black played 1...♗xf2? and lost. However, he could have won easily with **1...♕xh2+! 2 ♔xh2 ♖h8+ 3 ♗h6 ♖xh6#**, using a mating pattern that we already know.

The Queen

We all know that the queen is the strongest piece in chess. Can you remember its range? No fewer than 27 squares from a central position! Thanks to its great mobility, it can create many threats. For this reason, a nearby queen can be quite dangerous for the opponent's king. The fact that it is the only piece capable of moving along ranks, files and diagonals leaves no doubt about its great importance in chess.

In the following eight positions you can see various mating patterns using the queen. The first four are queen mates without the help of any pieces except the ones that are blocking in their own king. The first two are characteristic of the mate known as **epaulettes**, as the shape is reminiscent of the shoulder decorations of the military dress uniform. As can be seen, the blocking pieces (rooks on a8 and c8 in the top left; h7- and h5-pawns in the top right) are useless for the defence, but quite useful for the attacking side!

In the last four positions, the queen mates with the help of a pawn, in some cases supporting it directly, and in others cutting off the possible escape-squares.

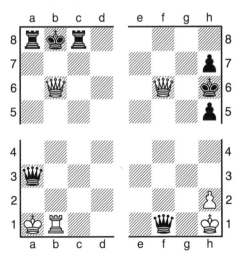

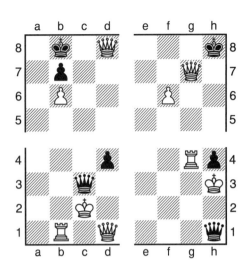

Let's now look at four cases in which the queen displays its full powers, producing mates reflected in the above patterns.

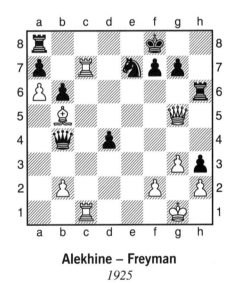

Alekhine – Freyman
1925

White detected a back-rank weakness, even though the c8-square is controlled by two black pieces at present. The game ended as follows:

1 ♖c8+! ♖xc8 2 ♖xc8+ ♘xc8 3 ♕d8#

In reality, White's three major pieces were all attacking the back rank and the queen could finally penetrate, once Black's knight was **deflected** (see the chapter on combinations).

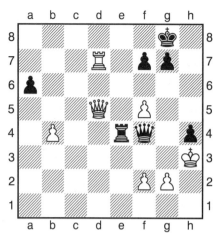

Tarjan – Karpov
Skopje 1976

Retaining the visual images of the mating patterns can make things easier when we find ourselves in positions such as this, in which a simple but elegant move put an end to the fight:

1...♖e3+! 0-1

White had to resign in view of 2 fxe3 (or 2 f3) 2...♕g3#.

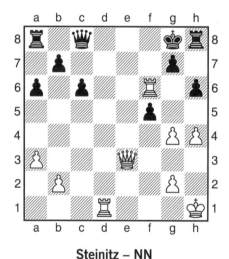

Steinitz – NN
1861

In this classic position the key to the combination is **deflecting** the black queen from the e6-square, so that its white counterpart can deliver an **epaulettes mate**.

1 ♖d8+!
Very elegant.
1...♕xd8 2 ♕e6+ ♔h7 3 ♖xh6+!!
This essential follow-up had to be foreseen.
3...gxh6 4 ♕f7#

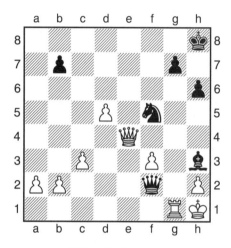

NN – Anderssen
1872

Here is another classic position in which, from the point of view of material, White has the advantage (9+5+6=20 vs 9+3+3+3=18). However, the position is loaded with dynamite, and a master as brilliant as Anderssen could not fail to discover an impressive mate.

1...♗g2+!!
Wasn't this square protected?
2 ♖xg2 ♕f1+ 3 ♖g1 ♘g3+!
and this one?
4 hxg3 ♕h3#

Questions

46) What are the moves that constitute the Ruy Lopez?

47) What are the moves that constitute the Giuoco Piano?

48) What are the moves that constitute the King's Gambit?

49) Is it advisable to set opening traps? Why?

50) What are the three stages of the game called?

51) What do we call the rule that allows us to calculate whether a king can reach a pawn before it arrives at the promotion square?

52) Can a pawn be promoted to a queen if there is still a queen of the same colour on the board?

53) Can a pawn be promoted into an enemy piece?

54) What do we call the situation in which both kings are facing each other with an odd number of squares between them?

55) In a ♔+♙ vs ♚ ending, can a black pawn on the a-file be promoted if the white king is on a1?

56) Position: w♔f6, ♙f7; b♚f8; Black to move. What should be the result?

57) In which corner of the board can two bishops force checkmate, with the help of the king?

58) A bishop attacks an enemy rook. Is it forced to capture it?

59) The black queen is attacked by a rook, which is protected by a pawn. Is the only defence to move the queen away from this attack? What other possibilities are there?

60) Black can capture a white rook, but in exchange would lose a knight and three pawns. Which side comes off best from this exchange?

Exercises

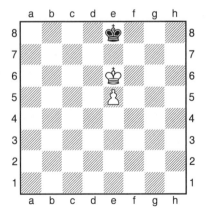

61) What should be the result of this endgame if: a) White is to move; b) Black is to move?

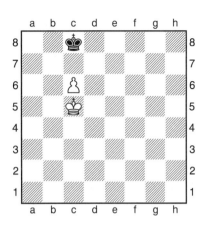

62) What should be the result: a) if it's White to move; b) if it's Black to move?

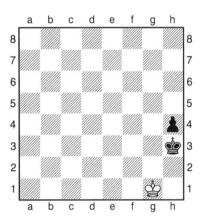

63) Can the black pawn be promoted?

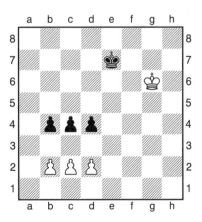

64) Is there a winning method for Black? What is it?

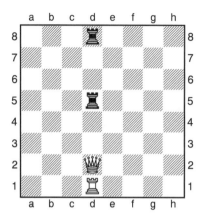

65) Should White capture the d5-rook? What is your calculation?

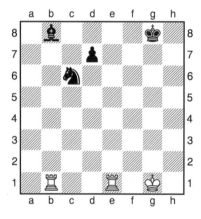

66) Should the b1-rook capture the bishop? Why?

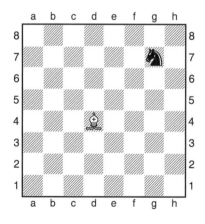

67) What is the most logical move for the knight, which is being attacked by the bishop?

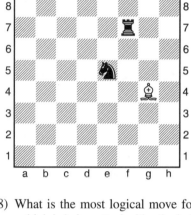

68) What is the most logical move for the bishop, which is being attacked by the knight?

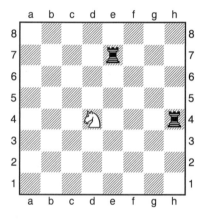

69) What is the best move for the knight?

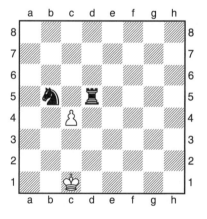

70) What move is the best for Black, considering that his two pieces are attacked by the c4-pawn?

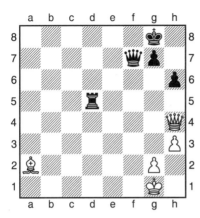

71) Can Black save his rook? How?

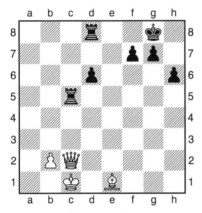

72) The black rook on c5 is threatening the white queen, which cannot leave the c-file. Is there a way to avoid the loss of the queen?

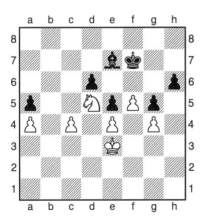

73) This position is about the relative scope of the pieces, i.e. their respective mobility. White can exchange his knight for the opponent's bishop. Should he do it? Explain.

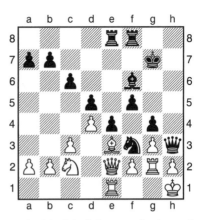

74) The black knight can win the exchange (taking the e1-rook). Is this best? Explain.

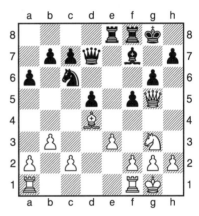

75) The c6-knight can be exchanged for the d4-bishop. Is this swap useful for Black? Why?

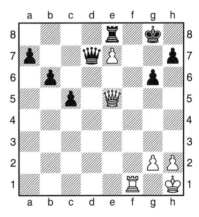

76) White has a very strong pawn on the seventh rank. Black's major pieces have it duly blockaded. Do you see a way to promote the pawn?

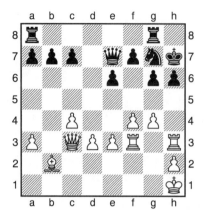

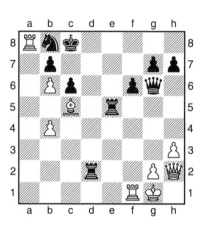

77) The queen and bishop on the long a1-h8 diagonal should attract your attention here. Also the fact that the black king is placed in the same file as White's h3-rook. Can you see a way to force mate?

79) Here the b6-pawn plays a significant role, but it is not easy to see how White can finish off the game. If you can see it, then you win the two points for this exercise.

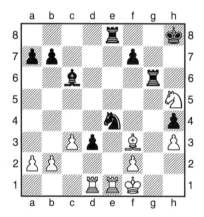

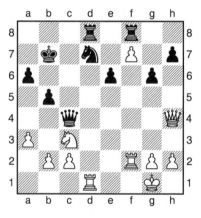

78) Erik Lundin, Black in this position, won the Swedish Championship several times. Here he will show us how to exploit the more active position of his pieces. How can Black win?

80) The f7-pawn is the key factor in the position. However, it is blocked and all the black pieces control the promotion square (f8). Can White promote his pawn? How?

Further Tips

You should play **Open Games** with your club-mates.

It is useful to practise exchanges of pieces on the board, i.e. setting up positions and establishing contacts among the pieces.

Practise the mate with two bishops until you can execute it in an almost mechanical way.

Practise pawn endgames (with only one or two pawns each side) and try to master the 'opposition'.

Revise basic technical concepts, such as why two bishops theoretically are superior to two knights, and whether a rook's pawn can promote if the opponent's king controls the promotion square.

Examine positions in which the minor pieces might be superior to the rooks. Try to use your own judgement.

5 Strategy and Tactics

You now know the rules and moves of the pieces and the basic ideas about the opening moves and the centre. Now you can start playing. Play a lot! Chess is a game, so you need to play it! And enjoy doing it! Only practice can make you familiar with the typical positions and manoeuvres and equip you with the skills necessary to take part in competitions.

With this book you will have a head start. You cannot jump straight into competitions, knowing nothing about the theory and technique of chess. This information is essential. Once you have absorbed the information, you can develop your own ideas and explore the richness that chess can offer you. You can never have too much enthusiasm. Play and play again. But never underestimate technical knowledge, as without this, even if you were the most intelligent person in the world, you would need many years to learn what can be learnt with a good book in three months.

You should study, yes, but try to spend at least twice as much time on practical play as on study. It's an offer that you can't refuse: for each hour of study, I recommend you to spend at least two hours playing!

Strategy

The general theory of chess is divided into two disciplines: **strategy** and **tactics**.

Strategy is the deep layer of the game. It concerns **what** to do, leaving to tactics the question of **how** to do it.

Strategy is the art or science of evaluating the features of the position and consequently making **plans** for playing the game.

Planning is essential to our game. Every position that you meet on the board needs to be handled according to a plan, from the simplest to the most complex. The most complex could well be the initial position, which mankind has been trying to decipher for many centuries. The simplest could be, for instance, a position in which you can mate on the next move. In that case, the plan should be not failing to mate!

A plan is a project of play and, as with all projects, it is composed of several stages. The difficult thing about playing chess lies in the fact that you don't play on your own, so to succeed with your plan you need to overcome your opponent's resistance, which can sometimes be very stubborn!

To make a plan we need to take some decisions: Should we improve the situation of our pieces? Should we attack the opponent's king? Should we strengthen our king's defences? Should we try to exchange pieces, to weaken the opponent's threats?

Once the relevant decision or decisions are taken, tactics will take charge of translating this into actual moves on the board.

A plan is not necessarily linear; even if we formulate an ideal plan, this does not mean that it should be executed in all its points. Our plan will come into conflict with our opponent's plan, which might then oblige us to rethink ours, or supplement it with further planning. These are matters that you will learn little by little as you deepen your understanding of the difficulties that may arise in every concrete game.

In the following section I shall briefly describe the fundamentals of chess strategy, a deeper study of which should be left to a higher level in your chess training.

Strategic Elements

Although we shall not enter into a deep strategic discussion here, I ought to provide you with some essential ideas about the technique of the game, since these will also be useful for understanding the language of chess.

The main strategic ideas are related to the following factors:

• King safety
• Material advantage
• Positional advantage
• Pawn-structure

Let's now examine these essential concepts.

King Safety

This is absolutely fundamental. We have already encountered this factor and we shall come back to it again, later in the book. The fact that checkmate puts an end to the game makes chess essentially different from most other games of strategy. If one side's king is checkmated, any material or positional advantages that side may have accumulated will be of no use at all. Thus the factor of king safety underpins the whole strategy of the game, and we must consider it before all else.

Attack, Defence and Counterattack

In the Romantic period of chess, the focus of the game was an attack on the opponent's king. It was a fight to the death. The American master Frank Marshall (champion of the USA on many occasions) explained his chess style precisely in boxing terms: "I am like Jack Dempsey: looking for the K.O. from the first round." Maybe Marshall was the last Romantic in chess.

Afterwards, by natural evolution, getting at the opponent's king became harder and, on the other hand, the players became wary of risking everything on a dubious attack. Nowadays attacks are usually well prepared, and are not always directed against the king, but can also be positionally motivated, directed against weak points in the opponent's camp.

Material Advantage

Direct attacks against the king or positional attacks do not always achieve their objectives but can still be partially successful. The attack might reach a dead end, but nevertheless the attacking side might have obtained some material advantage, an extra pawn for instance.

Or maybe the defence is so well conducted that the defender is the one left with a material advantage. In such cases the game enters in a new stage, generally the endgame, in which the **attacker** (the side with the advantage) will try to impose his material advantage.

Positional Advantage

Chess is a game in which we look for material advantage, the maximum possible material advantage, with the aim of destroying the opponent's resistance, giving superiority to our forces. But as we have already said, material is not everything. If the position contains features that allow a decisive attack on the king, the defender's material advantage will be of absolutely no use.

It may also happen (and this is the most usual case between players of similar strength) that neither side has a material advantage, but one of them has its pieces better placed, and this is another kind of advantage: a positional advantage. The deployment of the pieces is very important, since a clear positional superiority almost always leads to a material advantage.

Pawn-Structure

Weak Point

A square that cannot be protected by a pawn is considered a **weak point** or a **weakness**. When such a square is occupied by a pawn, then this is a **weak pawn**.

In the top diagram overleaf we have an example: the d6-square cannot be protected by a pawn, and so it's a weak point in Black's camp.

In the lower diagram the white pawn on d3 is a weak pawn.

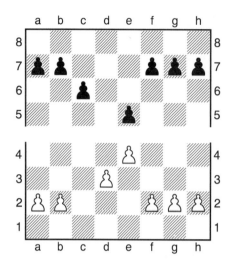

Pawn-Chain

When one side's pawns are arranged diagonally in such a way that they defend each other, this is called a **pawn-chain**.

The last pawn (link) is called the **base** pawn, as all the others in the chain depend on this one. A great theorist of the game, Aron Nimzowitsch, maintained that a pawn-chain should normally be attacked at its base, since if this pawn falls, then all the rest of the chain is weakened.

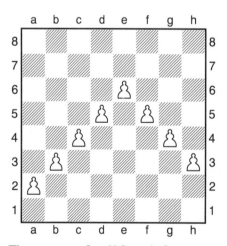

The pawns on a2 and h3 are the **base** pawns.

Doubled Pawn

A pawn is doubled when there is another one of the same colour on the same file. Doubled

pawns are generally not weak in themselves, but they lack mobility and can prove ineffective in an endgame since they may not be able to generate a passed pawn.

When doubled pawns are also isolated, then they tend to be a severe weakness.

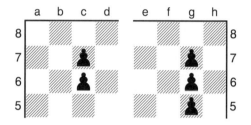

On the left-hand side we have an example of doubled isolated pawns on the c-file. On the right, the black pawns are tripled and isolated on the g-file, an even more important strategic weakness.

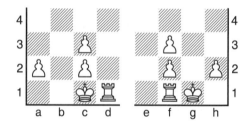

Here you can see doubled isolated pawns in front of the king, castled on the queenside and kingside respectively. This constitutes a serious weakening of the king's position, as it creates vulnerable squares near the king which can be occupied by enemy pieces (for example, a3 in the left-hand diagram and h3 in the right-hand one).

Isolated Pawn-Couple and Hanging Pawns

An isolated pawn-couple is an 'island' of two pawns, connected together but separated from the rest of their side's pawns, with no enemy pawns facing them along their files. The c3- and d4-pawns in the next diagram are an isolated pawn-couple.

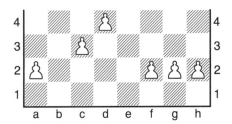

If White advances his pawn to c4, then they would be called 'hanging pawns'. Then the pawns would be more exposed to attack, but also pose more of a threat to the opponent.

Isolated Queen's Pawn (IQP)

This is self-explanatory. It's a d-pawn (i.e. the queen's pawn) that has become separated from the rest. This situation is of great strategic interest, as it may constitute a weakness (as an object of attack), but its particular situation in the centre can also give it a special dynamism, so the IQP is a topic worthy of study in manuals of strategy. If you are wondering why this particular one has been more intensively studied than other types of isolated pawn, then it is because it naturally arises from a wide variety of popular opening lines.

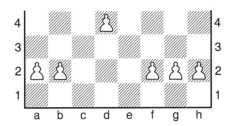

The d4-pawn constitutes an isolated queen's pawn.

Passed Pawn

A **passed pawn** is a pawn with no opposing pawns in front of it, nor on an adjacent file, controlling squares that the pawn needs to cross to be able to advance safely. It cannot be expressed better than with a graphical example.

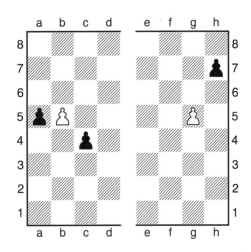

On the left, the b5-pawn is passed because, although there are black pawns on the adjacent files, these have already been left behind and, consequently, the white b-pawn has no obstacles in its way. However, on the right, the g5-pawn is not passed, since there is the black pawn on h7 that controls the g6-square.

The passed pawn is a fearsome weapon and, together with the attack on the king, it is one of the factors that most frequently decide the outcome of the battle. Accordingly, it's very important to take full advantage of it (for the side possessing the passed pawn) or to restrain its advance (for the side fighting against it).

Blockading the Passed Pawn

Blockading a passed pawn means physically preventing its advance. For the defender, merely controlling the square(s) ahead of the passed pawn may not be enough: sometimes it must be completely immobilized.

On the left-hand side of the diagram overleaf, the c6-pawn cannot safely advance, because two black pieces control the c7-square. Nevertheless, particular factors in any given position might still allow that advance at the right time. Even though the c7-square is controlled twice, the c-pawn is not blockaded and this pawn might become a strong weapon, thanks to its latent dynamism.

On the right side, the black pawn is perfectly blockaded and by the best **blockading piece**:

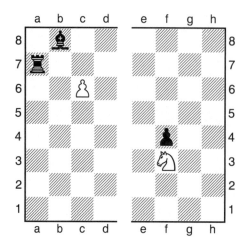

the knight. Why? If we blockade the pawn with a major piece (queen or rook), this piece might be attacked by minor pieces, forcing it to retreat and freeing the pawn to advance. For this reason, the minor pieces (bishop and knight) are the best blockaders, as they can't be attacked by opposing pieces of lesser value, so instead of having to retreat, the blockader can be defended by another piece.

Pawn-Majority on One Flank

This is a strategic factor whose importance grows as the game approaches the endgame.

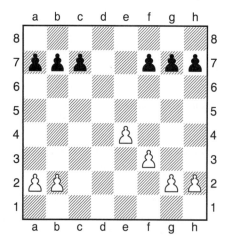

We can see that Black has three pawns on each flank, whereas White has two pawns on the queenside and four on the kingside. Thus, Black has a majority on the queenside and White on the kingside.

Which majority is better? This depends on many factors in the position and is subtly linked to the location of the kings. If a pawn-majority can become well-advanced in the middlegame, while the enemy king is far away on the other wing, then this majority could become a fearsome weapon in the endgame. On the other hand, in the middlegame, a majority may be useful in an attack, or it might provide excellent shelter for its king while the pieces carry out other tasks (such as attacking the enemy king that has less pawn-cover). Furthermore, there is a type of middlegame plan known as the minority attack, in which a minority is advanced against a majority with the aim of creating weaknesses within it.

Tactics

We already said a few words about this chess discipline. **Tactics** is the interplay between the pieces. Tactics cannot exist without strategy. Even if you use your pieces skilfully, this will not suffice if you cannot create adequate targets, if you don't know what plan to adopt.

By this very reasoning, strategy cannot do without tactics either. Making a perfect plan, with well-established aims, might not be enough if we don't know how to execute it with the precise moves that the plan requires.

Although it seems logical to start by learning the secrets of strategy, since a plan takes precedence over the concrete moves that form part of it, nevertheless most authors assert that studying tactics should come before studying strategy, as the elements of the game (the manoeuvres of the pieces) are tactical in nature, and it is necessary to acquire skill in playing the pieces before delving deeply into the secrets of strategy.

Let's start then with the study of tactics. Firstly, we should define the concept of a **manoeuvre**.

Manoeuvres

A series of moves with a common aim is a manoeuvre or tactical sequence, something like a skirmish within a battle. A plan may contain several different manoeuvres. Short-term plans, such as the ones you will try to execute successfully, are, as we have already said, of a tactical nature: Can I win that piece? Can I save my attacked piece? Can I win material thanks to this or that move? Can I attack the king?

Before exploring the topic of planning, I consider it best to become better acquainted with the strength and scope of the pieces. To build upon the study initiated in the previous chapter, we shall now examine how two pieces can operate together in **tandem**.

Tandems

Now we shall deal with the capacity of pieces acting as two-man tactical teams, as well as examining the different mating patterns they can achieve by working together. We shall call these two-man teams **tandems**.

We shall study the following tandems:
- Queen + Rook
- Queen + Bishop
- Queen + Knight
- Rook + Rook
- Rook + Bishop
- Rook + Knight
- Bishop + Bishop
- Bishop + Knight
- Knight + Knight

Queen + Rook

The combined strength of queen and rook gives rise to a tremendous team, since both are, as we know, major pieces, and have a similar effect to the artillery pieces in real war. In our war game though, unlike real artillery, they can also operate over a short distance, which makes them more fearsome still.

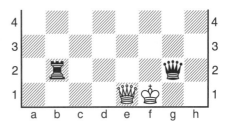

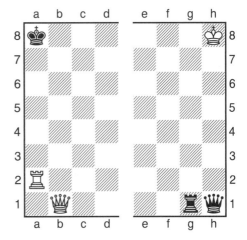

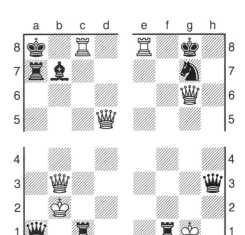

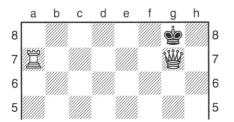

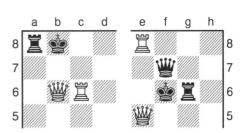

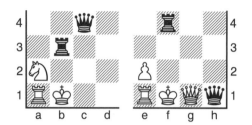

The diagrams above show a variety of mating patterns involving this terrifying duo.

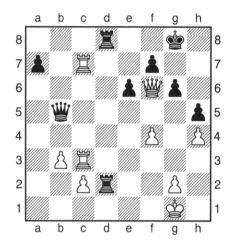

Lisitsyn – Bastrikov
USSR 1955

Here we shall see how Black's tandem of ♛+♜ executes a perfect attacking manoeuvre, ending in mate, following the sacrifice of one of his rooks:

1...♜xg2+! 2 ♔xg2 ♛e2+ *(D)*

3 ♔g3
3 ♔g1 allows 3...♜d1#.
3...♛g4+ 4 ♔f2 ♜d2+ 0-1
In the event of 5 ♔f1, Black plays 5...♛d1#, while if 5 ♔e3, 5...♛e2#.

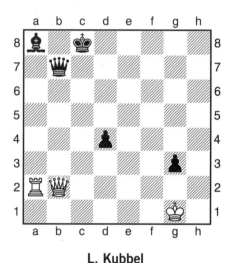

L. Kubbel
150 Endspielstudien, 1925

Despite being the exchange (rook for minor piece) up, White is apparently in a difficult situation, due to the fearsome black queen and bishop, lined up menacingly on the long diagonal, and the two black pawns. However, White has an effective manoeuvre that enhances the cooperation of his tandem of major pieces:
1 ♛c2+ ♔d8
Or 1...♔d7? 2 ♛a4+, winning the bishop, or 1...♔b8? 2 ♜b2.
2 ♛h7!!
A very beautiful move: the white queen defends against the mate on h1, keeps control of the b1-square and threatens 3 ♜xa8+; there is only one mystery: why not take it?
2...♛xh7 3 ♜xa8+
Now after the king moves, White plays 4 ♜a7+ and 5 ♜xh7. Splendid! Note that this is a 'study' (a composed position).

Queen + Bishop

The team of ♛+♝ can control a number of diagonals and, sometimes, the combined strength

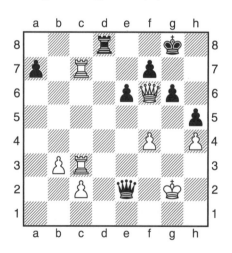

of the queen on ranks or files together with the bishop posted on a diagonal can create havoc in a direct attack on the enemy king.

The following diagrams show some mating patterns with this tandem.

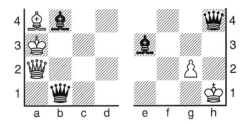

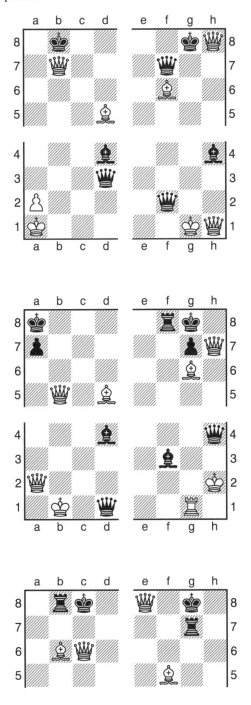

In the following typical position we can see perfect cooperation between queen and bishop, in their attack on the black king, whose defences have been weakened by the absence of the g-pawn.

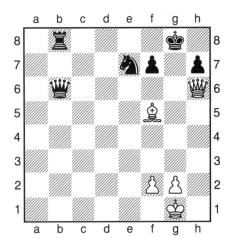

White wins with:
1 ♗xh7+ ♔h8 *(D)*

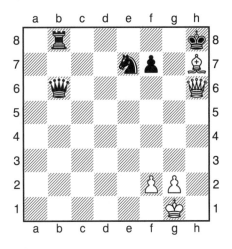

2 ♗g6+

The bishop must be played to this square and to no other, because:

a) the white queen is attacked; and

b) White needs the bishop to attack the f7-square.

2...♔g8 3 ♕h7+ ♔f8 4 ♕xf7#

The student should note that all the black king's moves are forced.

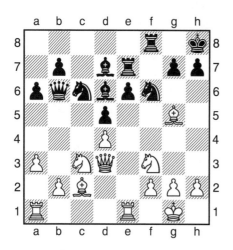

Trebula – Nemergut
Slovakian Team Ch 2012/13

White's queen and bishop are lined up against the h7-square. The decisive sequence is:

1 ♗xf6 gxf6 *(D)*

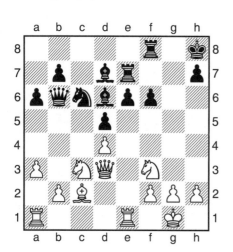

A forced move, to keep the h7-point protected by the e7-rook.

2 ♘xd5!

White wins. The main point is 2...exd5 3 ♖xe7.

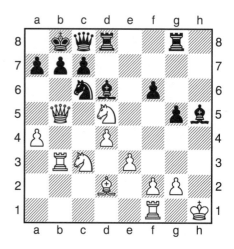

Manov – Khairabedian
1962

This position is more difficult. White exerts strong pressure along the b-file and has a wonderful knight on d5, but his own castled position is seriously weakened (the lack of the h-pawn leaves the h-file open) and there are no pieces protecting his king. Black found a winning sequence, key to which is to sacrifice no fewer than three pieces!

1...♗e2!

To clear the h-file. Black can also play his moves in reverse order, i.e. 1...♖h8!, with a deadly discovered check to follow, and meeting 2 ♔g1 with 2...♖h2+ 3 ♔xh2 ♗f3+! 4 ♔g1 ♖h1+! 5 ♔xh1 ♕h3+ 6 ♔g1 ♕xg2#.

2 ♘xe2

2 ♕xe2 does not change anything.

2...♖h8+ 3 ♔g1 ♖h1+! 4 ♔xh1 ♖h8+ 5 ♔g1 ♖h1+!

These successive sacrifices of the black rooks were necessary to clear the back rank and the h-file for the queen, which now comes into play decisively to force mate.

6 ♔xh1 ♕h8+ 7 ♔g1 ♕h2#

Now you can see the coordination between queen and bishop that you were expecting! The d6-bishop was not a mere spectator!

Queen + Knight

The peculiarity of the knight's move combined with the power of the queen make the combined action of these two pieces very effective. This tandem can create a number of mating possibilities and the experts consider the duo ♕+♘ mildly superior to ♕+♗. In the following diagrams you can see some standard mating patterns.

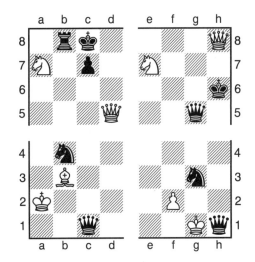

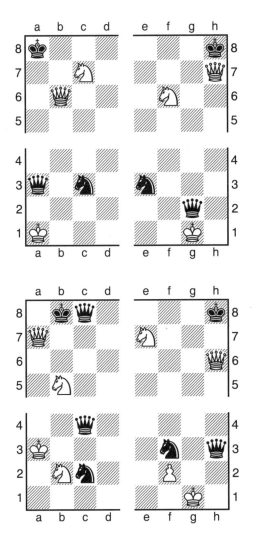

If there is one spectacular finish, it has to be **Lucena's Mate** (also known as **Philidor's Legacy**), executed by the knight, thanks to the magnanimous sacrifice of the queen, which we have already seen in Chapter 4, and whose final position is the one shown in the next diagram.

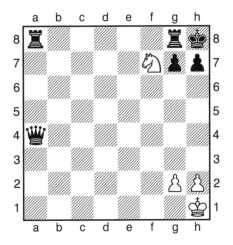

This is an example of a *smothered mate*: a knight checks the enemy king, all of whose potential flight-squares are occupied by 'friendly' pieces.

The following position appears to be won for White, thanks to his f7-pawn, but the three black pieces are very active and their coordination allows an attack on the white king.

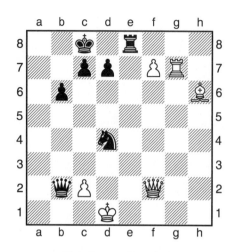

Vatnikov – Borovoi
1957

1...♕b1+ 2 ♗c1 ♖e1+! 0-1

White resigned in view of 3 ♔xe1 ♕xc1# and 3 ♕xe1 ♕xc2#.

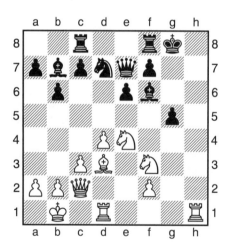

Rater – Belver
1940

Black's castled position is severely weakened and the white pieces are very active, which gave White the idea of a winning combination:

1 ♗a6!

To clear the b1-h7 diagonal and thus make it possible for the queen to invade the black camp.

1...♗xa6

Or 1...♗xe4 2 ♕xe4, with threats to h7 and c8.

2 ♘exg5! ♖fd8

Mate was threatened on h7.

3 ♖h8+!

An excellent rook sacrifice, decoying the king to a fatal square.

1-0

After 3...♔xh8 White mates with 4 ♕h7#.

Rook + Rook

Two rooks acting as a team are very menacing when operating on the same rank or file, in which case they are said to be 'doubled'. **Doubling** rooks is a term that you will see frequently in chess books and magazines, when both rooks are placed on the same file or rank.

The following diagrams show various typical mates with two rooks.

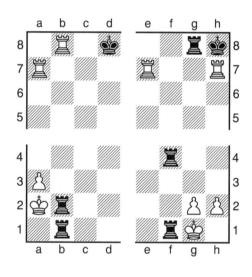

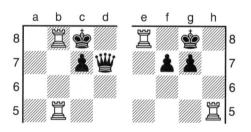

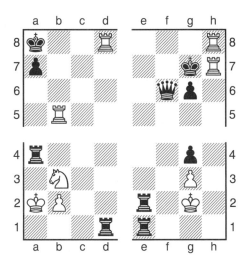

White has just played 1 f5??, attacking the g6-rook, and if it moves to f6, then possibly ♖g2. However, although everything seems under control, Black could have exploited the open lines for his pieces, and won the game on the spot with **1...♕f3+!**. If 2 ♖xf3, Black mates with 2...♖b1+. Note how the black rooks control the b- and g-files, a decisive factor. However, Black missed this golden opportunity and even went on to lose the game.

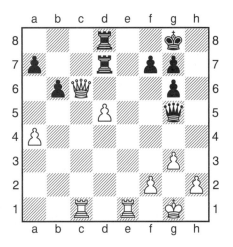

Alekhine – Colle
Paris 1925

Alekhine detected a combination to enable his rooks to work together, exploiting the weakness of Black's back rank:

1 ♕xd7! ♖xd7 2 ♖e8+ ♔h7 3 ♖cc8 *(D)*

Next we shall look at some cases in which you can appreciate the combined strength of the two rooks.

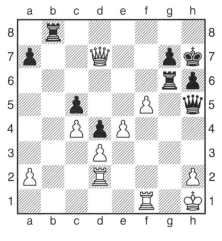

Barcza – Tarnowski
Szczawno Zdroj 1950

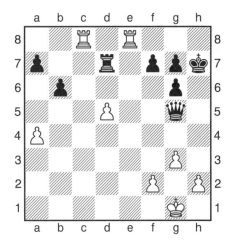

Black cannot avoid mate, except by giving up his queen, since both the g6-pawn and the black queen are blocking the possible escape-squares for the king.

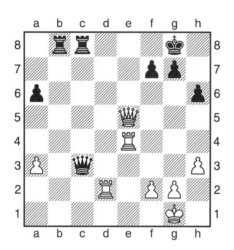

Palatnik – Sveshnikov
Leningrad 1976

White can finish off the fight with a manoeuvre which is rather more difficult than the previous ones, but still relatively straightforward:

1 ♖d8+ ♔h7

The rook cannot be taken, as the black queen would be captured, so Black is forced to move his king.

2 ♕f5+ g6 3 ♕xf7+ ♕g7 (D)

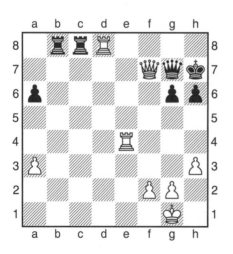

The attack seems to have reached a dead end, since exchanges seem unavoidable, but...

4 ♖e7! (D)

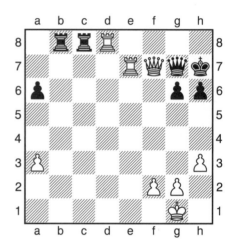

1-0

White forces one of our standard mating patterns.

Rook + Bishop

This is also a fearsome team which, in some aspects, reminds us of the ♕+♗ duo. The combined action of rook and bishop on open lines can trap the enemy king in a mating-net. Here are some mating patterns:

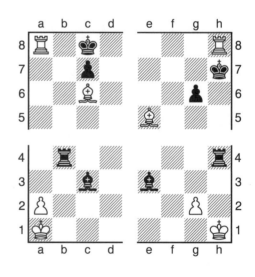

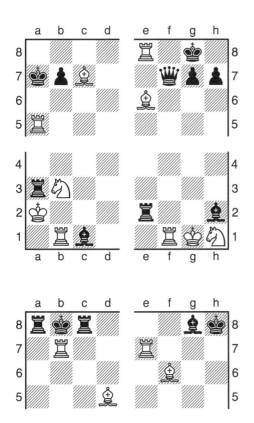

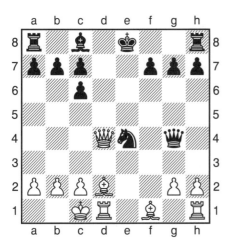

Let's now look at some positions that have arisen in practice:

Maczuski – Von Kolisch
Paris 1864

Black has two extra pawns, but... his king is still in the centre! If it were his move, with 1...0-0 all his problems would be solved and, most probably, his material advantage would be decisive.

But it's White to move:

1 ♕d8+!!

A surprising **decoy** sacrifice, a theme that we shall study in the next chapter.

1...♔xd8 2 ♗g5++!

A double check, which forces the king to move, since it is attacked simultaneously by the d1-rook and the g5-bishop.

2...♔e8 3 ♖d8# (1-0)

Here again you can see a mating pattern shown in an earlier diagram.

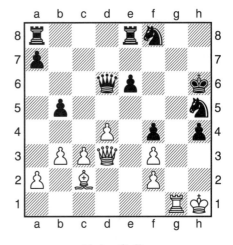

Høi – Gulko
Thessaloniki Olympiad 1988

Here White has a very simple combination, but... you have to be able to see it! Black has two extra pieces but the remaining white ones are very active: the queen, bishop and rook control a lot of squares, and they are all pointing at the black king. All you have to do is appreciate one more detail:

1 ♕h7+! 1-0

This one! With the queen sacrifice the black knight is deflected from the control of the g6-square and, at the same time, occupies h7, depriving the king of this escape-square: 1...♘xh7 2 ♖g6#. It should be mentioned that the more mundane 1 ♖g6+ would also have won comfortably.

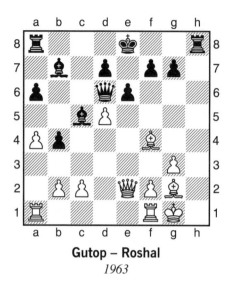

Gutop – Roshal
1963

White is better developed and apparently has some threats. For instance, the retreat 1...♕e7? allows White to build up his central control with 2 ♖fe1 (but note that 2 d6? fails to win the b7-bishop due to 2...♗xg2! 3 dxe7?? ♗d5 with mate on h1 to follow, as in the game). If the queen meekly moves aside with 1...♕b6?, White can play 2 a5 ♕b5 and now 3 ♕e5 or 3 ♕g4, with complications. Or even 3 ♕xb5 axb5 4 dxe6 ♗xg2 5 exf7+ ♔xf7 6 ♔xg2, with the black king exposed in the centre. However, Black plays the surprising **1...♕xd5!**, capturing the white pawn. After **2 ♗xd5 ♗xd5** *(D)*, White has no defence against the mate on h1, as the f2-pawn is **pinned**.

Conclusion: the key factor in this position is the control of the h-file by the h8-rook. Try to memorize this mating pattern.

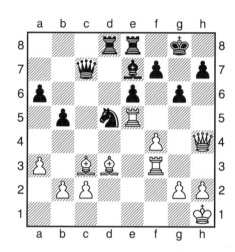

Ravinsky – Petriaev
1962

All the white pieces are very active, but with his last move Black seems to have solved his main problems, as the d5-knight threatens to capture the c3-bishop, which exerts latent pressure on the long a1-h8 diagonal. White, however, is in a position to resolve the struggle in dramatic fashion:

1 ♕xh7+!

A **decoy** sacrifice to draw out the black king.

1...♔xh7 2 ♖h5+ *(D)*

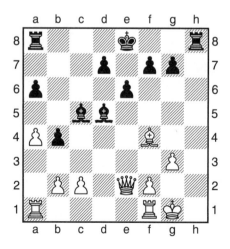

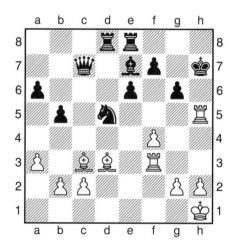

Exploiting the fact that Black's g6-pawn is pinned.

2...♔g8 3 ♖h8#

A similar mate to the previous one and a new display of the power of the ♖+♗ tandem, although with the additional help of the d3-bishop that allowed the pin.

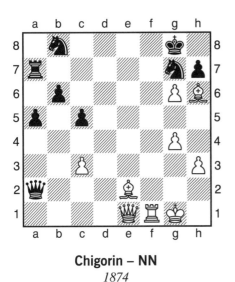

Chigorin – NN
1874

Here White saw a spectacular combination, in which he will sacrifice the queen and a bishop to reach one of the typical mates with ♖+♗.

1 ♗c4+!!

A clearance sacrifice.

1...♖xc4 2 ♕e8+! ♘xe8

The queen's capture opens the h6-f8 diagonal for the white bishop.

3 ♖f8#

Elegant!

Rook + Knight

The combination of the linear, direct force of the rook with the knight's leap gives this team a wide range of possibilities to attack the enemy king, above all when the rook is on the seventh rank. Keep in mind this expression: **rook on the seventh**.

In the following diagrams you can see the most characteristic mates of the ♖+♘ tandem.

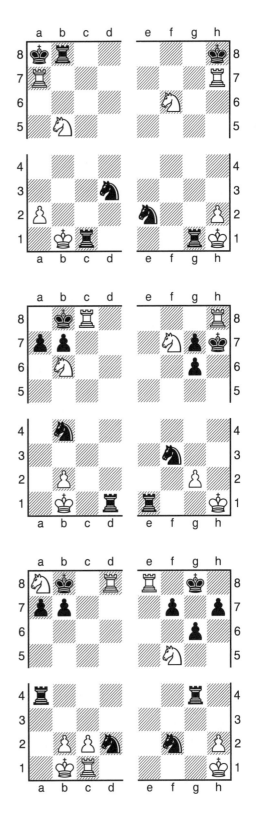

Now we shall look at some explosive positions that illustrate the splendid cooperation of these two pieces.

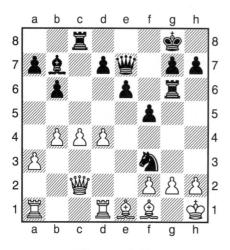

Winter – Colle
Scarborough 1930

White resigned here. Had he tried **1 d5**, then Black could have finished with **1...♕h4!**, exploiting the fact that the knight cannot be taken by 2 gxf3, as 2...♕g5 would follow, when White can't prevent the mate on g1. So **2 h3** is the only move, although it fails to prevent **2...♕xh3+! 3 gxh3 ♖g1#**. This is the **Arabian Mate**, which we have already mentioned.

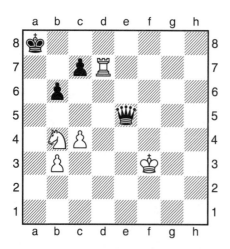

P. Stamma
Essai sur le Jeu des échecs, 1737

Here we see a position composed by the Syrian player Philip Stamma, one of the best masters of the 18th century. It is a good illustration of the fine coordination of rook and knight in some positions.

1 ♖d8+ ♔b7 2 ♖b8+! *(D)*

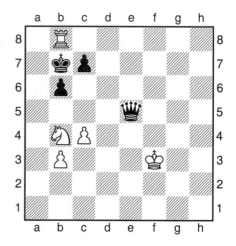

2...♔xb8
2...♔a7 3 ♘c6+ ♔a6 4 ♘xe5 is even worse.
3 ♘c6+
White wins queen for rook, reaching a winning endgame.

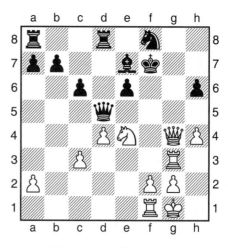

Korchnoi – Petersons
USSR Ch, Kiev 1964/5

White has sacrificed a piece for an attack on the opponent's king, but with his remaining pieces Viktor Korchnoi has more than enough to put an end to the battle:

1 ♕g7+ ♚e8 2 ♕xe7+!! 1-0

Black resigned in view of 2...♚xe7 3 ♖g7+ ♚e8 (the only move, as the d6- and f6-squares are attacked by the white knight) 4 ♘f6#. Optimal coordination by the ♖+♘ tandem.

Now we shall look at a position where everything seems to work as if by 'black magic', although it is White to play and win.

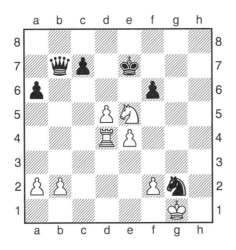

A. Troitzky
Deutsche Schachzeitung, 1910

Yes, rook and knight defeat queen and knight! It's a 'study' (composed position) in which the composer displays all his skill. I don't expect you to solve it, but I would hope that you will enjoy playing (slowly) through the solution. Imagine that you are playing with the white pieces and against your most hated opponent...

1 ♖b4!

The rook is protected indirectly by the knight fork.

1...♕c8

Or: 1...♕xb4 2 ♘c6+; 1...♕a8 2 ♖b8, winning the queen.

2 ♖b8! ♕h3

2...♕xb8 is met by 3 ♘c6+, when again the queen falls.

3 ♖h8! ♘h4

The only move.

4 ♖xh4! ♕c8

The rook is taboo once again.

5 ♖h8! ♕b7 6 ♖b8!

Black finally loses the queen, after returning, after five moves, to its initial position. In the meantime, the rook effected an incredible manoeuvre of **domination**, a round-trip that seems to defy all logic and the laws of physics. Do you get the impression that rook and knight might be good friends?

The Drawing Mechanism with ♖+♘

The ♖+♘ tandem can force a draw by perpetual check if the opponent's king is on an edge, and in positions such as this:

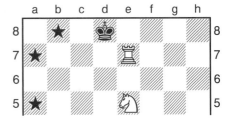

White can force a draw here with **1 ♘c6+ ♚c8 2 ♘a7+ ♚b8 3 ♘c6+ ♚c8** (not, of course, 3...♚a8?? 4 ♖a7#) **4 ♘a7+**, etc.

In the initial position the knight may be on another square, such as b8, a7, a5, b4 or d4; the important thing is that it can move to c6.

Bishop + Bishop

The pair of bishops is a force clearly inferior to the previous tandem. The numeric value gives us a rough idea: rook and knight equals eight points, whereas two bishops are only six. But that doesn't stop them being a mighty pairing, and stronger in most positions than ♗+♘ or ♘+♘.

In the positions that follow you can see the main mating patterns of this team. Let me remind you that when we study these tandems we assume that they don't have the support of any other friendly pieces and just, in some cases, the unwilling cooperation of the enemy pieces, blocking escape-squares for their own king.

In the case of the two bishops, for instance, there are many more mating patterns with the assistance of the king or even just a pawn.

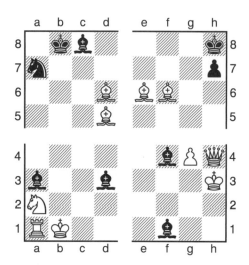

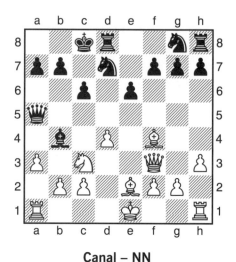

Canal – NN
Budapest (simul.) 1934

It's now time to see some spectacular positions featuring a mate with two bishops. There is a structure connected with queenside castling and with the pawns on a2, b2 and c3 (for White) or a7, b7 and c6 (for Black), where a piece sacrifice on c3 (c6) can give rise to this mate.

You might need to make a more determined effort to discover the mate in this position, as the material to sacrifice is considerably greater. But this example deserves the effort, so think about it for a few minutes. White is to move. Have you seen it? Check your solution with this one:

1 axb4!! ♕xa1+ 2 ♔d2 ♕xh1 *(D)*

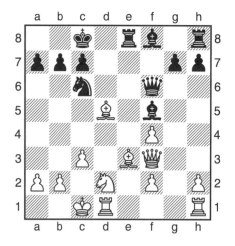

Schulder – Boden
London 1853

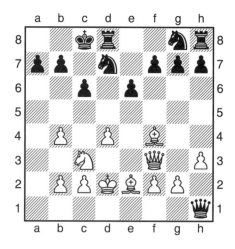

This is one of those cases. Black wins immediately with:

1...♕xc3+! 2 bxc3 ♗a3# (0-1)

Black's bishops control the three vacant squares around the white king, as well as the one on which it is placed.

White has given up both his rooks, but now it's his move again!

3 ♕xc6+! 1-0

3...bxc6 4 ♗a6#.

As you see, the mating pattern is the same as in the previous example and is worth memorizing.

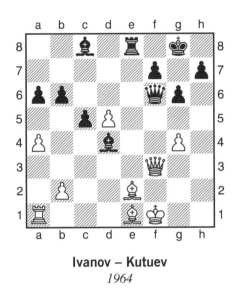

Ivanov – Kutuev
1964

Black has two extra pawns and it's his move. There is still one piece that so far has not moved: the c8-bishop. However, this piece will now become the executioner of the opponent's king. How? Very simple:

1...♗xg4! 2 ♕xf6 ♗h3#

Once more we can see that the bishops control the four critical squares.

Bishop + Knight

These minor pieces can produce some surprising combinations. A player should always be alert to the latent possibilities that may exist in each position, especially when the squares surrounding the king are controlled by one of these pieces, as this can be a trigger for a number of tactical sequences.

In the following diagrams you can see some typical mating patterns. Most of them are possible with the king castled or in a corner.

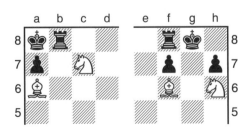

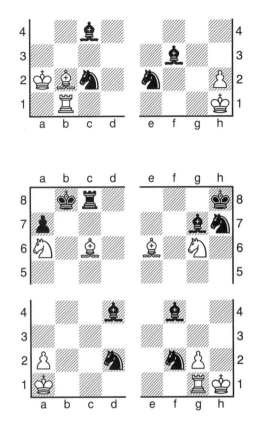

Let's start with a few simple positions that you should now be ready to solve.

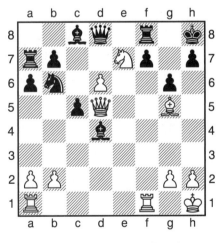

Barkwinkel – Djordjević
1975

In this first diagram we see a very dangerous white knight which has infiltrated to e7, attacking the g8-square. If you consider some of the previous patterns, if the white bishop could reach f6, it would be mate. Is that possible? Yes, and furthermore very easy:

1 ♕xd4+! cxd4 2 ♗f6#

The d4-bishop was the only piece defending against the mate.

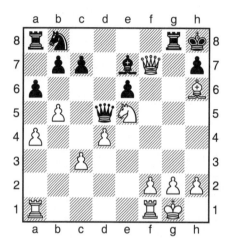

Semenov – Loginov
USSR 1952

This position is not difficult either. But you should be careful because, for instance, capturing the e7-bishop would be a fatal blunder (the black queen threatens mate on g2). Is there any effective continuation? All it needs is to **clear a space**:

1 ♕f6+! ♗xf6 2 ♘f7# *(D)*

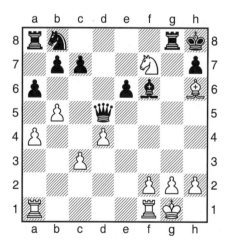

The knight mates on the square vacated by the queen, while the bishop controls the g7-square.

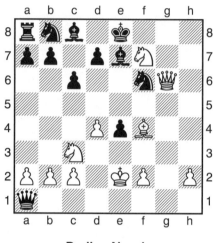

Borik – Novak
Čihak 1969

The finish in this position is quite spectacular. Can you find it? Let's imagine that you have three minutes to solve it. Don't get nervous and... find the mate!

1 ♘d6++! 1-0

Double check, a tactic that we have already met in the section on ♖+♗, but now with ♕+♘. I know that we are studying the ♗+♘ team. Be patient and you will see: 1...♔d8 (the only move) 2 ♕e8+!! (an incredible case; the black knight is decoyed to e8, which takes away the e8-square from the king) 2...♘xe8 3 ♘f7# *(D)*.

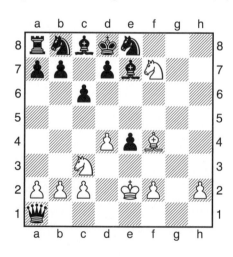

Now the bishop's role is obvious: not as passive as it looks, since it controls the escape-square c7.

It should be mentioned that, while beautiful, this isn't the only way to mate. 1 ♗c7 covers the flight-square d8 and is an efficient path to checkmate.

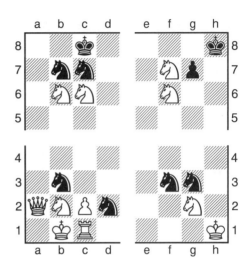

B. Horwitz
The Chess Monthly, 1882

Now let's look at a brilliantly composed study, in which the ♗+♘ team will dominate the opponent's king and queen. Black's king is very 'active', in contrast to the 'hidden' queen. White's minor pieces, on the contrary, occupy dominant positions and are going precisely to exert a relentless domination over the enemy pieces. Solution:

1 h3+ ♚h5
Or 1...♚g5 2 ♗e3+, winning the queen.
2 ♘f6+ ♚g5 3 ♗f8!!
The queen has nowhere to go. If 3...♛xf8, 4 ♘xh7+ wins the queen and the game.

Knight + Knight

This tandem can create strong threats only when operating close to the opponent's king. The combination of two such jumping pieces can sometimes give rise to an unusual finish. The two knights can take good advantage of any self-blocking by the opponent's pieces.

In the diagrams that follow you can see eight mating patterns.

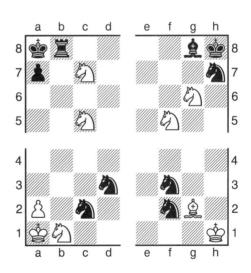

Once again taking some examples from tournament practice, we shall explain some explosive positions in which the pair of knights has a leading role.

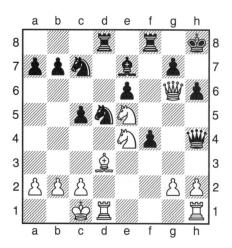

In this first position White ends the game in spectacular fashion with a double check which leaves the two knights controlling all three squares in Black's king's corner.

1 ♕h7+! ♔xh7 2 ♘f6++

Double check by the knight and the bishop.

2...♔h8 3 ♘g6#

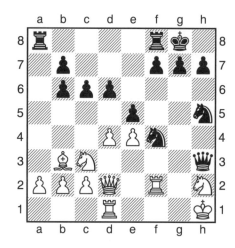

Egenberger – Schumacher
1959

In this position, if you can see an important **deflection**, the problem will be solved. To start with, please observe the active positions of both white knights (the one on f5 cannot be taken, because the e6-pawn is pinned). Besides these details, think about how to exploit the fact that the important f7- and e7-squares

are protected only by Black's king and queen, respectively.

The solution is not so difficult:

1 ♕d2!

A queen sacrifice that cannot be refused.

1...♕xd2 2 ♘e7+

Now the e7-square is no longer defended.

2...♔h8 3 ♘f7#

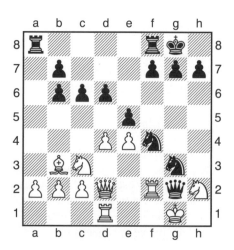

NN – Blackburne
1902

Here we have another case, relatively easy, in which the two knights decide the outcome with the help of the queen, all three pieces being in aggressive posts. Black, the English master Joseph Henry Blackburne, played:

1...♘g3+ 2 ♔g1 ♕g2+! *(D)*

Decoying the rook, with a forced self-blocking of the g2-square.

3 ♖xg2 ♘h3#

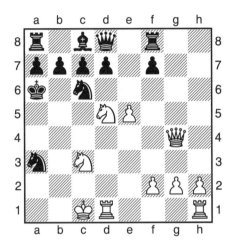

I. Zaitsev – Skotorenko
USSR 1970

This position is absolutely winning for White, given the exposed situation of the black king. But the final combination will allow us to see a curious and attractive mating position. Just as in the previous example, White also makes use of the decoy tactic, forcing one of the black knights to occupy a potential escape-square for the king.

1 ♕a4+ ♘a5 2 ♕b5+! ♘xb5 3 ♘b4+ ♔b6 4 ♘a4# (D)

The final position deserves a new diagram.

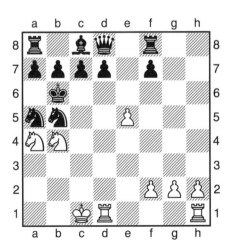

Mate with Bishop and Knight

The mate with bishop and knight is the most difficult of the basic mates, but not as difficult as most amateurs think. It's a matter of understanding and memorizing the mating procedure, for which several methods are possible.

Here we shall use the method based on *Delétang triangles*.

In order to mate, we have to establish good coordination between the attackers' three pieces, driving the defender's king to a corner of the same colour as the bishop, i.e. if the bishop moves on dark squares, then the opponent's king should be pushed to the a1 or h8 corner.

In the next diagram we have a position in which, since the bishop moves on light squares, the black king must be forced to the a8 or h1 corner. In this case, the given position of the pieces suggests it is better to plan the mate on h1.

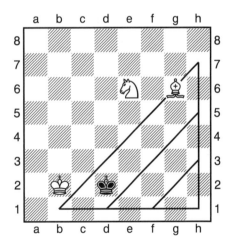

The method consists of progressively restricting the black king, locking him inside three triangles, as described in the above diagram. Thus, the first triangle is defined by the squares b1-h7-h1, the second by d1-h5-h1, and the last one, f1-h3-h1.

As you can see, the bishop is placed in the hypotenuse of the first triangle. Now what you have to do is go on restricting the black king, locking him into the second and third triangles. The attacker's king has to harass his black counterpart. The ideal position for the white pieces is knight on c4 and bishop on c2 in the first triangle and knight on e4 and bishop on e2 in the second one. Let's cut to the chase:

1 ♗c2

The domination of the king, i.e. the campaign to deprive it of squares, is slow and patient. The bishop has taken away the d1-square from the black king and soon the white monarch will be able to collaborate in the manoeuvre to push the enemy king towards the corner.

1...♔e3 2 ♔c1 ♔e2 3 ♗g6 ♔e3 4 ♔d1 ♔f2 5 ♔d2 ♔f3

As you can see, the black king is already very near the corner, but some manoeuvres are still required to lock him inside the last triangle.

6 ♔d3 ♔g4 (D)

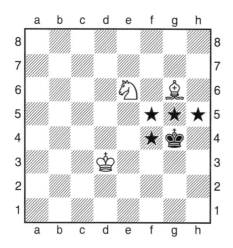

We can see the barrier that bishop and knight create, not allowing the black king to cross the squares f4, f5, g5 and h5. The knight should be deployed on a square of the same colour as the bishop, in order to cover the opposite-coloured squares.

7 ♔e3 ♔h4 8 ♔f4 ♔h3 9 ♗h5

The bishop locks the black king inside the second triangle (d1-h5-h1).

9...♔g2

If 9...♔h4, 10 ♗e2 ♔h3 11 ♘g5+ ♔g2 12 ♘e4, reaches the next diagram position more quickly.

10 ♔e3 ♔g3 11 ♗e2 ♔h4 12 ♔f4 ♔h3 13 ♘g5+ ♔g2 14 ♘e4 (D)

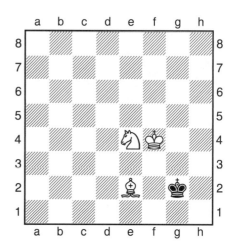

This is the ideal position (knight on e4 and bishop on e2), as now the black king is locked inside the second triangle.

14...♔h3 15 ♔g5 ♔g2 16 ♔g4 ♔h2

If 16...♔g1, 17 ♔g3 ♔h1 18 ♘f2+ ♔g1 19 ♘h3+ ♔h1 20 ♗f3#.

17 ♗f1

Locking the king inside the third triangle (f1-h3-h1).

17...♔g1 18 ♗h3 ♔h2 19 ♘c3 ♔g1 20 ♔g3 ♔h1

Now everything is ready for the mate.

21 ♗g2+ ♔g1 22 ♘e2# (D)

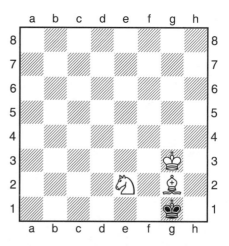

The reader should practise this mate which, as you may have seen, is not so much difficult as long and laborious. It should be achievable in less than thirty moves, even if the initial position is unfavourable. A few inaccuracies might not matter, but you should take into account the **50-move rule**, that stipulates that if fifty moves have been played without a capture or a pawn move, then either player can claim a draw.

Questions

61) What is strategy?

62) What is a plan?

63) Is a mating attack the only kind of attack?

64) How would you define counterattack?

65) Which is the most important strategic factor in chess?

66) What is meant by tactics?

67) What is a manoeuvre?

68) What is a passed pawn?

69) What is meant by a pawn-chain?

70) What is a weak point or a weakness?

71) What is the only weak point in a pawn-chain?

72) What is a doubled pawn?

73) Which is the best blockading piece?

74) What is meant by a tandem?

75) In which corner of the board is mate by bishop and knight carried out?

Exercises

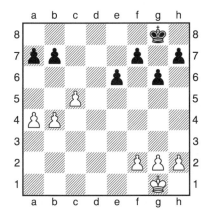

81) Which side has a positional advantage here?

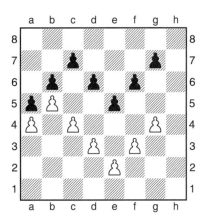

82) Which are the weak points of the two pawn-chains?

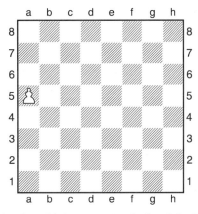

83) On which square (excluding b6, a7 and a6) could a black pawn be placed, to prevent White's pawn from being a passed pawn?

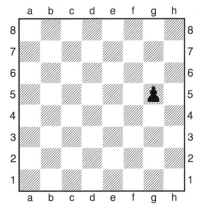

84) On which squares (excluding f4, h4, g2 and g3) could a white pawn be placed to prevent Black's pawn from being a passed pawn?

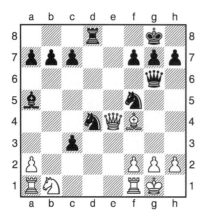

85) Black found a truly magical move that forced immediate resignation. What was it?

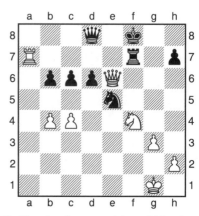

88) The dominant position of his pieces allows White to win material. How?

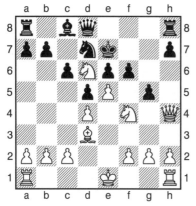

86) Black has just made a blunder with the advance of his g-pawn and now White can finish off the game. How?

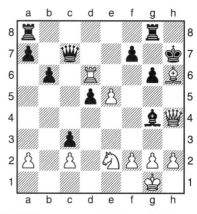

89) White to move. This is an ideal position for the ♖+♗ tandem to show what they can do. What would you play?

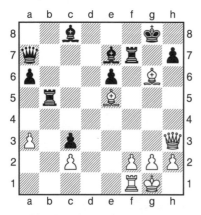

87) White has just captured the g6-pawn, since 1...hxg6?? isn't possible owing to the mate on h8. But a surprise awaited him. What would you play as Black here?

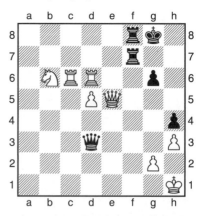

90) The doubled white rooks on the sixth rank are a serious threat against Black's king, but they won't have time to act. How can Black bring the game to an end?

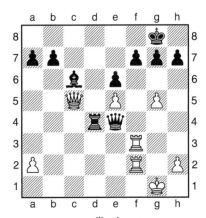

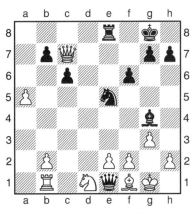

91) The lined-up ♕+♗ and the open lines around White's king position seem to give Black the advantage, but... It's White to move! Find the solution; it's easier than you might think.

94) White has a theoretical advantage in material but a serious positional disadvantage, and his position is now ready to collapse like a house of cards. What do you suggest for Black?

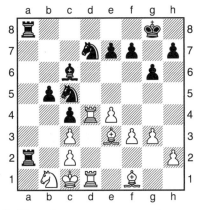

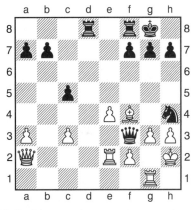

92) The c4-pawn exerts annoying pressure on the white position, but it's not easy see how to penetrate. Can you find the way? Black to move.

95) In this game between two grandmasters, Black found the winning move, and you can do the same if you concentrate on the position.

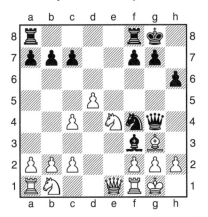

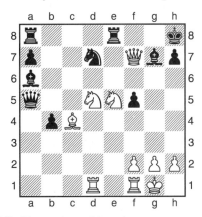

93) Another wave of the magic wand; Black finishes elegantly. How?

96) The active white pieces are menacing the black king. What would you do as White?

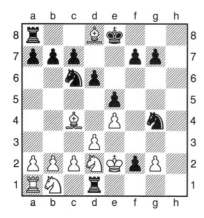

97) Here the position is winning for Black, whose pieces are most threatening. Analyse the position and find the winning sequence.

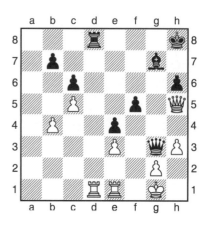

99) One move only is all it takes to win. But you need to put two and two together. Black to move.

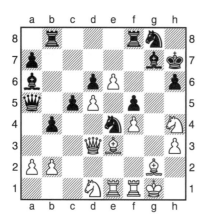

98) White's position is more harmonious and he also has a protected passed pawn on e6. However, with his last move Black seems to be winning the exchange. How would you solve White's problems?

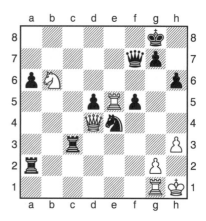

100) Notice the activity of both black rooks and the e4-knight. The only problem for Black seems to be the d5-pawn, but what if he ignores it? Calculate precisely a winning sequence. It's Black to move.

Further Tips

Revise the basic strategic principles and try to gain a thorough grasp of the concepts of **king safety**, **pawn-structure** and **material** and **positional advantage**.

Study carefully the different kinds of pawns. Place some positions on the board with material equality but with passed pawns, and play these positions out with a friend.

Practise blockading passed pawns.

Try to understand why doubled isolated pawns are a serious (and double) weakness.

Practise the mates involving 'tandems', memorizing the corresponding mating patterns.

Practise the bishop and knight mate until you can execute it with relative ease. (But you shouldn't become obsessed with this, as you won't meet this endgame every day.)

And, last but not least... play, play and play again!

6 Endgame Play and Further Openings

Endgames are treated exhaustively in specialist manuals such as *Fundamental Chess Endings*, and here we shall only outline some general recommendations, as well as studying a few basic endgames and useful manoeuvres.

Minor-Piece Endings

In the endgame, besides material, i.e. the respective forces, an important factor is the pawn-structure, since this can influence the activity of the pieces. For instance: if most of the pawns remain on the board, the position is usually blocked and, in such a case, if one of the sides has a knight and the other a bishop, the knight will usually be superior to the bishop, given its ability to jump over the pawn-barriers. The bishop, to the contrary, will be superior on a half-empty board, as the absence of pawns will allow the bishop to move easily around the board. Another factor that favours the knight is that it can attack (and defend) squares of both colours, whereas the bishop can only move to squares of the same colour. If we place our pawns on squares of the same colour as our bishop, it can surely protect all of them, as long as we stay alert to developments in the game, but then those very pawns will create a barrier which will considerably reduce the bishop's scope. Hence the experts say that we should place the pawns on squares of the opposite colour to our bishop. On the other hand, the knight moves slowly and its transfer to the other flank will require some time.

Endgames with *opposite-coloured* bishops, i.e. where each side's remaining bishop moves on squares of a different colour, are very hard, precisely because one of them controls (or may control) the 32 light squares and the other the 32 dark ones. This means that the attacker (with one or two extra pawns) will have great difficulty in winning if the opponent can set up a blockade on 'his' squares. Often the defender is able to draw, even two pawns down.

In endgames of bishop vs bishop or knight vs knight, if one of the sides has a material advantage, the logical and simple technique should be to exchange pieces to force a win in the pawn endgame. The defender, on the contrary, should try to keep pieces on, and extract the maximum possible activity from his piece.

Generally speaking, the fewer pawns that remain on the board, the greater the drawing chances. In the endgame, the relation of forces may seem paradoxical, in comparison with what we see during the rest of the game, where the superior side looks for simplifications to increase his advantage. It is obvious that eight pieces against seven is not the same as two against one. In the first case, the advantage may be important, but in the second it's enormous. In the endgame that reasoning is still valid as regards pieces, but not as regards pawns.

In the case of the pieces, you should take care not to 'strip' the board excessively, as there is the risk of insufficient material to mate, and for this reason the pawns' disappearance may give rise to drawing possibilities. Conversely, by retaining a number of pawns, the superior side may be able to promote one of them.

Bishop + Rook's Pawn vs King

This is a peculiar endgame in which you must take into account that if the defender's king can control the promotion square (which, by definition, must be on one of the a- or h-files), while the bishop moves on squares of opposite colour to the promotion square, then the endgame is a draw. In other words, if, for instance, the promotion square is a1 (a dark square) but the bishop moves on light squares, the endgame is drawn.

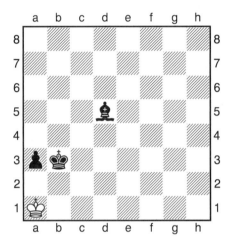

The black pawn will never reach a1, as the white king will oscillate between b1 and a1, and Black can do nothing to prevent this, since the bishop only controls light squares. Black can stalemate White, but he cannot win.

Rook and Pawn Endgames

Rook and pawn endgames are the most common type of endgame. However, they are sometimes very difficult to play, and to master them it is necessary to study a number of typical positions and often complex manoeuvres that have no place in an introductory book such as this.

Here I shall only show some useful positions and other basics that you should aware of.

Rook vs Two Pawns on the Sixth Rank

Can a rook stop two enemy pawns that are united on their sixth rank, like in the following diagram?

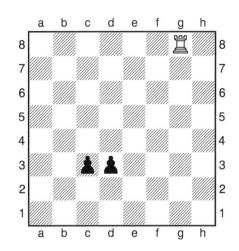

Unless the rook can immediately take one of the pawns, it cannot prevent one or other of the pawns from queening, even if it is White's turn to move. Whichever pawn the rook attacks, that pawn advances and the rook is then tied to preventing it from promoting; e.g., 1 ♖d8 d2 2 ♖d3 c2 3 ♖xd2 c1♕. A similar situation occurs with, e.g., pawns on d2 and c4; then 1 ♖d8 is answered with 1...c3. But if the pawns had been any further back, then the rook would have been able to capture them both.

You should keep this pattern and this concept in mind, since it is a type of situation that is not that unusual in normal competitive games.

How to Support a Passed Pawn

The rook should support a friendly passed pawn from behind, rather than from the front.

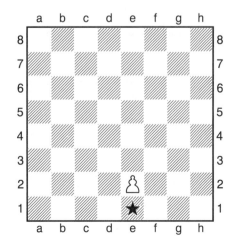

Where should a white rook be placed to support the advance of the e2-pawn? Strange as it may seem, the optimal square is e1. From the back (remember the artillery) the rook has great dynamism, supporting the pawn's advance. If the rook is in front, it is frequently an obstacle for the pawn. For a black rook seeking to hinder the pawn's advance, e1 is also the best place for it to be.

How to Attack a Backward Pawn

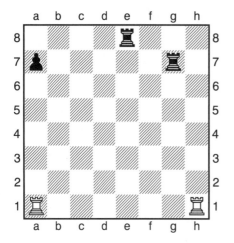

In this position (in which both kings are missing, as well as other pieces) let's suppose White has decided to double rooks on the a-file to attack the backward a7-pawn. Consequently, the rook on that file should be moved to make room for the other rook. The question is: where to place the first rook? At first sight it may seem that any move on that file will do, since in any case both rooks will be doubled on the a-file. But it is not so. There is only one good move: **1 ♖a6!**. The rook should be played precisely to this square, blocking the backward pawn. If you think a bit about this move, you will see that it makes complete sense. As in shooting, it's always easier and more effective to shoot at a fixed target (target practice) than a moving target (clay pigeon shooting).

The Lucena (or Bridge) Manoeuvre

In an endgame of ♖+♙ vs ♖, when the pawn has reached the seventh rank and the attacker's king

occupies the promotion square, the winning method is *Lucena's Manoeuvre*, also known as *building a bridge*:

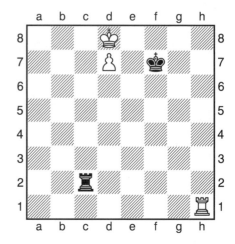

Black's king and rook are making it difficult for White to promote the pawn. The black rook can harass the white king with checks from behind every time it tries to free the promotion square, while the black king gets as close as it can to the action, to prevent the white king from moving to one of the sides.

With the Lucena manoeuvre, all the problems are solved:

1 ♖f1+

The first step is to drive the black king away.

1...♔g7

1...♔e6 was not possible, because after 2 ♔e8! the pawn promotes.

2 ♖f4!

Only here, on its fourth rank! We shall soon see why.

2...♖e2

Black cannot do more than await events.

3 ♔c7 ♖c2+ 4 ♔d6 ♖d2+

The usual defensive method: Black continually checks the white king.

5 ♔c6 ♖c2+

Temporizing with the king will not achieve anything either. For instance:

a) 5...♔g8 6 ♖f5!, followed by 7 ♖d5.

b) 5...♔g6 6 ♖f8 ♖c2+ 7 ♔b5 ♖b2+ 8 ♔a4 ♖a2+ 9 ♔b3.

6 ♔d5 ♖d2+ 7 ♖d4

The key to the whole manoeuvre: the white king has evaded the checks by zigzagging, 'knowing' that the rook will provide cover at the decisive moment. Now Black cannot prevent the pawn from reaching the eighth rank.

Queen vs Pawn on the Seventh

When a queen has to fight against a pawn on its seventh rank, supported by the king, the queen wins if the pawn is on one of the central files (d-, e-) or knight's files (b-, g-). If the pawn is on a rook's (a-, h-) or bishop's file (c-, f-) the endgame is usually drawn. Later we shall explain why.

The Winning Method

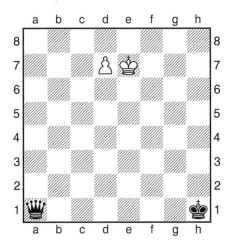

Here we see a white pawn on d7, supported by the king, against Black's queen and king that are far away. It is Black to move.

The winning method consists of checking the white king, forcing him to occupy the promotion square, in order to gain a tempo. At that moment the pawn cannot progress, so the black king can advance. The process will then be repeated as many times as necessary.

1...♕e5+ 2 ♔f8 ♕d6+! 3 ♔e8

This is the target position for the attacker, with only one rank between the queen and the white king, and with the pawn under attack.

3...♕e6+! 4 ♔d8 *(D)*

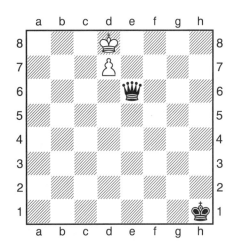

The first stage of the plan: the white king has been forced to occupy the queening square, blocking the advance of the pawn, and now Black can bring his king closer to the action.

4...♔g2 5 ♔c7

White again tries to promote, this time from the other side.

5...♕e7

The queen pins the pawn.

6 ♔c8 ♕c5+ 7 ♔b7 ♕d6! 8 ♔c8 ♕c6+!

We have again reached this key position, in which the defender's king is forced to block the pawn. The rest consists of applying the same technique again and again, until the black king reaches the pawn.

9 ♔d8 ♔f3 10 ♔e7 ♕c7 11 ♔e8 ♕e5+ 12 ♔f8 ♕d6+ 13 ♔e8 ♕e6+ 14 ♔d8 ♔e4 15 ♔c7 ♕e7 16 ♔c8 ♕c5+ 17 ♔b8 ♕d6+ 18 ♔c8 ♕c6+ 19 ♔d8 ♔e5 20 ♔e7 ♕e6+ 21 ♔d8 ♔d6

Now the pawn falls and we reach the position of a basic mate that we have already studied.

When is it a Draw?

We already mentioned that this endgame is drawn (with just a few exceptions that we shall not cover in detail here, but essentially the attacker's king needs to be already near enough to assist with mating ideas) when the pawn is on its seventh rank on the a-, h-, c- or f-file. What is the mysterious reason for this?

It is actually quite simple. See the following positions, in which a black pawn is on its seventh rank (c2 in the first case, and h2 in the second).

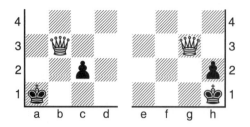

If the pawn is on the c- or f-file, when the queen gives the 'decisive' check, the defender's king, instead of blocking the promotion square, moves to the corner and the pawn cannot be captured as this would be a draw by stalemate. Consequently the attacking side is unable to win.

If the pawn is on one of the edge files (a- or h-), when the queen gives the critical check, the king moves in front of the pawn and now, since the defender has no moves, to avoid stalemate the queen must withdraw from the b- or g-file, and the attacker can make no progress.

In both cases, the endgame is drawn.

Semi-Open Games

The Rationale for an Asymmetrical Response to 1 e4

In the Open Games there are not only violent attacks and counterattacks. There are often also frequent exchanges of pieces, a consequence of the rapid clashes in the opening which, in many cases, can result in multiple exchanges and drawish positions. This is where **Semi-Open Games** come on to the scene. Fighting for the centre, yes, but preserving the possibility of playing for a win (a strategy of counterattack), by avoiding early exchanges of pieces.

The most important of these Semi-Open Games are:

• French Defence (1...e6)
• Caro-Kann Defence (1...c6)
• Sicilian Defence (1...c5)
• Alekhine Defence (1...♘f6)
• Pirc Defence (1...d6)
• Scandinavian Defence (1...d5)

French and Caro-Kann Defences

The basic idea of the French and Caro-Kann Defences is to contain the white expansion in the centre by playing 2...d5.

In the French Defence, for instance, Black answers 1 e4 with 1...e6 *(D)*.

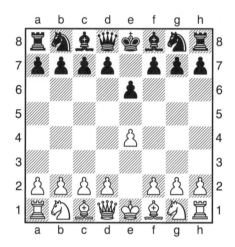

The idea is to meet 2 d4 with 2...d5. The first black move might appear timid, but after his second move we see that Black tries to create a strong point on d5, provoking either the advance of the opponent's pawn to e5, or an exchange on d5. In any case, Black forces his opponent to pay attention to his e4-pawn and, if he decides to protect it with a piece, then Black will have another option: maintaining the pressure or exchanging the pawns, so that he would have put a stop to White's 'arrogant' ambitions of central superiority.

Something similar happens in the Caro-Kann Defence, where Black plays 1...c6 *(D)*.

2 d4 will again be met by 2...d5. As you can see, the treatment is similar to the French Defence, where the advance ...d5 was supported by the e-pawn. The only difference is that the advance is supported by a different pawn here.

What are the advantages and disadvantages of one system or the other?

In favour of the Caro-Kann is the fact that the c8-bishop is not blocked in by the pawn-chain (as happens in the French, where the e6-pawn is blocking the bishop's diagonal)

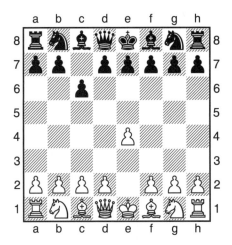

and, consequently, could be developed immediately, for instance, to f5. The disadvantage is that usually in both defences Black needs to play ...c5 to fight for the centre and, once effected, this advance would cost two tempi to Black in the Caro-Kann, whereas in the French Defence it can be executed in a single move.

Which system is better? It is not possible to say. In modern chess, once symmetry has been renounced, each side looks for compensation, i.e. small advantages in return for other concessions. A player needs to learn to consider these factors at any given moment.

Let's consider now some basic variations of both these systems.

In the French Defence, after 1 e4 e6 2 d4 d5 (D), White may choose from three different approaches, which lead to different plans:

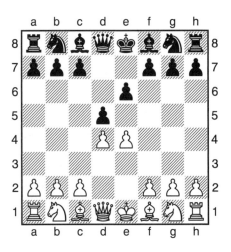

- Releasing the central tension by exchanging pawns: 3 exd5 exd5
- Advancing the e-pawn, gaining space in the centre: 3 e5
- Protecting the e4-pawn: 3 ♘c3 or 3 ♘d2

Exchange Variation

The first case, 1 e4 e6 2 d4 d5 3 exd5 exd5 (D), is a variation with the reputation of not being ambitious, as White exchanges his e-pawn, simplifying the position which now becomes symmetrical, and opening the c8-h3 diagonal for Black's queen's bishop.

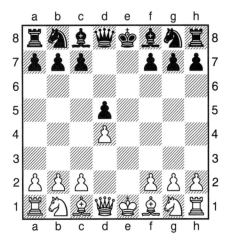

The only advantage White has is that it is now his move. A sample continuation is 4 ♗d3 ♗d6 5 ♘e2 ♘e7 6 0-0 0-0, etc. Black has a fairly comfortable game as he can develop his pieces without difficulty.

Advance Variation

After 3 e5 White has gained space and this pawn is cramping the opponent's position (at this moment a black piece cannot move to f6 or d6), but he has also presented Black with a clear plan, consisting of attacking the base of White's pawn-chain (d4) and later perhaps the e5-pawn. White might have difficulty preserving his central pawns, and if he has to exchange them he will lose his space advantage.

A typical continuation is 3...c5! 4 c3 ♘c6 5 ♘f3, with two main lines: 5...♕b6 and 5...♗d7. In both cases, White needs to keep a close watch on his d4-pawn.

Main Line: 3 ♘c3

The development of the knight to c3 on the third move gives rise to a number of variations, since Black can choose from:
- 3...dxe4 – Rubinstein Variation
- 3...♗b4 – Winawer Variation
- 3...♘f6 – Classical Variation

In the Rubinstein Variation, 3...dxe4 (D) the white centre is broken up.

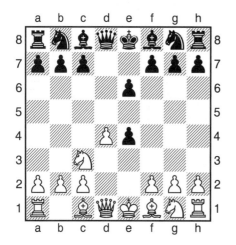

White can try to exploit the space advantage he is left with following the exchange on e4 in a line like 4 ♘xe4 ♘d7 intending ...♘gf6.

The sharp Winawer Variation, 3...♗b4 (D), however, is perhaps the acid test for deciding how good 3 ♘c3 is against the French Defence.

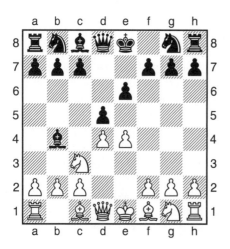

In this variation White has a number of options (such as 4 e5, 4 a3, 4 ♕g4, 4 ♗d2 or 4 ♘e2), but so does Black.

The Classical response 3...♘f6 has, after a long period of neglect, been very popular among strong players in recent years and has consequently seen a huge expansion in its theory following both 4 e5 (Steinitz's move) and 4 ♗g5, after which play can diverge once more, depending on Black's response: 4...dxe4, 4...♗e7 or 4...♗b4.

Tarrasch Variation

This variation, 3 ♘d2 (D) is the most solid and flexible against the French Defence. To start with, it avoids the Winawer Variation and, in addition, it allows the possible advance of the c-pawn.

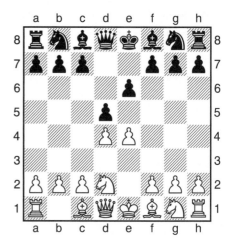

Black has three main answers: 3...c5, 3...dxe4 and 3...♘f6. The game usually follows paths in which White maintains a very slight advantage, and that is the reason for its adoption by many grandmasters, who keep one eye on the possibility of winning and the other on safety.

In the Caro-Kann Defence, Black is more able to control the type of play resulting from the opening. There are fewer variations and systems to look at. Here there is also the same strategic problem as in the French Defence: how should White react after 1 e4 c6 2 d4 d5 (D)?

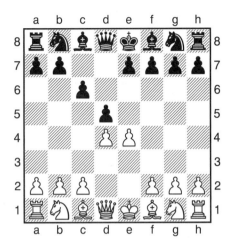

Exchanging, advancing or protecting the e-pawn?

Let's examine the main options:

- 3 exd5 cxd5 4 ♗d3 – Exchange Variation
- 3 e5 – Advance Variation
- 3 ♘c3/3 ♘d2 – Classical and Modern Variations
- 3 exd5 cxd5 4 c4 – Panov-Botvinnik Attack

The Exchange Variation, 3 exd5 cxd5 4 ♗d3 *(D)*, might at a glance be evaluated similarly to its French Defence counterpart.

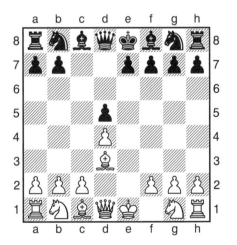

However, the asymmetrical pawn-structure makes it a good deal less drawish. Nevertheless, it is not considered a critical test of the Caro-Kann, and it appears only rarely at grandmaster level, despite a fair following among club players.

For a long time, the Advance Variation was thought to be less complex than some lines of its French counterpart.

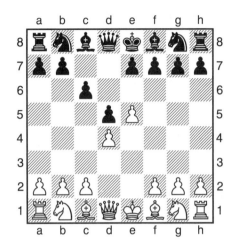

White wins space with the e-pawn and gives the play a closed character. It might seem that Black should not have too many problems equalizing since he can develop his bishop actively at f5 (unlike in the French). However, White has a variety of aggressive ways to question this simplistic view, for example 3...♗f5 4 ♘c3 e6 5 g4 ♗g6 6 ♘ge2. Currently it is one of the most popular systems vs the Caro-Kann, with much experimentation of new ways for White to organize his pieces.

With the moves 3 ♘c3 dxe4 4 ♘xe4 *(D)* the play is more open.

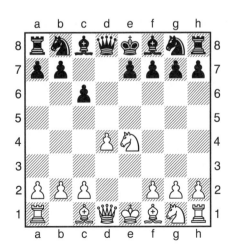

Black generally chooses between 4...♗f5 (Classical Variation) and 4...♘d7 (Modern Variation).

In the first case, 4...♗f5, the queen's bishop is developed with tempo, as it attacks the e4-knight. Of course, White can convert his attacked piece into an attacking one by playing 5 ♘g3, but in so doing he retreats the knight from its central position.

In the second case, with 4...♘d7 Black prepares the development of his king's knight, proposing an exchange that does not damage his own pawn-structure.

There is also the possibility of 4...♘f6, inviting doubled pawns after 5 ♘xf6+. Then 5...gxf6 (Bronstein-Larsen Variation) is a sharp idea only practised by experienced players who know all its intricacies, while 5...exf6 is safer but leaves Black with less counterplay.

The Panov-Botvinnik Attack, 3 exd5 cxd5 4 c4 (D), is based on a completely different strategic idea from that of the Exchange Variation.

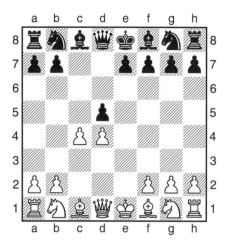

White exchanges his e-pawn but with the aim of immediately attacking the d5-pawn with c4, creating great central tension and opening lines, so that all his minor pieces have natural development squares and can frequently launch a direct attack on Black's castled position. The play often resembles lines of the Queen's Gambit, with an isolated queen's pawn a standard feature.

Sicilian Defence

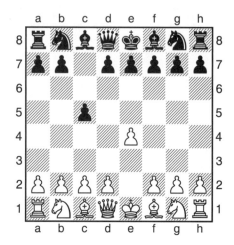

The Sicilian Defence (1...c5) is a very old opening, but nevertheless it is still one of the most modern and flexible systems against the king's pawn opening, with a huge following at all levels of chess. In fact, it is far and away the most popular single chess opening.

The basic idea of the Sicilian is simple, but very consistent. As White has occupied the e4-square, Black is refusing to allow his opponent to place another pawn in the centre on d4. If White prepares this advance with a piece, then when the d4-pawn moves to d4 it will be taken (...cxd4).

The Sicilian has withstood the test of time and resisted all attempts at refutation, such as 2 ♘c3 (Closed Variation), renouncing an early d4 advance, 2 c3 (Alapin Variation, preparing the d4 advance), and 2 f4, which also renounces an early d4 advance. All these possibilities are less worrying for Black than the lines resulting from the Open Sicilian (2 ♘f3 followed by 3 d4).

Another advantage the Sicilian offers to the player who wants to fight for the initiative and is not happy with a quiet game is that usually there are not many exchanges in the opening, which means that a considerable part of each side's army will be available to fight in the middlegame. The game also tends to be highly unbalanced in terms of pawn-structure, thus reducing the chance of sterile equality.

After 1 e4 c5 2 ♘f3, Black can choose from a number of options, the main ones being:

- 2...e6 – Taimanov, Paulsen, Scheveningen and other variations
- 2...d6 – Najdorf, Scheveningen, Classical, Dragon
- 2...♘c6 – Classical, Sveshnikov, Accelerated Dragon
- 2...g6 – Hyper-Accelerated Dragon

The Sicilian, more than any other Semi-Open system, allows a large number of transpositions, i.e. reaching the same variation by a different move-order. For example: the Classical Sicilian consists of the moves 1 e4 c5 2 ♘f3 d6 3 d4 cxd4 4 ♘xd4 ♘f6 5 ♘c3 ♘c6 *(D)*.

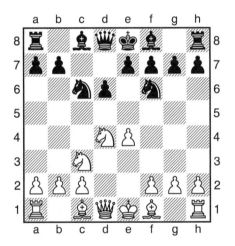

But this same position can be reached by swapping round Black's 2nd and 5th moves, i.e. 1 e4 c5 2 ♘f3 ♘c6 3 d4 cxd4 4 ♘xd4 ♘f6 5 ♘c3 d6.

Transposition of moves is a matter of some importance in today's openings, although we cannot really cover it in any detail in this book. Occasionally, transpositional ideas are rather venomous, but in other cases they are purely mechanical and harmless.

Alekhine, Pirc and Scandinavian Defences

At the beginning of the 20th century, several masters who were very interested in opening theory investigated some answers to 1 e4 which are apparently paradoxical, such as 1...♘f6 *(D)* and 1...d6. These days the Alekhine and Pirc

Defences are regularly seen in tournament play.

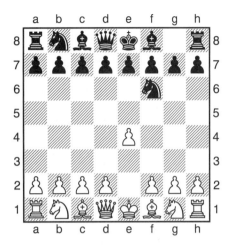

The Alekhine Defence tries to provoke the advance of the white e-pawn, as Black considers that such an advance weakens the white centre and afterwards can be attacked or exchanged by playing ...d6.

Conversely, the Pirc Defence, 1 e4 d6 *(D)*, has the idea of playing 2...♘f6 without allowing e5 in response.

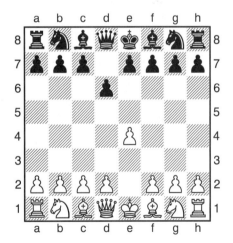

Black generally follows up with a **fianchetto** (i.e. flank development) of his king's bishop (3...g6 and 4...♗g7), creating a flexible structure, having in mind an eventual counterattack, once the opening is finished. This opening avoids an immediate fight in the centre and is

based on a strategy of *reculer pour mieux sauter*, i.e. taking a step backwards in order to be better able to advance later on.

The Scandinavian Defence, 1 e4 d5 *(D)*, is an immediate aggression against White's central pawn.

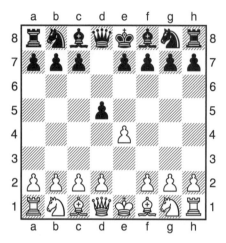

This seems to go against the general principles of chess, as after 2 exd5 ♕xd5, White can gain a tempo by attacking the black queen with 3 ♘c3 and, once it retreats, it is once again White to move. But principles and rules, although it is necessary to know and, in general, to follow them, do not always have a precise application to the game. Today the Scandinavian Defence is at least as popular as the last two defences mentioned above and is frequently seen, even at high levels of competition.

On the other hand, after 2 exd5, Black can also choose to gambit the pawn with 2...♘f6, an interesting positional variation. If White defends the pawn he can have problems and it is better to give it back. For instance: 3 d4 ♘xd5 4 c4, etc.

Traps and Tricks in the Semi-Open Games

In Chapter 3 we saw some examples of traps in the Open Games. The concept of the trap is the same in all kind of openings. Let's see some examples within this group of openings.

Caro-Kann Defence

1 e4 c6 2 ♘f3 d5 3 ♘c3 dxe4 4 ♘xe4 ♘d7

Now White plays an innocent-looking move...

5 ♕e2

...blocking in his bishop but preparing a trap by inviting Black to continue with his plan, which consists of developing the king's knight, without incurring doubled pawns on f6, since now he would recapture with the other knight.

5...♘gf6??

After this blunder Black will receive a great surprise.

6 ♘d6# *(D)*

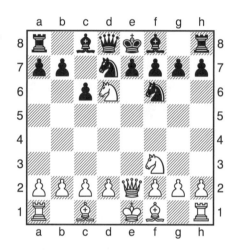

A 'smothered' mate of the black king, as the e7-pawn is pinned by the white queen. If Black had thought about the move 5 ♕e2, he would have discovered the motivation and found a way to neutralize it. One way is to play 5...e6 before continuing with the planned 6...♘gf6, while another is to change course with 5...♘df6, which has the advantage that the c8-bishop can still be developed freely. Then the queen might not look so clever on e2.

Let's now look at a trap that can arise in the 4...♘d7 Variation of the Caro-Kann Defence, if Black is not aware (be especially careful in rapid or blitz games!):

1 e4 c6 2 d4 d5 3 ♘c3 dxe4 4 ♘xe4 ♘d7 5 ♗c4

This is an aggressive response to Black's plan, by which White seeks to avoid exchanges.

5...♘gf6 6 ♘g5 e6

The best defence against the threat to f7. Sometimes 6...♘d5 has been played.

7 ♕e2 *(D)*

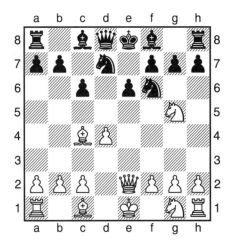

White sets a trap which, in this case, does not damage his own position, even if Black discovers it.

Another way of looking at it is that White makes a threat which causes Black some inconvenience. Indeed, it is a logical follow-up to his last two moves, which might end up looking rather pointless otherwise.

7...h6?

Black does not see any reason not to repel the knight, thus falling into the trap. The correct move is 7...♘b6, attacking the c4-bishop as well as protecting e6.

8 ♘xf7! ♔xf7

Now the black king will be the victim of an irresistible direct attack.

9 ♕xe6+ ♔g6 10 ♗d3+ ♔h5 11 ♕h3#

Another trap arises in the Fantasy Variation, in which White reinforces his e-pawn with f3.

1 e4 c6 2 d4 d5 3 f3

This is the Fantasy Variation. Supporting the e4-pawn has its logic – White wants to maintain his pawn-centre, since after any exchange on e4 White keeps two central pawns on the fourth rank. On the other hand, it weakens White's kingside.

3...dxe4!? 4 fxe4 e5

Trying to refute the variation directly does not work, although Black's play so far is OK.

5 ♘f3

White avoids 5 dxe5? ♕h4+, after which the black queen creates havoc (6 ♔e2 ♕xe4+; 6 g3 ♕xe4+). The text-move develops a piece and activates White's game.

5...exd4 6 ♗c4!

In obvious gambit style, justified by Black's lagging development.

6...♗b4+? 7 c3 dxc3 *(D)*

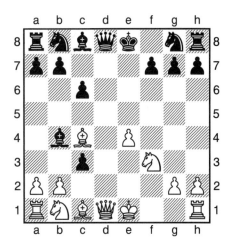

This is a case of a 'hunter hunted', as both players think they are being cleverer than their opponent. White thinks that Black has not seen that he will lose his queen, and Black thinks that, after the capture of his queen, he will have a winning position, as he can recover it.

8 ♗xf7+! ♔xf7 9 ♕xd8 cxb2+ 10 ♔e2 bxa1♕ *(D)*

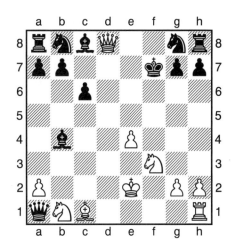

Now Black, with an extra rook and bishop, seems to have a decisive advantage. However, it is White who saw farther, appreciating that the black king is very exposed and there is now a forced win.

11 ♘g5+ ♚g6 12 ♕e8+ ♚h6

If 12...♚f6, 13 ♕f7+ ♚e5 14 ♗f4+! (not 14 ♕xg7+ ♘f6) 14...♚d4 15 ♕xg7+, winning the queen.

13 ♘e6+ g5 14 ♗xg5#

The Levenfish Trap

In the Dragon Variation of the Sicilian Defence, White can set an attractive trap by playing the Levenfish Attack. However, Black has a few ways to neutralize it.

Nezhmetdinov – Ermolin
Kazan 1946

1 e4 c5 2 ♘f3 d6 3 d4 cxd4 4 ♘xd4 ♘f6 5 ♘c3 g6

This is the Dragon.

6 f4

With this move, which characterizes the Levenfish Attack, the trap is set. Black's safest reply is 6...♘c6!.

6...♗g7!?

Black opts for this natural move, ignoring the trap.

7 e5 dxe5?!

7...♘h5 is best.

8 fxe5 ♘d5??

One instructive variation runs 8...♘g4?! 9 ♗b5+! ♚f8?? (9...♗d7? allows 10 ♕xg4! winning a piece; 9...♘c6! is best, but White can keep some advantage after 10 ♘xc6 ♕xd1+ 11 ♘xd1! a6! 12 ♗a4 ♗d7! 13 h3! ♘h6 14 ♘xe7!) 10 ♘e6+! winning the queen with an unusual double attack. 8...♘fd7 keeps Black in the game.

9 ♗b5+ ♚f8

As you can see, there is no better answer. 9...♘c6 would lose material after 10 ♘xc6, and both 9...♘d7 and 9...♗d7 would be met by 10 ♘xd5.

10 0-0 ♗xe5 11 ♗h6+ ♚g8

If 11...♗g7, 12 ♗xg7+ ♚xg7 13 ♘xd5 ♕xd5 14 ♘f5+!, winning the queen.

12 ♘xd5 ♕xd5 *(D)*

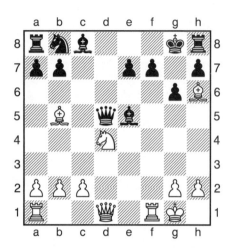

13 ♘f5 ♕c5+ 14 ♗e3 ♕c7 15 ♘h6+ 1-0

White will mate with 16 ♖xf7#.

In the Pirc Defence a very simple trap can arise:

1 e4 d6 2 d4 ♘f6 3 ♘c3 g6 4 ♗c4 ♗g7 5 ♘f3 ♘bd7?

This is a mistake, as Black has not prevented the e5 advance.

6 e5! ♘g8 *(D)*

If 6...dxe5 7 dxe5 ♘g4, 8 ♗xf7+! ♚xf7 9 ♘g5+ wins.

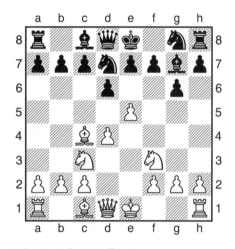

7 ♗xf7+! ♚xf7 8 ♘g5+

Black loses his queen after 8...♚f8 9 ♘e6+ with a fork, or 8...♚e8 9 ♘e6, 'smothering' the queen.

Semi-Open Miniatures

Let's see some short victories (known in chess as 'miniatures') in the Semi-Open Games, so that you can get used to these types of positions.

Botvinnik – Spielmann
Moscow 1935
Caro-Kann Defence

1 c4 c6 2 e4 d5 3 exd5 cxd5 4 d4

The opening that started as an English Opening, is now by transposition a Caro-Kann Defence, Panov-Botvinnik Attack.

4...♘f6 5 ♘c3 ♘c6 6 ♗g5 ♕b6 7 cxd5 ♕xb2??

This capture leads to disaster. Black had to play 7...♘xd4!.

8 ♖c1!

Protecting the c3-knight and also the c2-square.

8...♘b4 *(D)*

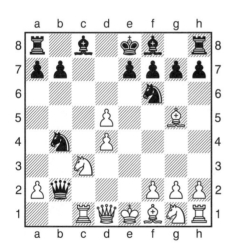

9 ♘a4! ♕xa2 10 ♗c4 ♗g4 11 ♘f3 ♗xf3 12 gxf3 1-0

Black resigned as he cannot avoid the loss of his queen. If 12...♕a3, 13 ♖c3. It is incredible how such a strong grandmaster as Rudolf Spielmann, known as *King of the Attack*, could be beaten in only twelve moves, something that should make us reflect upon the dangers of the opening.

The following game was played by Mikhail Tal in a simultaneous exhibition. A couple of years later Tal would conquer the world championship.

Tal – NN
Stuttgart (simul.) 1958
Sicilian Defence

1 e4 c5 2 ♘f3 ♘c6 3 d4 cxd4 4 ♘xd4 g6 5 ♘c3 ♗g7 6 ♗e3 d6 7 ♕d2 ♘f6 8 f3

We have transposed from an Accelerated Dragon to the Dragon Variation; despite the names, the latter usually gives rise to sharper fights. White has adopted a set-up called the Yugoslav Attack.

8...♗d7 9 0-0-0 ♕a5 10 ♔b1 ♖c8 11 g4

White starts immediate action on the kingside to dissuade the black monarch from castling there.

11...h6?

This advance weakens the kingside and not only fails to prevent the further advance of the white pawns, it even makes it easier, as it creates a 'hook' for a pawn-break on g5.

12 h4 a6?! 13 ♗e2 ♘e5

A typical manoeuvre in the Dragon Variation. The black knight heads for the c4-square, to force the exchange of one of the white bishops, often followed by doubling Black's rooks on the c-file.

14 g5! hxg5 15 hxg5 ♖xh1 *(D)*

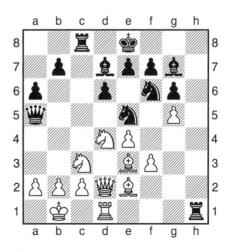

16 gxf6!!

In defence of the player with the black pieces, we should say that this was, to say the least, a complete surprise!

16...♖xd1+

16...♗xf6 17 ♖xh1 leaves White a piece up.

17 ♘xd1!!

The paradoxical key to the combination. Now both the black queen and the g7-bishop are threatened (a double attack). Yet the white queen can be taken! What does White have in mind?

17...♕xd2 18 fxg7! *(D)*

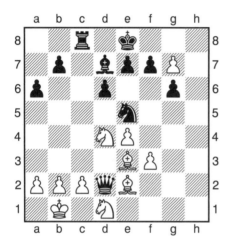

1-0

Pure magic! All the white pieces are defending each other. Tal is again threatening a sort of double attack: the black queen is attacked and the pawn is ready to queen on g8. There is no defence; after 18...♗e6 19 g8♕+ ♔d7 20 ♕xc8+ ♔xc8 21 ♗xd2 it is clear that further resistance is futile. A brilliant demonstration of how a combinative sequence can turn the board upside-down.

The following game is mentioned by some authors as a trap, but in fact White did not plan any trap. Simply, Black failed to see a decisive combination in the opening.

Fischer – Reshevsky
USA Ch, New York 1958/9
Sicilian Defence

1 e4 c5 2 ♘f3 ♘c6 3 d4 cxd4 4 ♘xd4 g6 5 ♘c3 ♗g7 6 ♗e3 ♘f6 *(D)*

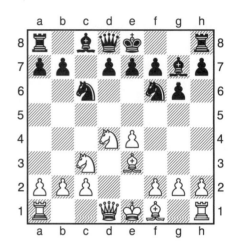

This is similar to the Dragon Variation which we saw in the previous game, but when Black does not play an early ...d6, it is called the *Accelerated Dragon*.

7 ♗c4 0-0 8 ♗b3 ♘a5?

Black is anxious to eliminate the dangerous b3-bishop, and so he commits an unusual blunder for a grandmaster as experienced as Samuel Reshevsky. Today it is considered that Black should play 8...♕a5, 8...a5 or 8...d6. Now it's instructive to see how Fischer will exploit this mistake. By the way, Bobby was then only 15 years old.

9 e5! ♘e8 *(D)*

9...♘xb3 10 exf6 ♘xa1 11 fxg7 gives White a clear material advantage.

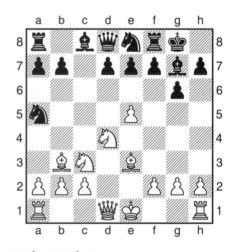

10 ♗xf7+! ♔xf7

If 10...♖xf7, 11 ♘e6!, winning the queen.

11 ♘e6! dxe6

The main point of White's combination is that after 11...♔xe6 12 ♕d5+ the black king will be mated in a few moves.

12 ♕xd8

And Reshevsky played on stubbornly, before finally resigning after White's 42nd move.

What a wonderful combination!

The following game was considered the best in the first part of 1976 by the jury of experts in the *Informator* periodical.

Reshevsky – Vaganian
Skopje 1976
French Defence

1 e4 e6 2 d4 d5 3 ♘d2

The Tarrasch Variation. The knight protects the e4-pawn, and this has the advantage that White can avoid the pin by the bishop (which can happen after 3 ♘c3), and it also allows the c-pawn to advance in the fight for the centre.

3...♘f6 4 e5 ♘fd7 5 f4 c5 6 c3 ♘c6 7 ♘df3 *(D)*

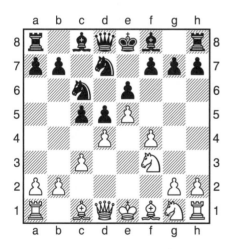

This move, artificial at first sight, since it hinders the development of the g1-knight to this square, provides in a single move two additional defences to the d4-pawn. The other knight will be developed on e2.

7...♕a5 8 ♔f2

Initiating a manoeuvre known as 'castling by hand' or 'artificial castling', to be followed by

♖e1. The king seems to be safe, thanks to the cluster of pieces surrounding it, and, especially, White's pawn-chain.

8...♗e7 9 ♗d3 ♕b6 10 ♘e2 f6 11 exf6 ♗xf6 12 ♔g3 *(D)*

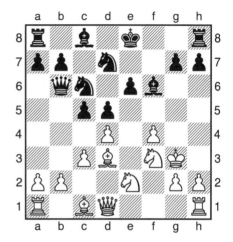

The king moves off the black queen's diagonal, since its position on f2 would allow Black to break with ...e5.

12...cxd4 13 cxd4 0-0

Practically nothing remains of the once-impressive white pawn-centre. Black has castled and opened new lines towards the opponent's king, such as, for instance, the f-file.

14 ♖e1?! *(D)*

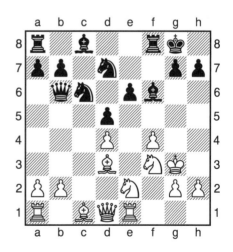

14...e5!

A spectacular and unexpected pawn-break, as the e5-square is controlled by the f4- and d4-pawns, but other factors should be considered, such as the exposed position of the white king.

15 fxe5?! ♘dxe5!

A brilliant piece sacrifice, which blows up the white defences.

16 dxe5 (D)

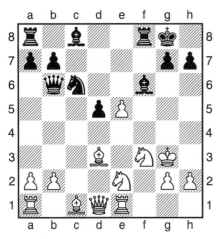

16...♗h4+!!

And this is now a masterly move. Reshevsky, a very experienced grandmaster, has been trapped by Vaganian's ultra-dynamic play. Now all the black pieces (except the a8-rook) will concentrate on the king-hunt.

17 ♔xh4

Naturally not 17 ♘xh4? due to 17...♕f2#.

17...♖xf3!

The fireworks go on. This move is the consequence of the previous one. The rook cannot be captured, since after 18 gxf3 ♕f2+ 19 ♔g5 h6+ (not 19...♕xh2?? 20 ♗xh7+!) the white king will be mated.

18 ♖f1 ♕b4+ 19 ♗f4 ♕e7+

The black queen has great mobility and zooms around the whole board.

20 ♗g5 ♕e6!

The queen threatens mate on g4, and 21 gxf3? would allow 21...♕h3#.

21 ♗f5 ♖xf5

If 21...♕xf5, 22 ♕xd5+ ♗e6 (or 22...♔h8) 23 ♕xf3.

22 ♘f4 ♕xe5 23 ♕g4 ♖f7 24 ♕h5 ♘e7!

Threatening 25...♘f5+, and 25 ♗xe7? loses to 25...♖xf4+!.

25 g4 ♘g6+ 26 ♔g3

26 ♘xg6 allows 26...♕xh2#.

26...♗d7

Calmly completing development.

27 ♖ae1 ♕d6 28 ♗h6 ♖af8 0-1

A memorable display by Vaganian!

Let's see now how a future world champion played, at the age of fourteen.

Kasparov – West

USSR – Australia (telechess olympiad) 1977
Sicilian Defence

1 e4 c5 2 ♘f3 ♘f6

This is the Nimzowitsch Variation, a rare and provocative line.

3 ♘c3

Rather than being provoked into playing 3 e5, Kasparov invites a transposition back into the normal paths of the Open Sicilian.

3...e6 4 d4 cxd4 5 ♘xd4 ♗b4

Called the Pin Variation for obvious reasons, this is a risky line, but seen from time to time in international tournaments.

6 e5 ♘d5 7 ♗d2 ♘xc3 8 bxc3 ♗f8

This retreat seems artificial, but Black is already starting to have problems. If, for instance, 8...♗e7, 9 ♕g4 could have followed, when White could meet 9...0-0 with 10 ♗h6, winning the exchange.

9 ♗d3 d6 10 ♕e2 ♘d7? (D)

Black had not developed a single piece, so he is anxious to catch up, but this move is a mistake, as the young Kasparov will demonstrate.

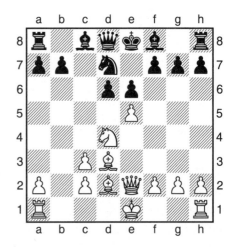

11 ♘xe6!

A decisive sacrifice. The knight cannot be taken as White wins after 11...fxe6? 12 ♕h5+ g6 13 ♗xg6+ hxg6 14 ♕xg6+ ♚e7 15 ♗g5+.

11...♕b6 (D)

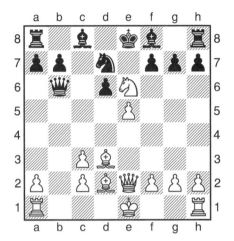

Now we shall see the simplicity with which White puts an end to the game.

12 ♘c7+! 1-0

After 12...♕xc7, the discovered check 13 exd6+ wins the queen.

Questions

76) In a rook endgame, where do the king and pawn of the attacking side need to stand, so that the *Lucena Manoeuvre* is possible?

77) In which cases can the queen (usually) not win against a pawn on its seventh rank?

78) If we are thinking of doubling rooks to put pressure on an enemy pawn, to which square should we normally move the first rook?

79) From where should the rook usually support the advance of a passed pawn?

80) In an endgame with blocked pawn-chains, which piece is superior: the bishop or the knight?

81) Can a rook stop two connected passed pawns on the sixth rank, when neither of them is attacked?

82) In a knight endgame with two pawns against one, which is better for the attacker: exchanging pawns or preserving them?

83) Name three Semi-Open Games, indicating the moves that define them.

84) With which move does Black avoid the Levenfish Trap?

85) What advantages has 3 ♘d2, in the French Defence, in comparison with 3 ♘c3?

86) Give two reasons for playing a Semi-Open Game.

87) After 2 exd5 in the Scandinavian Defence, does Black have to recapture on d5 right away?

88) What should Black play after 1 e4 c5 2 ♘f3 e6 3 d4?

89) What is the main disadvantage of the French Defence, compared with the Caro-Kann?

90) What is the initial purpose of the Alekhine Defence?

Exercises

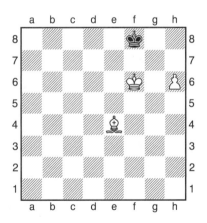

101) Black to move. Can White promote his pawn?

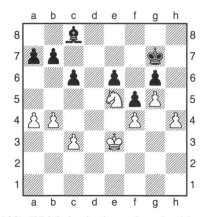

102) Which is the best piece in this end-game? Why?

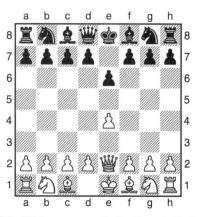

105) White answered the French Defence with 2 ♕e2. Should Black play now 2...d5, as usual? Why?

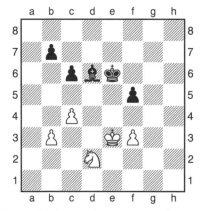

103) Which is the better minor piece in this endgame? Why?

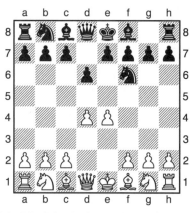

106) Black is playing a Pirc Defence. Is the advance 3 e5 good now? Why?

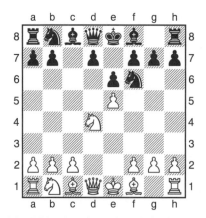

104) White has just played 5 e5. Is this a good or a bad move? Why?

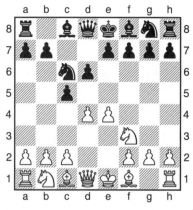

107) Black has answered 3 d4 with 3...♘c6. Is this a good reply, in the spirit of the Sicilian Defence? Explain.

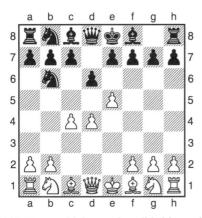

108) From which opening did this position result? Can you reconstruct the opening moves?

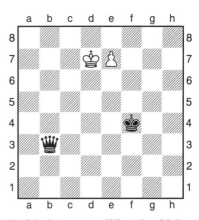

111) Black to move. What should be the result of this endgame be? Indicate a sample line.

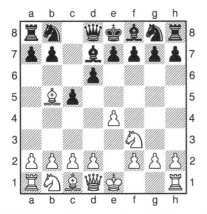

109) From which opening did this position arise? Can you reconstruct the opening moves?

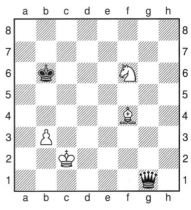

112) Revision exercise. White to move. What is the best move?

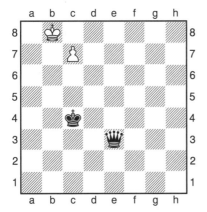

110) Black to move. What should be the result of this endgame be? Why?

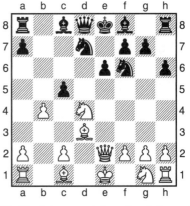

113) Revision exercise. In this position White wins with a forceful combination. How?

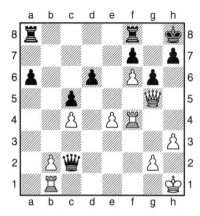

114) White's major pieces, together with the f6 pawn-wedge, are able to win by force. Can you see how?

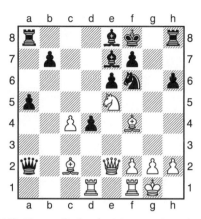

117) Try to find a decisive continuation involving both white bishops. What is the winning line?

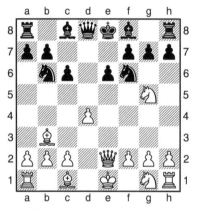

115) Why is the capture on d4 not good for Black?

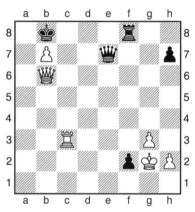

118) Theme: pawn promotion. White to move. Can you find a winning sequence?

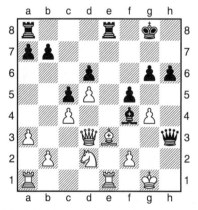

116) Black is a piece down, but is threatening the white king. How can he finish off the game?

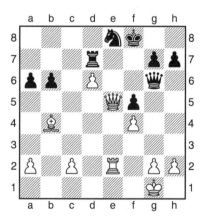

119) Theme: pawn promotion. The d6-pawn looks securely blocked, but White has a stunning combination to win the game. Can you find it?

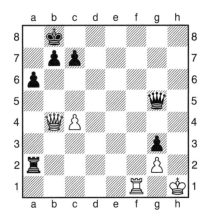

120) This position seems hopeless for White, threatened with mate and apparently with no adequate defence. However, White has a brilliant manoeuvre to force a draw. Can you see it?

Further Tips

Against club mates of around the same level as you, play out some endgame positions involving bishop vs knight, with pawns. Evaluate, in each case, which is the better piece in the initial position.

Practise playing opposite-coloured bishop endgames, with one side having one or two extra pawns, to get used to the difficulties of this type of endgame.

Practise the **Lucena (Bridge) Manoeuvre** in rook endgames.

Practise the endgame with queen vs pawn on the seventh rank.

Practise playing some Semi-Open Games as Black and gain a first impression about which ones you do, or do not, feel comfortable playing. Use openings books to look up the lines with which you don't feel comfortable.

Now you should be ready to appreciate the games of the great players. Play through such games from books, magazines or chess news websites and discuss them with your chess-playing friends.

7 Combinations and Tactical Themes

* Combinations * Fork and Double Attack * Pin * Discovered Attack * Removing the Guard * Interference * Deflection * X-Ray * Decoy * Self-Blocking * Clearance * Questions * Exercises * Further Tips *

Combinations

a forced manoeuvre, which usually includes a material sacrifice, and gives the position a surprising and unexpected twist.
LUDEK PACHMAN

Grandmaster Pachman was talking about **combinations**. While there has been a fair amount of rather academic discussion of how best to define a combination (with a major point of contention being whether a sacrifice is strictly essential), there is no doubt that a combination is a very dramatic turn of events on the chessboard. A player sees a chance to turn the game in his favour, calculates the tactics, assesses the position at the end of each variation and, once he is sure he hasn't missed anything vital, takes the plunge.

We should examine some terminology:

A **forcing variation** means a sequence of moves where one side's moves oblige the opponent to reply with one or more forced ('only') moves.

A **sacrifice** is the willing offer of one or more pieces, in exchange for material of lesser value, or no material at all.

A combination should have a **purpose**, such as achieving checkmate, a decisive material advantage, or a draw. Or the aim might be simply to clarify the position. And a combination is generally based on one or more tactical themes...

Tactical Themes

We are going to classify combinations by themes, illustrating them with a number of examples, so that you get used to the types of combinations that a given position might contain.

A combination can on its own decide the outcome of a game; hence the importance of studying them.

Combinations can be classified according to the theme on which they are based. The following themes are the most frequent ones:
• Fork and double attack
• Pin
• Discovered attack
• Removing the guard
• Interference
• Deflection
• X-ray
• Decoy
• Self-blocking
• Clearance

When studying **tandems** we have seen some combinations, most of them based on one or more of the above themes.

Now we shall examine combinations produced in real tournament games. The chance to play a combination should not be missed, as it can bring down the opponent's position like a house of cards.

Fork and Double Attack

As the name suggests, a **double attack** is any move that simultaneously attacks two of the opponent's pieces. A **fork** is a special case, where one piece makes both threats. Knights are particularly good pieces for making forks, as they move differently from all the other pieces; sometimes they fork more than two pieces at once, as we shall see. But all pieces can fork, even pawns and kings, and of course queens often attack several targets at once. A further reason why the knight is an ideal forking piece is its relatively low value. When a knight attacks a queen or rook, it is a major threat, even if the piece is defended, but the reverse is not true.

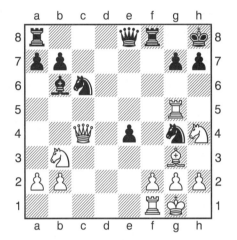

Kapengut – Kupreichik
USSR 1976

Here we shall see a very simple fork in a game between masters. Material is equal and Black wants to advance his e-pawn, with three pieces (queen, bishop and knight) in support, but ...e3 cannot be played immediately, as the g4-knight is attacked. However, that 'magic' square can be occupied immediately by the knight, forking the queen and the f1-rook:

1...♘e3! 2 fxe3 ♗xe3+ 0-1

A new fork, this time on the king and the g5-rook. White resigned since 3 ♔h1 is met by 3...♗xg5.

In the next diagram the good set-up of the white pieces seems to be compensated for by Black's strong queen and bishop.

If the white queen now meekly moves aside, the bishop can take the b2-pawn, equalizing the material. But White found a forking combination, based on the active position of his pieces and the weakness of Black's back rank.

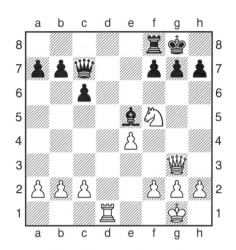

Capablanca – Fonaroff
New York 1918

1 ♘h6+ ♔h8 2 ♕xe5! ♕xe5 3 ♘xf7+! 1-0

The knight cannot be captured, as the back rank would then be unprotected (3...♖xf7 4 ♖d8+ and mate), so White wins a piece and a second pawn.

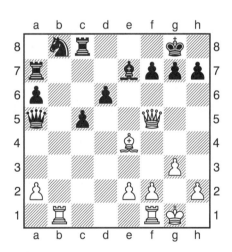

Here the white queen is forking two targets: the h7-square (mating with 1 ♕xh7+ ♔f8 2 ♕h8#) and the c8-rook.

In the next diagram we have the position that could have resulted in the previous one.

1 ♘c8!

White is looking for a fork: if 1...♖xc8, then 2 ♕f5, reaching the position we already know.

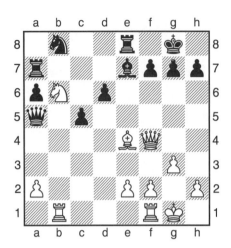

Kasparov – Ligterink
Malta Olympiad 1980

1...♘c6 2 ♘xa7 ♘xa7 3 ♗d5 1-0

If 3...♗f6 there would follow 4 ♖b7 (a new fork, attacking the a7-knight and the f7-square), with a decisive advantage.

You will soon see that White's a7-rook stands in a threatening position, in immediate contact with the d7-knight and also in potential contact with the f7-rook. If you look further, you will appreciate that the white queen is also in a threatening position, in potential contact with the black king and the f7-rook, along the same diagonal (a2-g8). The strong d5-knight does not threaten anything at the moment, but has in his sights the squares b6, c7 and, especially, e7 and f6. And if we think about it a little more, we can see that the f7-rook is in an insecure position, indirectly pinned by the white queen.

Thus we arrive at the conclusion that White has a dominant position and that there might be a forced win. And there is: after **1 ♖xd7!**, if the queen captures the rook (1...♛xd7), then 2 ♘f6+ exploits the pinned rook to win the queen with a knight fork, whereas the capture with the rook, 1...♖xd7, would allow 2 ♘e7++! ♚g7 3 ♛g8+ ♚f6 4 ♘d5#. The powerful knight has delivered mate from the square it occupied a few moves ago! Consequently, after 1 ♖xd7! Black resigned.

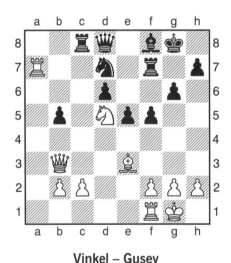

Vinkel – Gusev
USSR 1964

Consider for a moment the various contacts between pieces in this position. For instance: the white queen attacks the b5-pawn. But for the moment it's quite difficult to see, for instance, any possible contact between the f8-bishop and the white king. However, I'd like you to look a bit deeper into the position.

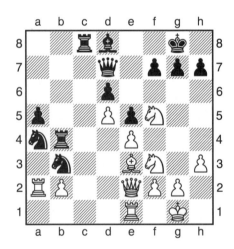

Kudrin – Ivkov
Lone Pine 1981

The b4-rook and the two black knights seem very active, but for the moment there is not much that they can attack on the queenside (since the b2-pawn is protected twice), but the attack on e4 is unpleasant. A passive defence would involve moving the e3-bishop or retreating the f5-knight.

Please remember the golden rule regarding threats: a threat that is hard to defend against should, if at all possible, be answered with a stronger counter-threat.

Now I'd like you to think again about this position. The f5-knight is very strong, but will need the help of some other pieces to create threats against the black king. The queen, for instance. Dreaming costs nothing. Imagine that you are White and that your queen is already on g4. In that case White would have a fork a bit like a parcel bomb, threatening both mate on g7 and a discovered check (♘h6+) that would win the black queen.

But let's come back to reality: the white queen is not on g4 but on e2, and the f3-knight blocks its passage to g4. Can we solve this? Well, the knight is not fixed to f3: it can move. How can we move it, without losing any time? By threatening something. But how? It's not so difficult:

1 ♘xe5!

Attacking the black queen.

1...♕e8

1...dxe5 is met by 2 ♕g4, with the above-mentioned double threat.

2 ♕g4!

Anyway!

2...♕xe5

2...♗f6 is met by 3 ♘d7!.

3 ♘h6+ ♔f8 4 ♕xc8

White is the exchange and a pawn up, while after 4...gxh6 5 ♕xd8+ ♔g7 6 ♕d7 he has powerful threats.

Pin

In a **pin**, a piece immobilizes an enemy piece, since if the latter moves, his side would lose a more valuable piece. A pin may be **absolute** or **relative**.

An **absolute pin** is when a piece is completely immobilized because the more valuable piece 'at the end of the line' is the king.

A **relative pin** is when the pinned piece can legally move, since although it is shielding a piece of superior value, that piece is **not** the king.

Here are some examples of pins:

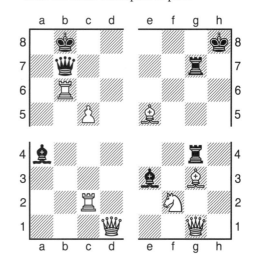

The top two are absolute pins and the lower two are relative pins. In the bottom right there are even two pins, as the knight is pinned by the black bishop, and the white bishop by the rook.

Let's now look at some positions from tournament play.

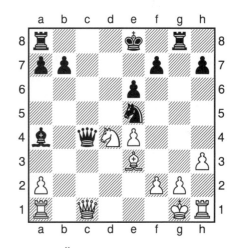

Šubarić – Trifunović
Yugoslav Ch, Zagreb 1946

Black wins immediately with a very clear tactical sequence, exploiting the fact that the g2-pawn is pinned by the g8-rook:

1...♕xd4! 0-1

Mate follows after 2 ♗xd4 ♘f3+ 3 ♔f1 (the only legal move) 3...♗b5+.

pin on the f2-pawn by Black's c5-bishop. Now the threat is 3...♖xg3+. White played **3 ♖xg8** but after **3...♕xc3** Black went on to win.

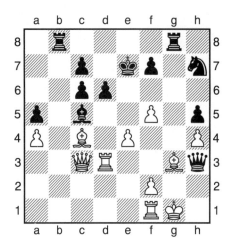

Gendel – Suskevich
USSR 1956

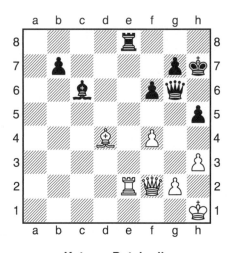

Kotov – Botvinnik
USSR Ch, Leningrad 1939

Here the solution is not so obvious, but should not present too many difficulties, bearing in mind the combinative theme we are studying. Black won as follows:

1...♖xg3+! 2 ♖xg3 ♖g8!! *(D)*

Here we will see something very simple which, nevertheless, happened in a game between two grandmasters. Black wins the exchange in simple fashion:

1...♕xg2+! 2 ♕xg2 ♖xe2 0-1

The pin by the c6-bishop is absolutely decisive.

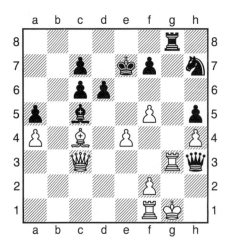

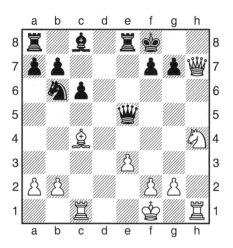

Abrahams – Thynne
Liverpool 1932

An excellent move, a sacrifice exploiting a **cross-pin**, which is in effect a double-pin: the white rook is pinned on the g-file (to the king) and on the third rank (to the queen). At the same time, the whole sequence depends on the

This position also contains a winning combination. White exploits the great activity of his pieces:

1 ♕g8+! ♔e7

The idea is 1...♔xg8? 2 ♘g6!, and thanks to the pin by the c4-bishop, mate with ♖h8# cannot be prevented.

2 ♕xf7+ ♔d8

and White won easily, attacking a king in the centre with extra material.

The magic of the pin is well illustrated in the next example.

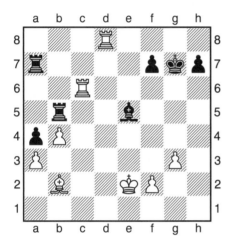

Panno – Ja. Bolbochan
Villa Gesell 1971

White produced a display of geometrical possibilities:

1 ♖b8! ♖d5!

This is practically the only move, because 1...♖xb8 loses a piece after 2 ♗xe5+. Here, in addition to the pin, the fork plays a role. Panno insisted on his linear assault:

2 ♖d6! ♗xb2

After 2...♖xd6 3 ♗xe5+ ♖f6, White needs to be a little careful, since the obvious 4 ♖b6?? is bad due to 4...♗e7. Instead, 4 ♗xf6+ ♔xf6 5 ♖b5 followed by 6 ♖a5 leads to a winning ending, while 4 ♔d3 (pin avoidance!) is also very good.

3 ♖xd5 ♗xa3 4 ♖a5 1-0

The endgame is losing for Black thanks to White's extra material.

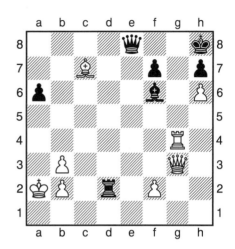

Nunn – Murshed
Commonwealth Ch, London 1985

White found a spectacular finishing touch:
1 ♗e5!!

Defending b2 and both pinning and attacking the f6-bishop at the same time.

1...♖xf2

It was not possible to play 1...♗xe5 because of 2 ♖g8+! ♕xg8 3 ♕xe5+, mating.

2 ♖e4

There are several ways to win now; e.g., 2 ♗xf6+ ♖xf6 3 ♕c3 (or 3 ♖e4!).

2...♗xe5 *(D)*

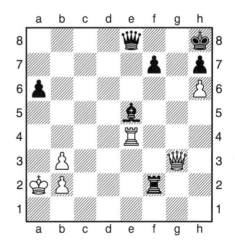

Now the bishop is pinned against the queen.
3 ♕g7+!! 1-0

Black resigned in view of 3...♗xg7 4 ♖xe8+ ♗f8 5 ♖xf8#.

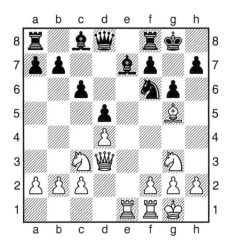

Spielmann – Wahle
Vienna 1926

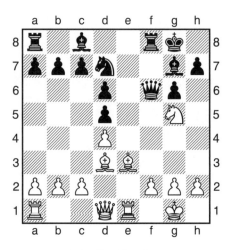

Todorčević – Jean
Paris 1969

White is more active and is fully developed, whereas Black still has to mobilize his queenside. White is ready to carry out a winning combination:

1 ♖xe7!

Removing the guard, in order to exploit the pin.

1...♕xe7 2 ♕f3 ♔g7 3 ♘ce4! *(D)*

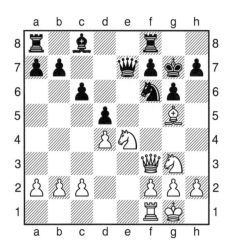

A fresh sacrifice, but the piece will be recovered with a well-calculated sequence.

3...dxe4 4 ♘xe4 ♕e6

Even the desperate 4...♕xe4 fails to help after 5 ♕xf6+ ♔g8 6 ♗h6, followed by mate on g7.

5 ♗xf6+ ♔g8 6 ♕f4 1-0

If Black is allowed to chase away the white knight with ...h6, then he could complete his development (for instance, with ...♘b6 and ...♗f5), but it is White to move and he has a decisive combination:

1 ♘xh7! ♔xh7 2 ♕h5+

Possible thanks to the pin by White's d3-bishop.

2...♔g8 3 ♗xg6 ♖f7 4 ♕h7+ ♔f8 5 ♗h6!

The 'game of pins' continues: the threat is 6 ♕h8#.

5...♗xh6 6 ♕xh6+ ♕g7 7 ♖e8+! *(D)*

This 'sham sacrifice' wins the game.

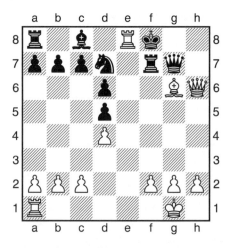

After 7...♔xe8, 8 ♕xg7, the f7-rook is pinned by the bishop.

Discovered Attack

A **discovered attack** consists of revealing an attack on an enemy piece by moving another of your own pieces out of the way. The more important the attacked piece, the more effective will be the discovered attack.

We saw some cases of discovered attacks (or checks) when we were studying tandems. Now we shall look at some other positions which are good examples of this theme.

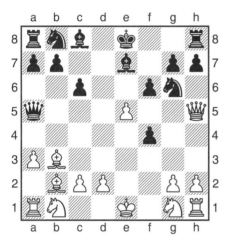

Katalymov – Ilivitsky
Frunze 1959

Here we are still in the opening. The white e5-pawn is pinned (both queens are on the fifth rank), but White found a little combination that wins a piece:

1 ♗f7+! 1-0

Black resigned, since 1...♔xf7 2 e6+ **unpins** the pawn with check and **discovers** an attack on the black queen, while if 1...♔f8, simply 2 ♗xg6.

In the following position the black knights are at least as strong as the white bishops and what's important is that it is Black to move and he now has a forced winning sequence, exploiting the unprotected white queen:

1...♘f3+! 2 gxf3 ♕g6+! 3 ♔h1

The only move, but now the two queens lie on the same diagonal.

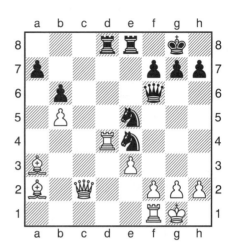

Liublinsky – Baturinsky
Moscow 1945

3...♘g3+!
and Black won.

A similar idea arose in the next example:

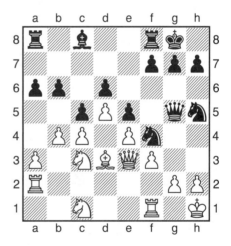

Belliard – Nevednichy
Moscow Olympiad 1994

1...♘g3+! 2 hxg3 ♕h6+ 3 ♔g1
The only move, but it allows a decisive discovered attack.

3...♘h3+!
winning the white queen.

The next position is somewhat more difficult.

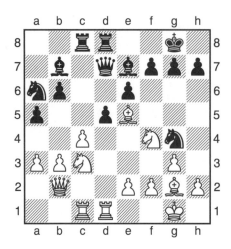

Ehlvest – Ki. Georgiev
Komotini 1992

The opening is over and the sides are contesting the first rounds of the middlegame. The black knight has just created an unpleasant threat against the e5-bishop, but the fact that White's queen is on the same diagonal as his attacked bishop gives White the idea of a combination based on a discovered check:

1 ♗xg7! ♔xg7

Or: 1...♗c5 2 ♗d4; 1...e5 2 ♘fxd5 ♔xg7 3 ♘e3.

2 ♘cxd5+ *(D)*

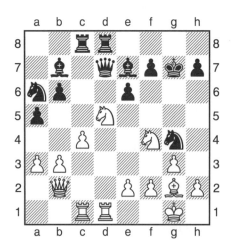

Now the white pieces really display their activity, especially the queen, which seemed hidden behind this knight.

2...♗f6

2...♔g8 is met by 3 ♘h5, and 2...♔f8? with 3 ♕h8#.

3 ♘h5+ ♔f8 4 ♘hxf6 ♘xf6 5 ♘e3! 1-0

Black resigned due to 5...♕e7 6 ♗xb7 ♕xb7 7 ♕xf6, with a winning position.

Next is a position where the terrific strength of the white pieces allows him not only to ignore the fact that he is a piece down, but even to execute a decisive attack. We shall see that in this attack several combinative themes come into play, such as **pin-breaking** and **discovered attack**.

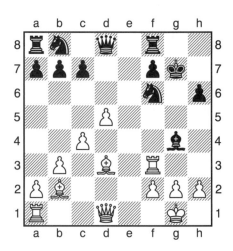

1 ♖xf6!!

When a pinned piece moves, sacrificing the piece behind it, this is known as 'pin-breaking'.

1...♗xd1

If 1...♕xf6, 2 ♕xg4+ ♔h8 3 ♗xf6#.

2 ♖g6++!

Double check by the rook and the b2-bishop.

2...♔h7 3 ♖g7++ ♔h8 4 ♖h7++!

Double check again... the b2-bishop resembles a powerful cannon!

4...♔g8

All Black's king moves are forced.

5 ♖h8#

We saw the pattern for this mate when we were studying the ♖+♗ tandem.

One of the most spectacular combinations involving the theme of discovered attack ever seen in an international tournament was played in

Moscow 1925, in the game between the young Mexican Carlos Torre and the great Emanuel Lasker.

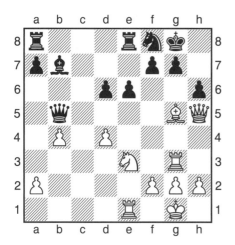

C. Torre – Em. Lasker
Moscow 1925

Lasker had just played ...h6 to exploit the pinned bishop, without appreciating the danger he was in. Torre created a sensation with an extraordinary move:

1 ♗f6!!

White attacks the black queen and the g7-square, but also offers his own queen as a sacrifice. Torre's idea, very precisely calculated, is to win material and then recover the queen. Let's see how he does it:

1...♕xh5 2 ♖xg7+ ♔h8 3 ♖xf7+!

First discovered check.

3...♔g8 4 ♖g7+ ♔h8 5 ♖xb7+

We see how the young master is sweeping pieces from the board, giving simultaneous checks by the bishop.

5...♔g8 6 ♖g7+ ♔h8

Here we should observe that this does not qualify as a draw by repetition, since although the manoeuvre is being repeated, the position is different; each time a new piece disappears from the board.

7 ♖g5+!

After having captured his booty of a bishop and two pawns, the rook goes big-game hunting.

7...♔h7 8 ♖xh5 ♔g6

Double attack by Black on rook and bishop, but it does not help.

9 ♖h3! ♔xf6 10 ♖xh6+

With three extra pawns, White duly won the endgame.

The theme of this famous combination, which is also an example of optimal coordination of the ♖+♗ tandem, is known as the **Windmill** (or the **See-Saw**).

Removing the Guard

There are two kinds of combinations based on the theme of **removing the guard** (also known, more dramatically, as **destruction**). The first consists of eliminating the piece that protects an important enemy piece (or square). The second consists of removing the pawn-barrier protecting the opposing king (also known as **annihilation of defence**).

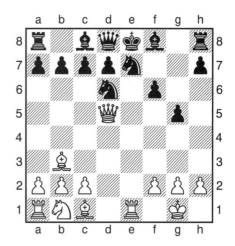

Here we have an example of the first kind. The white queen would threaten mate on f7 if this square were not defended by the d6-knight. The first idea is to try to eliminate this piece. The problem is how. The advanced black pawns on the kingside have weakened the king's position, which suggests **1 ♗f4!**, and Black is lost, as the bishop cannot be taken in view of 1...gxf4 2 ♕h5+ and mate. This position results from analysis of the Urusov Gambit in the Bishop's Opening, i.e. 1 e4 e5 2 ♗c4 ♘f6 3 d4 exd4 4 ♘f3.

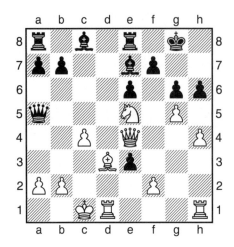

Tolush – Niemelä
Riga 1959

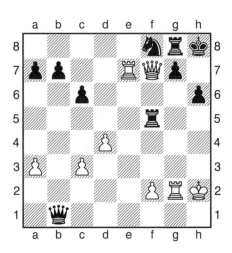

Alapin – Levitsky
St Petersburg 1911

This is a position of the second kind. We see three very active white pieces (queen, bishop and knight) and a weakened black castled position. The queen and bishop, lined up on the b1-h7 diagonal, are very menacing. The f7- and g6-squares are the sensitive points of the black position. Eliminating the defence of g6 would be a gigantic step. Thus, once the idea has been grasped, let's move into action:

1 ♘xf7!

This is stronger than 1 ♘xg6, as the queen now threatens an immediate invasion on g6.

Black now lost after 1...♗a3 2 ♕xg6+ ♔f8 3 ♕f6 1-0. The critical line is 1...♔xf7, when the white queen sacks the black king's fortress: 2 ♕xg6+ ♔f8 3 ♕xh6+ ♔g8 4 ♗h7+ ♔f7 5 ♕g6+ ♔f8 6 ♕g8#.

After the knight sacrifice, the ♕+♗ tandem carried out an efficient execution of the black monarch.

Now, to cheer us up, let's look at two mistakes committed by masters, although really there should be no consolation for our own mistakes in such *schadenfreude*. More seriously, chess is such a complex game that nobody should blame a player for a mistake, even if the player is a famous master.

In the following position, Black is a piece up, but, worried about the triple attack of the white major pieces on g7, believed that he could consolidate his position with his last move, ...♖f5, apparently forcing the retreat of the white queen. Alapin answered 1 ♕e8? and lost. However, he could have won with a simple combination:

1 ♕xg8+! ♔xg8 2 ♖exg7+

The capture must be with this rook, as 2 ♖gxg7+? gets White nowhere, because h7 is protected by the knight.

2...♔h8 3 ♖g8+ ♔h7 4 ♖2g7#

A pattern already seen when we studied the ♖+♖ tandem.

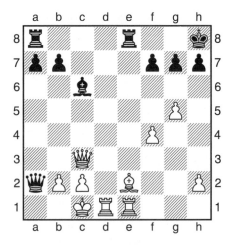

Blackburne – Süchting
Leipzig 1894

Here Black played 1...♕a1+?, and after 2 ♔d2 ♖ad8+? (2...♕a4 retains some advantage) 3 ♗d3, the game drifted towards a draw. However, if Süchting had detected the key defensive piece, he would have understood the need to eliminate it, and won as follows:

1...♖xe2 2 ♖xe2 ♕a1+ 3 ♔d2 ♖d8+ *(D)*

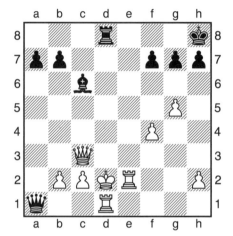

White loses the d1-rook and the game.

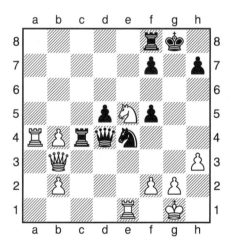

Liliedahl – Johannessen
Sweden-Norway 1976

Black has a serious weakness in his castled position, given the lack of the g-pawn. This, in addition to the active positions of his knight, queen and a4-rook, allows White to dream of a winning combination. The idea is similar to

what we saw in the game Capablanca-Fonaroff (see the section on the fork). If the white queen could reach g3, everything would be perfect. But the black knight is preventing it, so... let's get rid of the knight!

1 ♖xe4!

Now, any capture of this rook (e.g., 1...♕xe4) allows 2 ♕g3+ ♔h8 3 ♘xf7+! ♖xf7 4 ♖a8+ and mate.

1...♖c1+ 2 ♔h2 1-0

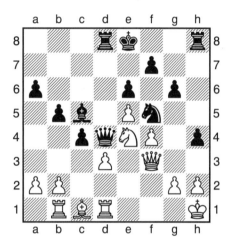

Wilhelm – Mayer
Mulhouse 1970

Here we see close cooperation between the h8-rook, the f5-knight, the h4-pawn and the queen and bishop, lined up on the a7-g1 diagonal. In other words, there is a mating pattern. As the g3-square is attacked by the h4-pawn, a check by the knight on g3 would force its capture by the h2-pawn, opening the h-file with mate! Black sees that 1...♘g3+ 2 hxg3 hxg3+ leads to mate, as the black queen controls the g1-square. However, there is a problem: the white knight also controls the g3-square. We would like very much to eliminate it, but it doesn't seem possible... But is there really no way? Let's be bold!

1...♕xe4!! 0-1

The move is so good that White resigned on the spot, in view of 2 ♕xe4 ♘g3+! 3 hxg3 hxg3# and 2 dxe4 ♖xd1+ 3 ♕xd1 ♘g3+ 4 hxg3 hxg3+, mating.

In the following example we have a position that seems complicated and difficult to evaluate at first sight. White has two pawns for the exchange, one of which (b6) is very dangerous.

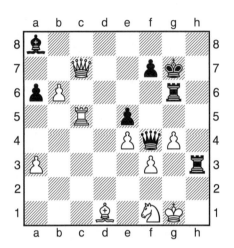

Barbulescu – Andonov
Dubai Olympiad 1986

On the other hand, Black has his three major pieces all aimed towards the opponent's king – considerable fire-power. The a8-bishop is out of play, since the little pawn-chain e4-f3-g4 is blocking it. Thinking a bit more, we can see that both e4- and g4-pawns depend on the little pawn at f3. Too heavy a task! We call such a piece **overloaded**. Can we exploit this? Maybe. What about a rook sacrifice on g4? It seems a big sacrifice and it's hard to see the light at the end of the tunnel... But the Bulgarian player Andonov could see it:

1...♖xg4+!

Destruction of the pawn-barrier.

2 fxg4 ♖h1+!!

Here is the key: **decoying** the white king into the corner.

3 ♔xh1 ♕xe4+! 0-1

The white king will be mated by ...♕g2#.

Interference

Interference is a theme based on forcing the obstruction of a vital line (or square), which will allow the execution of a decisive combination. In the following examples this idea will become perfectly clear.

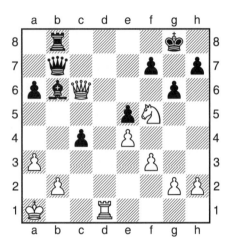

Zhuravliov – Semeniuk
USSR 1976

White won with a typical interference move:

1 ♖d8+! 1-0

Black had to resign, since if 1...♖xd8 he loses the queen (deflection), while if 1...♗xd8 (interference) the bishop would obstruct the defence of the back rank, allowing 2 ♕e8#.

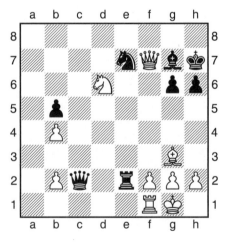

Keller – Nievergelt
Zurich 1960

White has a dominant position and two extra pawns, although it seems that Black will recover one at least. If the g7-bishop could not be protected, ♘e8 would be very strong, but the immediate 1 ♘e8 allows Black to hang on for the time being with 1...♕xb2, defending the g7-bishop. Thinking about the defence by the black queen on the long diagonal, and seeking a way to rule it out, White found the answer: an interference:

1 ♗e5! ♖xe5 2 ♘e8 *(D)*

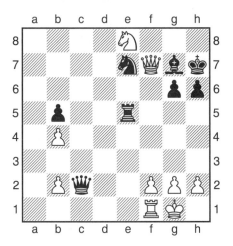

Now this works!

2...♘f5 3 ♘f6+

The secondary threat!

3...♔h8 4 ♕g8#

In the next position, the finish is really spectacular.

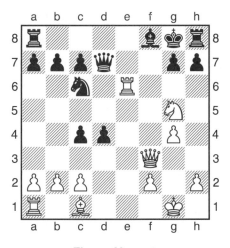

Finn – Nugent
New York 1900

The threats against f7 and along the a2-g8 diagonal make the black queen an overloaded piece. The aim of White is to deflect it from the defence, and he can succeed with...

1 ♖e7!

Now, if the rook is captured by the bishop (1...♗xe7) or the knight (1...♘xe7), then 2 ♕f7# would follow (interference), while after 1...♕xe7, now that the a2-g8 diagonal is open, White can play 2 ♕d5+ ♕e6 3 ♕xe6#. Black chose to give up his knight with 1...♘e5.

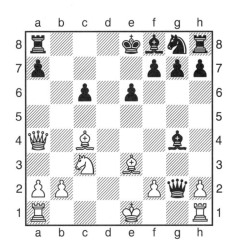

Janowski – Schallopp
Nuremberg 1896

Here we have a classic position in which Dawid Janowski solved his problems brilliantly. As you can see, the h1-rook is attacked and Black has two extra pawns. On the other hand, he is underdeveloped and his king seems to have been left to its fate. White can exploit all these factors with a move which attacks and defends at the same time.

1 ♗d5!

This sacrifice blocks the line g2-c6.

1...exd5 2 ♕xc6+ ♔d8

2...♔e7 would be even worse, in view of 3 ♘xd5+.

3 ♕xa8+ ♔d7 4 ♕b7+ ♔e6 5 ♕c6+ ♗d6 6 ♗f4 1-0

Black resigned in view of 6...♕xh1+ 7 ♔d2 ♕f3 (or 7...♕g2) 8 ♕xd6+ ♔f5 9 ♕e5+ ♔g6 10 ♕g5#.

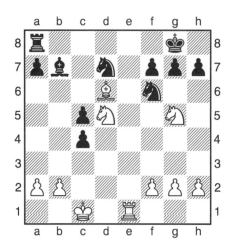

Karsa – Z. Nemeth
Harkany 1986

It seems strange that in a position with so few pieces as this, White can create threats against the opponent's king, but the four white pieces are near the black monarch and that allows a winning sequence:

1 ♘e7+ ♔f8

1...♔h8? 2 ♘xf7#.

2 ♘c8+!

The knight obstructs the black rook on the back rank – interference.

2...♔g8 3 ♖e8+!! *(D)*

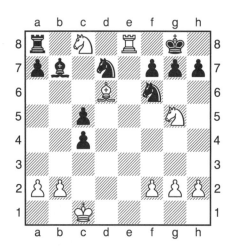

Lightning from a clear sky!

3...♘xe8 4 ♘e7+ 1-0

Black resigned due to 4...♔f8 5 ♘xh7# and 4...♔h8 5 ♘xf7#. The g5-knight, in cooperation

with his team-mates, became a real executioner.

The next position features Bobby Fischer in action.

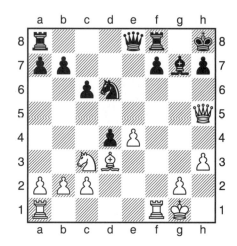

Fischer – Benko
USA Ch, New York 1963/4

Here we can clearly see a threat to h7 (queen and bishop), but Black has kept calm and if the white knight retires to e2, then, although it is risky, he will capture the e4-pawn. At first sight it seems that the immediate 1 e5, with a double attack on h7 and the d6-knight, wins, but that's not the case. Black can respond with 1...f5! and White will not be able to avoid exchanges, and 2 ♕xe8 ♘xe8 rescues the knight. So, what is the hidden key?

1 ♖f6!!

This move blocks the advance of the f-pawn and therefore prevents the black queen from being brought into the defence. This greatly increases the effectiveness of the e5 advance, which now cannot be prevented.

1...♔g8

After both 1...♗xf6 and 1...dxc3 White plays 2 e5!.

2 e5 h6 3 ♘e2!

Not fearing 3...♗xf6 on account of 4 ♕xh6, while if 3...♘b5 then 4 ♕f5! wins.

1-0

In that USA Championship, Fischer scored 100 percent.

Deflection

This tactical theme is based on forcing an enemy piece to abandon a key defensive position.

In the following diagrams we will see combinations inspired by **deflection**.

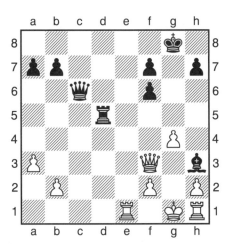

Wexler – Bazan
Mar del Plata 1960

White has just played g4, with the obvious intention of capturing the black bishop, but he has fallen into a trap:

1...♖d1! *(D)*

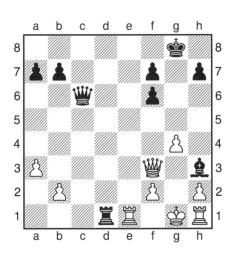

0-1

A deflection: if the queen captures the black rook (2 ♕xd1), then 2...♕g2#, while 2 ♖xd1 is

met by 2...♕xf3, and 2 ♕xh3 by 2...♖xe1+. In this combination the weakness of White's back rank also comes into play.

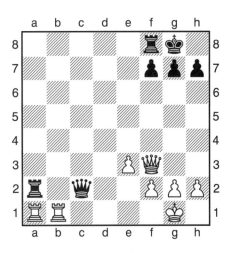

Füster – J. Balogh
Hungarian Ch, Budapest 1964

In this position too the major pieces play the leading roles, and the weakness of White's back rank is also a factor. Black wins with an unexpected move:

1...♕b2! *(D)*

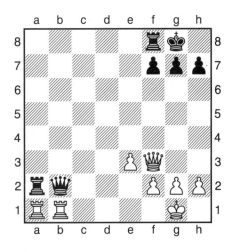

0-1

This increases the pressure on the a1-rook, and as you can see, neither queen nor rook can be captured because of the back-rank mate. The white queen is unable to participate in the defence, since 2 ♕d1 would allow 2...♕xf2+ 3 ♔h1 ♕xg2#.

Now, Black cannot avoid the mate on f8 by the rook. The immediate 1 ♔g5 would not have worked because of 1...♘xe4+. The key to this deflection lay in tightening the net around the black king, not allowing the slightest hole.

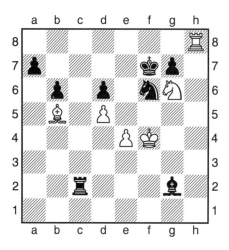

Bondarevsky – Ufimtsev
USSR 1961

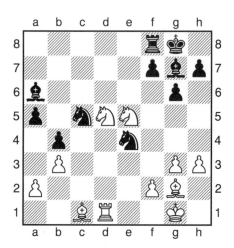

Given the scarce material on the board, it's difficult to believe that Black would not make his two extra pawns count in the endgame. But it is White to move and he finds an elegant deflection manoeuvre:

1 ♗e8+!

Starting with the spectacular sacrifice of a piece!

1...♘xe8 *(D)*

In this composed position, after **1 ♘e7+ ♔h8**, White can play the spectacular and unexpected **2 ♖d8!** to deflect the black rook from the defence of f7, so 2...♖xd8 would allow 3 ♘xf7#. This, in any case, is now a threat, since the black rook is pinned. Black must give up the exchange with **2...♖xe5 3 ♖xf8+**, when White has a won endgame.

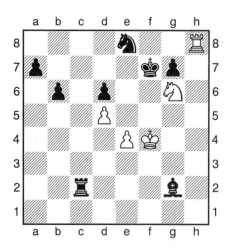

The only move.
2 ♔g5!

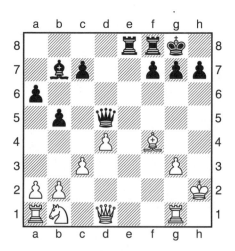

Belenky – Pirogov
Moscow 1957

Here a simple but beautiful deflection gives Black the win. The first element we see in the position is the power of the queen and bishop lined up on the long diagonal. The winning move is:

1...罝e1! 0-1

A double deflection, since 2 罝xe1 allows 2...豐g2#, while 2 豐xe1 is met by 2...豐h5#.

If White tries to offer resistance by 2 豐g4, then 2...豐h1+! is an X-ray, the tactical motif that which we shall study next. After 3 罝xh1 罝xh1# we have a familiar pattern of the 罝+皇 tandem.

In chess, as in thrillers, things are **never** what they seem to be. In the following famous position, for instance, Black's b3-knight occupies an advanced post, deep in the opponent's camp, but is it really a strong outpost?

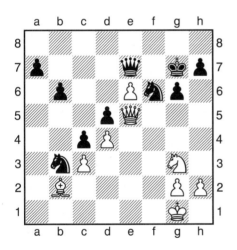

Botvinnik – Capablanca
Rotterdam (AVRO) 1938

In fact, it's completely out of the game. White wants to exploit his advanced passed pawn and pin on the f6-knight. What can he do?

1 皇a3!!

Deflection.

1...豐xa3

1...豐e8 loses simply to 2 豐c7+ 含g8 3 皇e7 ᐧg4 4 豐d7.

2 ᐧh5+!

Thanks to the pin.

2...gxh5 *(D)*

2...含h6 is met by 3 ᐧxf6 豐c1+ 4 含f2 豐d2+ 5 含g3 豐xc3+ 6 含h4! 豐xd4+ 7 ᐧg4+!, winning.

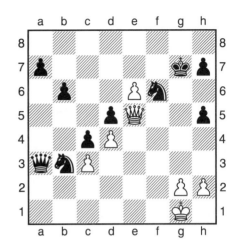

3 豐g5+ 含f8 4 豐xf6+ 含g8 5 e7
and White won.

Two great players reached the following position in a famous international tournament.

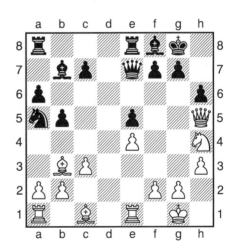

Geller – Portisch
Moscow 1967

At a glance we can see the active set-up of the white pieces (queen, knight, b3-bishop, even the other bishop, pointing at h6 in Black's castled position), but the a5-knight is attacking the dangerous bishop. If it retreats, Black will be able to consolidate. Consequently White should act without delay, in order to take advantage of his aggressive position:

1 &g5! &d7

The bishop cannot be taken: 1...hxg5? 2 ♘g6, with mate on h8; 1...♕xg5? 2 ♕xf7+ &h7 3 ♕g8#.

2 ♖ad1 &d6 (D)

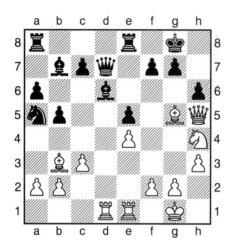

White has developed his two remaining pieces, driven the black queen away from the defence of its king, and the king's bishop is no longer on f8 to protect the king's pawn-barrier. The decisive moment has arrived. There followed:

3 &xh6! gxh6

3...♘xb3 4 &xg7! &xg7 5 ♘f5+ &g8 6 ♕g5+ and mate.

4 ♕g6+ &f8 5 ♕f6

Threatening mate in two with 6 ♘g6+ &g8 7 ♕h8#.

5...&g8 6 ♖e3 1-0

A new piece comes decisively into the attack.

X-Ray

An **X-ray** tactic occurs when a long-range piece (rook, bishop or queen) exerts pressure 'through' one of the opponent's pieces, indirectly attacking/threatening or defending something beyond it.

We have already seen one example of an X-ray tactic above (in Belenky-Pirogov). Now we shall look at some further examples.

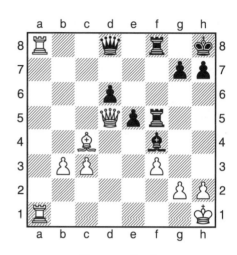

Pages – Gude
Correspondence 1980-2

White is a pawn up and is strategically winning, given the domination of his pieces on the a-file and the a2-g8 diagonal. Thanks to the bishop and queen on this diagonal and the potential attack of the a8-rook on the g8-square, Black must resign on the spot, since if his queen evades the attack by **1...♕e7**, for instance, it is mate in two with the help of the X-ray motif: **2 ♕g8+! ♖xg8 3 ♖xg8#.**

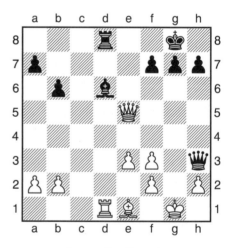

Csanadi – Pogats
Budapest Ch 1963

White has been tempted to try to exploit the pin on the black bishop by capturing on e5, but now he was surprised by an X-ray combination:

1...♕xh2+!

The d6-bishop attacks h2 *through* the white queen.

2 ♕xh2

Or 2 ♔xh2 ♗xe5+.

2...♗xh2+ 3 ♔xh2 ♖xd1 0-1

Black has won the exchange and has a winning endgame.

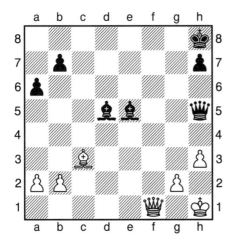

This is a neat composed position (based on one of Pillsbury's games, which we saw earlier in the book). Black has an extra piece and serious threats against the king (...♕xh3+), but there are two little details that will allow White not only to survive, but... even to win! First, the bishops confronting each other on the long diagonal, and second, Black's back-rank weakness. The devilish interconnection of queen and bishop seems easy when you see the X-ray:

1 ♕f8+ ♗g8

Forced.

2 ♕f6+!

Now that the black king's escape-square is blocked, this X-ray attack is lethal.

2...♗xf6 3 ♗xf6#

Once again we have seen that White's bishop attacked *through* Black's e5-bishop.

Now we shall look at an X-ray combination involving an attack by Black's three major pieces:

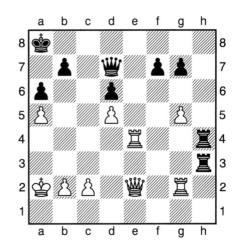

Tisdall – J. Polgar
Reykjavik 1988

1...♕a4+! 0-1

After 2 ♖xa4 (2 ♔b1 loses to 2...♖h1+) 2...♖xa4+ 3 ♔b1 (the two black rooks are well coordinated, as the second one controls the third rank, including the escape-square b3) 3...♖h1+ this rook is now charged with the task of mating on White's weak back rank.

The next position is only slightly more difficult.

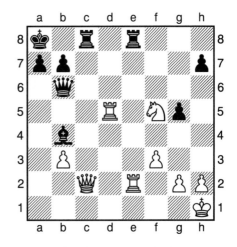

Teschner – Portisch
Monte Carlo 1969

Both black rooks are on the back rank, whereas the white ones have abandoned their back rank, creating a serious weakness there. This allows Black to launch a decisive queen invasion with:

1...♕f2!

The queen is, of course, immune from capture: 2 ♖xf2? ♖e1+ and back-rank mate follows.

2 ♘g3

The only move to cover both attacks, on the e2-rook and the f1-square.

2...♕e1+!

A winning X-ray tactic: the queen exploits the c8-rook's potential to give mate.

3 ♖xe1 ♖xe1+

and Black is winning.

However, in the game, Black did not see this idea and played 1...♕a6? instead; the game was eventually drawn.

Decoy

In a **decoy**, an enemy piece is made to move *to* a square or line that allows us to exploit its position there in some way. Maybe it sets it up for a fork or a pin, or a king might be lured into a deadly double check.

The following examples feature sacrifices to attract the king to a square that permits either a decisive attack or a draw in an apparently lost position.

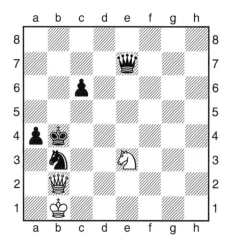

L. Kubbel (end of a study)
150 Endspielstudien, 1925

This diagram shows clearly the devastating effects of one such *fatal attraction*. White wins with the 'simple'...

1 ♕a3+!

Pure attraction!

1...♔xa3

Otherwise Black loses the queen to the **skewer** motif.

2 ♘c2#

Please observe that both the knight and the a4-pawn, acting as self-blocking elements, are what make this combination possible.

With just one position we can say that we now know how lethal the consequences of a decoy can be.

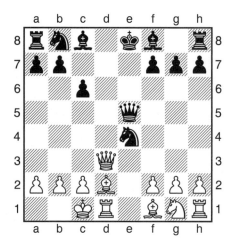

Réti – Tartakower
Vienna (offhand game) 1910

In the opening Black dared to open lines and grab material with his king still in the centre; in even a casual game between masters, that usually receives harsh punishment. Here even an excessive one:

1 ♕d8+! ♔xd8 2 ♗g5++

After this double check Black can only choose one of two mates.

2...♔c7

The other mate is 2...♔e8 3 ♖d8#.

3 ♗d8# (1-0)

We have seen here a decoy, a discovered attack and perfect coordination from the ♖+♗ tandem.

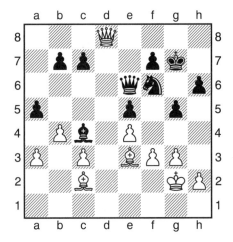

Andersson – Hartston
Hastings 1972/3

This example confirms the truth of the Latin proverb *errare humanum est*, as Ulf Andersson, one of the most solid players of the 20th century, was tempted by an incorrect capture:

1 ♕xc7??

He was presented with a dramatic surprise:

1...♕h3+!!

Decoy.

0-1

The main point is 2 ♔xh3 ♗f1#. 2 ♔f2 and 2 ♔g1 both allow 2...♕f1#, while 2 ♔h1 is mated with 2...♕f1+ 3 ♗g1 ♕xf3#. What a bishop!

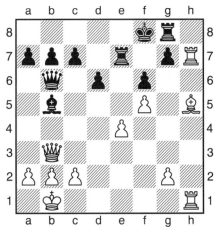

Krylov – Tarasov
Leningrad 1961

Here we can see the influence of the white queen along the a2-g8 diagonal, as well as the strength of the bishop that controls the only two squares 'available' to the black king (e8 and f7). The white rooks, doubled on the h-file, also attract our attention; their pressure on the h-file seems useless but it is not. All these interconnected factors enabled White to play...

1 ♕xg8+!!

A splendid decoy sacrifice.

1...♔xg8 2 ♖h8+!

A second decoy sacrifice, which can't be refused either.

2...♔xh8 3 ♗f7#

A discovered check that rounds off the combinative action with a new display by the ♖+♗ tandem.

The next position seems complicated, but White will show that, on the contrary, everything is crystal-clear.

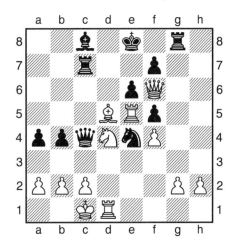

Katalymov – Mukhin
Kazakh Ch, Aktiubinsk 1976

Both queens are attacked and there are many contacts between the pieces. If you remember the game Réti-Tartakower (earlier in this section) and have drawn some conclusions, you will arrive at the same solution that White found:

1 ♗xe4 fxe4 2 ♕d8+!

Decoying the king to the fatal square.

1-0

The finish would be 2...♔xd8 3 ♘c6++! (the correct double check; 3 ♘xe6++?? doesn't work) 3...♔e8 4 ♖d8# – a flawless Arabian Mate, perfect and aesthetically pleasing.

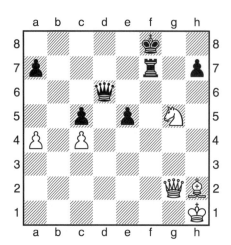

Petrosian – Simagin
Moscow Ch match (5) 1956

Here we see two heavyweights in action. White has two minor pieces for a rook and two pawns. Material is more or less equal, but the situation is uncomfortable... for both players! Both kings are exposed and the position is very open. Nevertheless, Tigran Petrosian (who seven years later would be crowned as world champion) was able to get his bearings on the chessboard like the best of navigators and here he even spotted a winning combination:

1 ♕a8+

If instead White captures the rook, Black can get perpetual check on the squares d1, f3 and h5.

1...♔g7

1...♔e7 2 ♕xa7+.

2 ♗xe5+!

A decoy and a fork.

2...♕xe5 3 ♕h8+!

Another decoy.

3...♔xh8 4 ♘xf7+ 1-0

Black resigned since White plays 5 ♘xe5, with an extra piece and a won endgame. We should add that the immediate 2 ♕h8+ is inferior, in view of 2...♔g6.

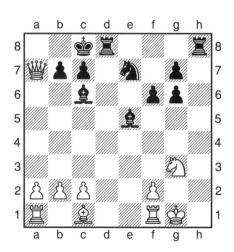

Schiffers – Chigorin
St Petersburg match (13) 1897

Black had a unique opportunity to achieve immortality (and please excuse me for such a big word). The reader should judge for himself:

1...♖h1+!!

Black instead played 1...b6? and the game later ended in a draw.

2 ♘xh1

Deflection.

2...♗h2+!! *(D)*

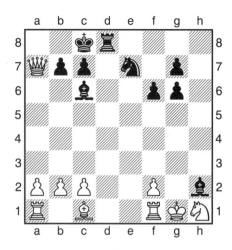

How is it possible that with only a minor piece for the white queen, Black can even sacrifice two more pieces?

3 ♔xh2

Decoy.

3...♖h8+ 4 ♔g3

4 ♔g1 ♖xh1#.

4...♘f5+ 5 ♔f4 ♖h4#

If you failed to enjoy this, I am sure that you should forget about playing chess and turn your attention towards some other game.

Self-Blocking

In a **self-blocking** combination, the attacker forces his opponent to occupy vital squares. In the case of a mating combination, those squares might have been the escape-squares for the king, or squares that a vital defensive piece could otherwise have used. It can be seen that this motif is closely related to decoy.

We should distinguish this tactical type of square-blocking from the positional concept of blockade, where a piece is placed in front of an enemy pawn to block its advance, or to control some key squares and so hinder some undesirable pawn-break or other.

Let's look at a few positions to clarify our understanding of this tactical motif.

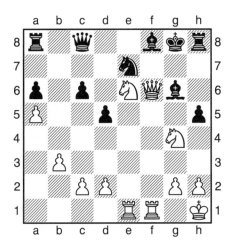

West – Booth
Melbourne 1993

White forced mate as follows:

1 ♕f7+! ♗xf7 2 ♘f6# (1-0)

This example involved a sacrifice not only to force the **self-blocking** capture on f7 but also to **clear** the f6-square for the decisive check.

The tactical sequence in the next example is surprising and, nonetheless, entirely logical.

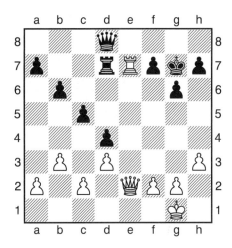

Kwilezki – Roslinski
Poland 1954

1 ♕e5+ ♔f8

The king cannot go to g8 in view of 1...♔g8 2 ♖e8+, winning the queen, while 1...♔h6 loses to 2 ♕f4+ since the black king cannot return to g7 on account of 2...♔g7 3 ♕xf7+, mating, but if 2...♔h5 White mates with 3 g4+ ♔h4 4 g5+ ♔xh3 5 ♕g3#.

2 ♕f6! (D)

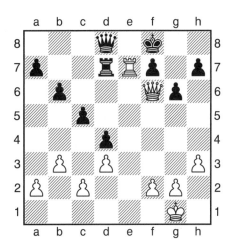

1-0

Black can only defend against the mating attack on f7 by taking the rook, but then the e7-square will be **self-blocked** and the white queen can mate on h8. Black resigned since if 2...♕xe7 (or 2...♜xe7), White mates with 3 ♕h8#.

1 ♖xg7! ♖xf6 2 ♔e5! *(D)*

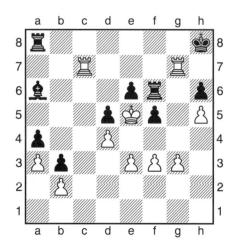

1-0

The only possible retreat-square for the f6-rook is f8 (2...♖ff8), where it would block the escape-square for his king, and the same in the case of 2...♖af8. White would deliver mate with 3 ♖h7+ ♔g8 4 ♖cg7#.

The next is a more modern position, with two outstanding grandmasters in action.

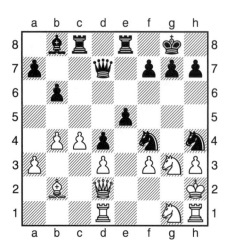

Tot – Asztalos
Ljubljana 1938

Black saw very clearly how to mate the opponent's king:

1...♕xh3+! 2 ♘xh3 ♘xf3# **(0-1)**

A spectacular mate involving the two black knights. A castled position with a pawn missing tends to be an unreliable shelter for a king.

The finish of the next position is simple but very elegant.

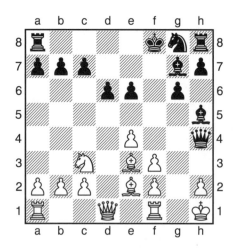

Dorfman – Romanishin
Cienfuegos 1977

Here too White has weakened his castled position, with doubled pawns on the f-file and none on the g-file. Black does not achieve anything from immediate aggression against h2

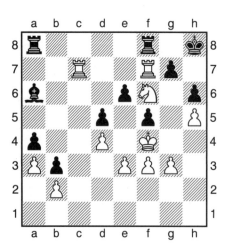

Alekhine – Yates
London 1922

with 1...♗e5, owing to the answer 2 f4. Grand-master Romanishin left nothing to chance:

1...♗xf3+! 0-1

This not only eliminates the defensive move f4, it also blocks the f2-pawn. Now there is no way to protect the h2-b8 diagonal: 2 ♗xf3 ♗e5.

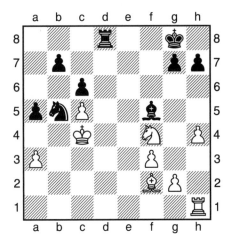

Kopylov – Karlson
Irkutsk 1961

Here we have an extraordinary position that illustrates the self-blocking motif perfectly. The white king can only move to one square (b3), since all the others are attacked by the enemy pieces (b5, d5, b4, d4, c3 and d3). This is a cause for worry but with so few pieces on the board, the danger does not seem so great. However...

1...♖d3!! (D)

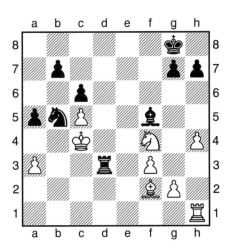

By threatening 2...♖c3# and 2...♘xa3#, Black provokes a decisive self-blocking.

2 ♘xd3 ♗e6# (0-1)

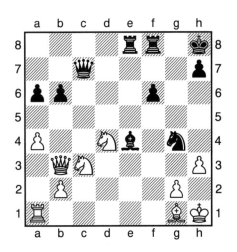

Poutiainen – Szabo
Budapest 1975

Black is the exchange up, but does not wish to abandon the attack by retreating his knight to h6, and so he conceives an aggressive sequence:

1...♗xg2+! 2 ♔xg2 ♖g8! 3 ♔h1 (D)

If 3 hxg4, 3...♖xg4+ 4 ♔f1 ♕g3 wins.

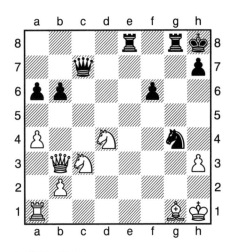

3...♕h2+!! 0-1

A ritual sacrifice: the queen immolates itself to reach a mating pattern with the ♖+♘ tandem: 4 ♗xh2 ♘f2#.

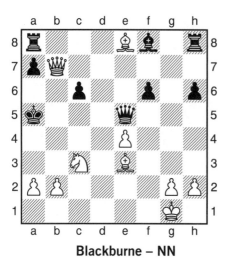

Blackburne – NN
Kidderminster (blindfold simul.) 1863

It's no secret that the players of old also knew how to make combinations. Here White exploits the general confusion among the opponent's pieces to finish off the black king in style:

1 b4+!

Decoy sacrifice to provoke self-blocking.

1...♗xb4 2 ♗b6+! *(D)*

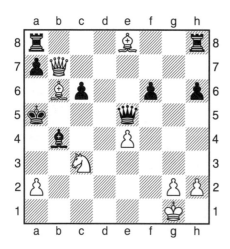

A second such sacrifice.

2...axb6 3 ♕xa8# (1-0)

Clearance

When lines or squares are cleared, incredible attacking ideas sometimes appear. Opening lines (whether ranks, files or diagonals) or vacating squares, generally by sacrificing material, is the theme of the combinative motif known as **clearance**.

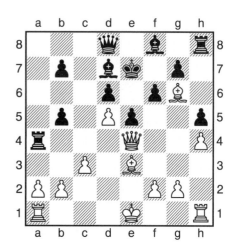

Terzić – Nurkić
Bosnia 1994

This is a peculiar position in which White has a simple mate in two moves. Naturally, you have to open lines against the black king:

1 ♕xe5+! *(D)*

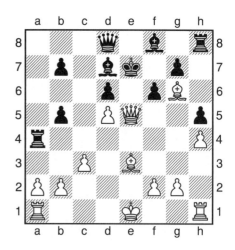

1-0

A **clearance sacrifice**, although it could also be considered an example of **removing the guard**. Now Black has a sad choice: from which square to be mated, and in the end he decided to resign in view of 1...dxe5 2 ♗c5# and 1...fxe5 2

♗g5#. A symmetrical mate by a colossal bishop, which looks composed but was not.

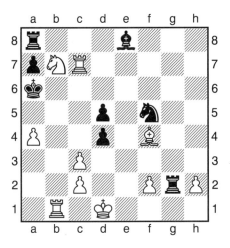

Ivkov – Portisch
Bled 1961

White convincingly exploited the awkward position of the black king:

1 ♖c6+! 1-0

Elegant **clearance** of the c7-square, so that the bishop can become the executioner. Black resigned due to 1...♗xc6 2 ♘c5+ ♔a5 3 ♗c7#. Optimal coordination between the three white pieces!

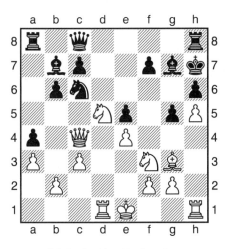

Ljubojević – Padevsky
Nice Olympiad 1974

Here White found a clear way to triumph:

1 ♘f6+!

Clearing a path to f7 for the queen.

1...♗xf6 2 ♕xf7+ ♗g7 *(D)*

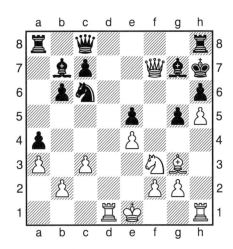

3 ♘xg5+! 1-0

A new **clearance** – also **removing the guard** – that breaches the black fortress. Black resigned since if 3...hxg5, 4 h6 is decisive.

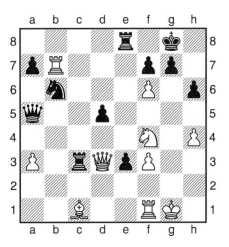

Bronstein – Geller
USSR Ch, Moscow 1961

In this position the white pieces seem unco-ordinated but nevertheless White can win with one 'simple' (but magical) move which seems to defy all logical rules:

1 ♕g6!! 1-0

Threatening mate in one and thus forcing the capture, and thus clearance of the seventh rank. 1...fxg6 is met by 2 ♖xg7+ ♔f8 (or 2...♔h8) 3 ♘xg6#. Acrobatics with no safety-net!

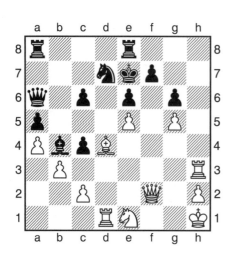

E. Vladimirov – Kharitonov
Alma-Ata 1977

Here we shall see a brilliant combination based on the theme we're studying. First, White surprisingly sacrifices the queen:

1 ♕f6+!! ♘xf6 *(D)*

Deflection of the knight. Now White makes another sacrifice to open the d-file (**clearance**) and thus cut off the escape of the black king:

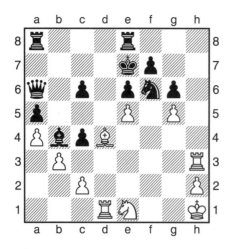

2 ♗c5+! 1-0
2...♗xc5 3 gxf6+ ♔f8 4 ♖h8#.

A simple (but not so simple!) opening of lines takes place in the next example, in which two Romanian stars are in combat.

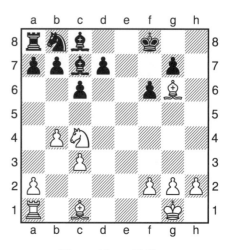

Gheorghiu – Uržica
Romania 1967

We can appreciate that three black pieces have not yet played any part yet and that the black king is in a very dangerous situation, as the white bishop controls the e8- and f7-squares. This conjures up the image of a mating pattern: if only a white rook could reach e8, that would be the end for Black.

1 ♗f4! ♗xf4 2 ♖e1!

All clear and direct but, of course, the bishop can retreat to e5, blocking the e-file.

2...♗e5 3 ♘xe5 *(D)*

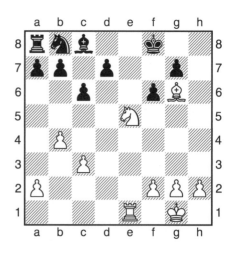

Calmly, since 3...fxe5 loses to 4 ♖xe5, when mate cannot be prevented.

3...d6

3...♘a6 is met by 4 ♘xc6.

4 ♘xc6!

Clearance of the e-file.

4...♗d7 5 ♘a5 1-0

Black resigned since both 5...♗c8 and 5...♗c6 are futile, and 5...b6 fails to 6 ♗e4.

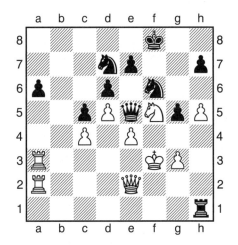

Ftačnik – Wolff
New York 1983

The white king is somewhat exposed, which combined with the invader (h1-rook) can create some tactical possibilities. But it's not easy to see a winning line, and even less to imagine that the white position could collapse in so short a time.

1...♖h2!!

Deflection. 1...g4+? is no good, on account of 2 ♔g2, attacking the black rook.

2 ♕d3

The offer could not be accepted. If 2 ♕xh2, 2...♕xe4+ 3 ♔f2 ♘g4+ 4 ♔g1 ♘xh2 5 ♖xh2 ♕b1+ 6 ♔g2 ♕b2+, winning.

2...♕b2!! 0-1

The key: this move **clears** the e5-square, which is needed for the culmination of the attack. White resigned in view of 3 ♖xb2 ♘e5+ 4 ♔e3 ♘fg4#. An excellent pair of knights, but the major pieces prepared the ground, doing all the dirty work.

Questions

91) Can you remember the moves of the Dragon Variation of the Sicilian Defence?

92) Which moves are characteristic of the Panov-Botvinnik Attack against the Caro-Kann Defence?

93) What is a transposition of moves in the opening?

94) Can we say that a game that starts with 1 ♘f3 d6 2 e4 c5 is a Sicilian Defence?

95) Imagine a game that starts with 1 e4 e6 2 d4 d5 3 ♘d2. What are the names of the opening and the variation?

96) What is a combination?

97) What is a sacrifice?

98) What is a variation?

99) What is the difference between a discovered attack and a double attack?

100) Is the aim of all combinations to mate or to win material? Is there another kind?

101) Name six types of combinative themes.

102) Which piece is most commonly decoyed in a mating combination?

103) With a black king on f6 and a black queen on f2, where on the board would you need to place a white rook, bishop, or knight in order to win the queen by a tactic such as a fork or a skewer? In each case assume that the white piece is working on its own.

104) Try to imagine a position involving a threat of discovered check by a bishop against a white king on g2. You must place a rook blocking the black bishop. Indicate the positions of both the rook and the bishop.

105) How many pieces take part in a combination based on the X-ray theme?

Exercises

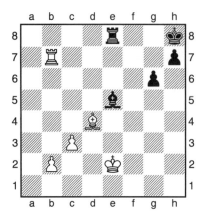

121) How can White exploit his dominant position? Themes: pin, decoy, fork.

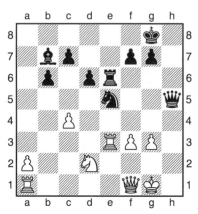

123) Black has a clearly superior position and can seek to exploit the fact that the e3-rook is loose. Your solution? Themes: fork and clearance.

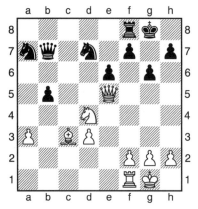

122) White exerts strong latent pressure on the long dark-squared diagonal. Can you profit from this? Themes: decoy, discovered attack.

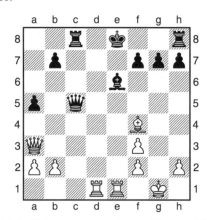

124) This game was solved with one of those tactical tricks that can arise on the board at any moment. White exploits the back-rank weakness and the exposed black king in the centre. What would you play? Theme: pin.

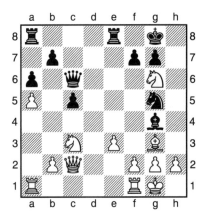

125) Here three black pieces are threatening the white king, protected only by the g3-bishop, which does not cover the key squares. What would you do? Themes: decoy, annihilation of defence.

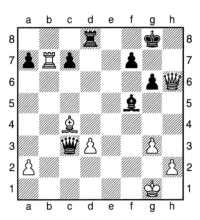

127) Think about a combination that will expose the black king and queen to a fork. How does White win? Themes: decoy, skewer.

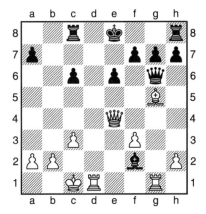

126) This game is barely out of the opening but is already almost over. White to move. Solution? Themes: deflection, back-rank weakness.

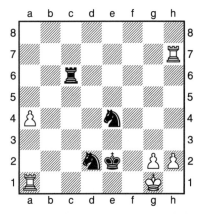

128) This is from an historic world-championship game. White is clearly at least OK from a material viewpoint. But it's Black move and his pieces are very active. Can you suggest a move? Themes: annihilation of defence, clearance.

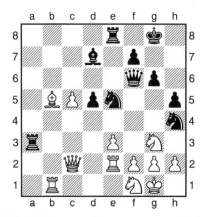

129) With a very nice move, ex-world champion Boris Spassky finished off the white king. What do you suggest? Themes: clearance, annihilation of defence.

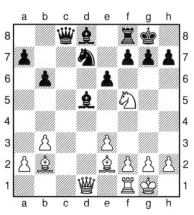

131) White has two active pieces (b2-bishop and f5-knight) and it's a pity that the queen cannot immediately join in the attack (if 1 ♕d4, 1...♗f6). On the other hand, the f5-knight is attacked. Can you find a brilliant finish? Theme: clearance.

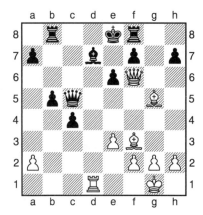

130) The black king is dangerously exposed in the centre and the four white pieces are very active. On the other hand, Black is the exchange up and has a threatening passed pawn on c4. Can you see a decisive sequence for White? Theme: deflection.

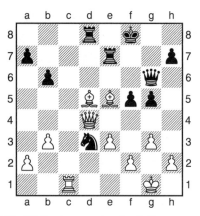

132) White has a simple little move that wins the game. Once you see the idea, the rest is easy. Notice the dominant bishops. Themes: clearance, pin.

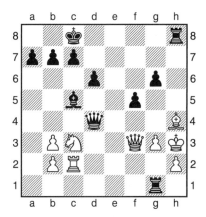

133) This tense position arose in a 'rapid-play' game. Black plays and wins, thanks to the optimal activity of his pieces. What can you see? Themes: annihilation of defence, clearance.

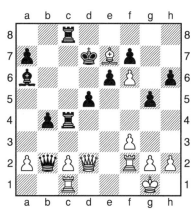

135) Here the skilful hand of Geller guides Black to victory. Notice the pressure of the major pieces on the c-file, as well as the relative weakness of White's back rank. Can you see the solution? Themes: deflection, X-ray.

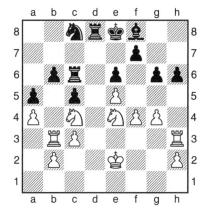

134) Playing a modest-looking trump-card, White brought the battle to a close. How? Theme: clearance.

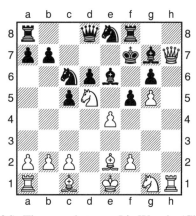

136) The game between Liu Wenzhe (China) and Donner (Holland) reached this explosive position. This was the first time the Chinese took part in a Chess Olympiad. Nobody dreamt that the Chinese board two could defeat an experienced grandmaster such as Donner. But that is precisely what happened. How? It's White to move and win. Themes: decoy, annihilation of defence, discovered attack.

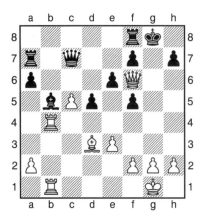

137) With a nice tactical manoeuvre, White applies the finishing touch to the game. How would you do it? Themes: clearance, fork.

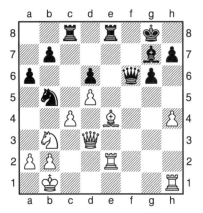

138) Kindly pay attention to the coordination between the five black pieces. Does it suggest anything to you? Analyse the position carefully, as it's more complicated than the previous ones. But if you persist you'll find the solution. Themes: deflection, annihilation of defence, fork.

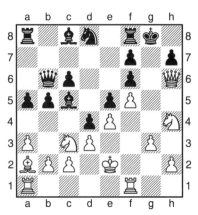

139) This is a classic game which White won with a series of brilliant moves. The key is how to incorporate more forces into the attack. Don't forget that your knight on c3 is attacked. Theme: clearance.

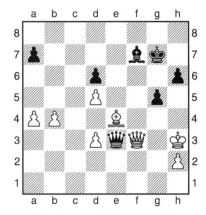

140) This is one of those position that reminds us that even great players make blunders. White has just played ♕f5-f3. Why was this a serious mistake? Themes: fork, skewer, decoy.

Further Tips

Analyse positions and/or games from books or major chess news sites that are based on combinations. Try to solve them and identify the combinative theme(s).

With your chess-playing friends, seek out famous attacking games by great players, ones that contain impressive combinations.

In every friendly game, be alert to the tactical possibilities that may be hidden. At times you'll discover that you can win quickly, just with a combination of imagination and concentration.

8 Attacking Play

Attacks against the Castled King

To start an attack in chess, as in war, you need superiority of forces in the sector where you intend to attack. If that is not the case, then your attack is doomed to failure in advance.

We also have to weigh other factors, such as our own king's safety and, in general, the solidity of our position.

Attacks against the castled position are usually characterized by the destruction of the pawn-barrier in front of the king, generally with the sacrifice of a piece or pieces. In this book we shall be primarily concerned with attacks led by pieces, rather than pawn-storms.

To start with, let us recall the usual set-up after castling. The first four quarter-diagrams represent quite normal set-ups, without any weaknesses. In the bottom left and right, the bishops have been developed by **fianchetto**, i.e. with the three pawns forming a triangle.

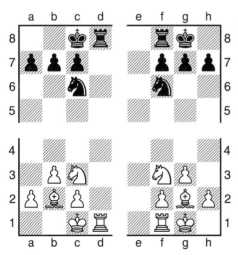

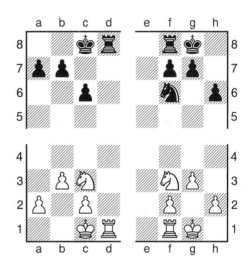

In these last positions, the pawn advances have produced weaknesses. During a game it's not uncommon to advance one of those pawns to give some *luft* (an escape-square, literally 'air') to the king. However, we should be aware that such an advance creates a weakness.

In the lower left and right, the disappearance of the bishops has left serious weaknesses (a3 and c3, and f3 and h3 respectively).

Typical Attacks with Queen and Rooks

An attack with major pieces is usually very dangerous, especially if the opponent's castled position offers some kind of weakness.

In the diagram on the following page, for instance, Black's h-pawn is no longer on the board and his f-pawn has been advanced to f5. We can also appreciate the strength of the white g6-pawn, which controls two important squares, f7 and h7. This brings us to a familiar mating pattern: if the white queen were on h7, that would

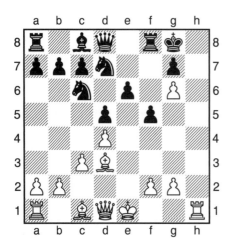

be mate. These factors, plus the fact that the white queen and rook have direct lines of access to the black kingside, allow us to launch a combination by means of a typical decoy sacrifice:

1 ℤh8+! ♚xh8 2 ♕h5+ ♚g8 3 ♕h7#

We were able to place the queen on h7 without loss of time. You should try to retain this image of this typical mate against a castled king.

The previous attack gives us clues as to the path to follow in our next example.

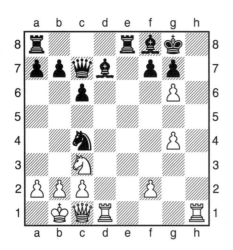

Some factors are similar: the h-pawn is missing, there is a white pawn on g6 and the h-file is open for the white rook. We lack only one thing to make our happiness complete: the white queen has no immediate access to the h-file. But the fact that it is not *immediate* does not mean that it's *impossible*.

If we use a bit of imagination we should find the solution:

1 ℤh8+!! ♚xh8 2 ℤh1+ ♚g8 3 ℤh8+! ♚xh8

Now you can see the finish...

4 ♕h1+ ♚g8 5 ♕h7#

We have sacrificed both rooks to reach the mate, but all the merit has to be credited to having stored the previous mating pattern in our memory. Once this was known, we just had to find a way to reach h7 with our queen, and without caring about material sacrifices along the way!

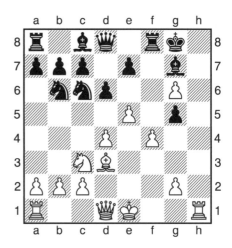

This new position offers another kind of difficulty. Here, queen, rook and pawn are placed on similar squares to the previous examples, but the g7-bishop complicates matters somewhat. The direct attack 1 ♕h5? does not work, as Black can answer 1...ℤxf4, and after 2 ♕h7+, the black king can move to f8, and then it's not easy to continue the attack.

Let's examine the position carefully (there is no clock running). The g6-pawn is very strong, and so is the h1-rook, and the queen can reach h5 in only one move. Is it really possible that there is no decisive combination here? No, it isn't. That combination *does* exist:

1 ℤh8+!! ♗xh8

Obviously not 1...♚xh8, which allows 2 ♕h5+ ♚g8 3 ♕h7# with our familiar mating pattern.

2 ♕h5

Now this is good! White is threatening mate in one, and 2...罩xf4 is met by 3 營h7+ 含f8 4 營xh8#. The difference is that the bishop was forced to move to h8 and to that purpose we sacrificed the rook. Black cannot avoid mate.

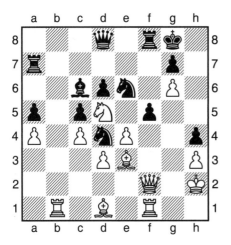

Botvinnik – Keres
USSR Team Ch, Moscow 1966

White is thinking about how to exploit his g6-pawn, surely recalling the themes we are studying. But there is no white rook controlling the h-file, and how could the queen reach h7? However, Black's h-pawn is protected only by the queen, which gives us a hint. Do we have some means to deflect the queen from the defence? At first sight, we don't. But by looking deeper we may discover a wonderful **deflection** move. Remember what you have studied... Yes, you've got it:

1 罩b8!! 1-0

Black cannot prevent the impending mate. After 1...營xb8 2 營xh4, Black's king is trapped in the spider's web created by the g6-pawn (controlling f7) and the d5-knight (controlling e7). Thus, not even moving the rook, e.g. by 2...罩d8, can save the king, as White mates with 3 營h7+ 含f8 4 營h8#, since the escape-squares are all controlled by white pieces.

In the next position the white queen and rooks create, with the invaluable help of a pawn, a mating-net for the black king.

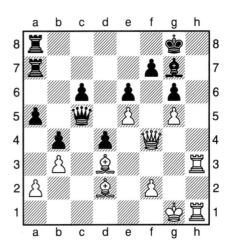

Szabo – Bakonyi
Hungarian Ch, Budapest 1951

1 營f6!! 1-0

The queen is sacrificed, with predictable results, since after 1...盒xf6 2 gxf6 Black cannot prevent the mate on h8. 1 營f6 creates an X-ray threat on h8 (do you recall this tactical motif?), *through* the black bishop: 2 罩h8+! 盒xh8 and now 3 罩xh8# or 3 營xh8#.

When the g- or h-file is controlled by a rook, the sacrifice of this piece can be conclusive. In the next two positions you can see mating patterns involving the major pieces.

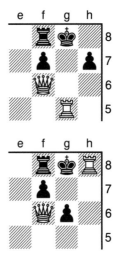

The following composed position illustrates the first of these patterns:

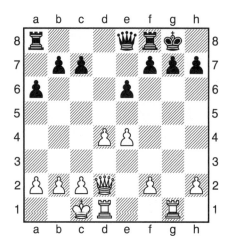

1 ♖xg7+! ♚xg7
1...♚h8 2 ♕h6.
2 ♕g5+ ♚h8 3 ♕f6+ ♚g8 4 ♖g1#

In the next position we can reach the second mating pattern, also by sacrificing the rook, this time on h7:

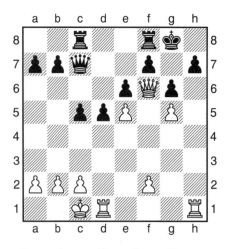

1 ♖xh7! ♚xh7 2 ♖h1+ ♚g8 3 ♖h8#
It is highly advisable to retain an almost photographic image of these typical patterns, to be able to detect the mate at once, should the opportunity arise.

Attacks with Queen and Other Pieces

Attacks against the castled king with queen, bishop and knight are usually very dangerous,

especially when the bishop and knight occupy active positions. Let's look at some typical cases.

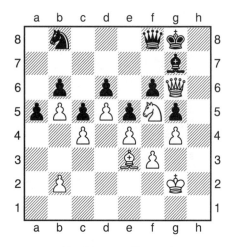

Pachman – Zomas
Cordoba 1959

The bishop is sacrificed not so much to destroy the pawn-cover as to bring the knight to a decisive invasion point:
1 ♗xg5! fxg5 2 ♘h6+ ♚h8 3 ♘f7+ ♚g8 4 ♘xg5
Now Black is lost, as any move of the queen (e.g. 4...♕e7) would be answered with 5 ♕h7+ ♚f8 6 ♘e6+, etc.

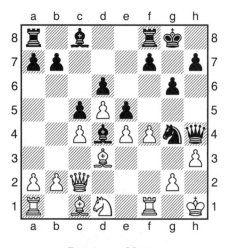

Peretsa – Motta
1937

Here White thought that the worst was over, as his knight protects the f2-square, but he did not expect...

1...♛g3!

The queen can play to this square with impunity, threatening mate on h2, owing to the tremendous strength of the d4-bishop. If 2 hxg4, the queen retraces its steps to mate with 2...♛h4#. The h-file is open and the white king lacks the protection of its pawns!

The above pattern is worth remembering if we find ourselves, for instance, in a position like the next diagram.

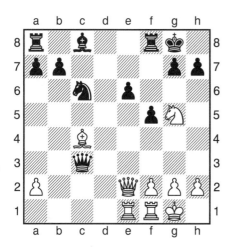

Lemachko – Merdinian
1976

Here we have the same elements which allowed the mate in the previous position. With 1 ♛h5, queen and knight would be on the same (equivalent) squares, but the bishop (also on the same diagonal) is blocked by the e6-pawn. How many white pieces are attacking that pawn? Well, you already have the basis of your action plan.

1 ♛h5 h6 2 ♖xe6!

The aim was to eliminate this pawn but at the same time retain the bishop, which is vital for our purposes.

2....♗xe6

2...♛xc4 was no use either, due to 3 ♖xh6! gxh6 4 ♛g6+ ♚h8 5 ♛h7#, while 2...hxg5 fails to 3 ♖h6+ ♛xc4 4 ♖h8#.

3 ♗xe6+ ♚h8 4 ♛g6!

We have reached an identical mating pattern to the previous one.

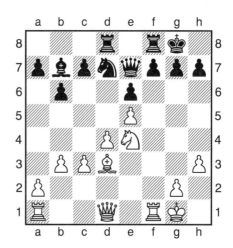

In this composed position we shall see another combination in which the same set of pieces as in the previous diagram (queen, bishop, knight and rook) take an active part, with the help of the e5-pawn.

1 ♛h5? is not very good, since with 1...f5 or even 1...♗xe4 Black can defend. However, there is an immediate and forceful sacrifice that destroys the kingside defences:

1 ♘f6+! gxf6

If 1...♘xf6, 2 exf6 wins easily.

2 ♛g4+

Not 2 ♛h5? f5.

2...♚h8 3 ♛h4!

We already have the ideal position. To prevent the mate on h7, Black would have to give up his queen with 3...f5. This was the reason for the check on g4, i.e. placing the queen on h4, threatening the mate and pinning the f6-pawn at the same time.

In the following diagram, White won by sacrificing the bishop on g7:

1 ♗xg7! ♚xg7 2 ♛g5+ ♘g6

Or 2...♚h8 3 ♛f6+ ♚g8 4 h6, with the same mating pattern.

3 h6+ 1-0

After 3...♚g8 4 ♛f6 there is no defence against the mate on g7.

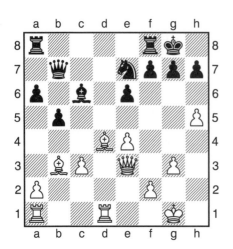

Spielmann – Grünfeld
Karlsbad 1929

Now we are going to see a small miracle, in which the main participants in the attack are the queen, the pair of knights and a 'Sleeping Beauty' (a rook).

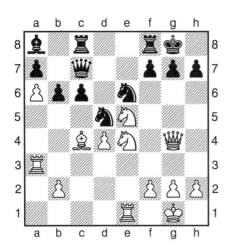

Rossolimo – Reissmann
Puerto Rico 1967

The white pieces occupy such active positions that they can carry out an extraordinary combination. To start with, let's analyse the position a little. Black's bishop is horrible and his two knights are the black king's best defensive trumps, particularly the one on d5 that covers the f6-square. Thus, White starts by eliminating this piece:

1 ♗xd5 cxd5 2 ♘f6+ ♔h8 *(D)*

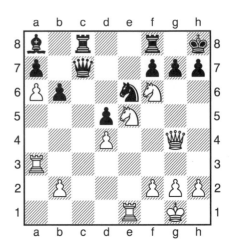

Now, the magician playing with White initiated a stunning tactical sequence:

3 ♕g6!!

What is this? White is threatening mate on h7, but the queen has moved to a square controlled by two enemy pawns! However, it cannot be captured by either of them. If 3...hxg6, 4 ♖h3#, while 3...fxg6 walks into 4 ♘xg6+ hxg6 5 ♖h3#.

3...♕c2

This is the only defence, providing X-ray protection for the h7-square, but...

4 ♖h3!!

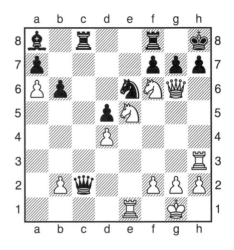

1-0

Now there is no defence against ♖xh7#. The white queen is on a square attacked by three black pieces, yet feels quite at home there!

The Greek Gift

We are now going to study some typical bishop sacrifices on h7 (or h2 by Black) as the key to an effective direct attack using the ♕+♘ tandem. This is known as the 'Greek Gift'.

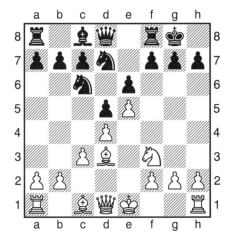

This type of position arises very frequently in practice, when the e5-pawn dislodges the f6-knight. This permits a technical mechanism that you should store in your memory, as a kind of 'loaded gun' in case the situation appears in one of your games. White wins as follows:

1 ♗xh7+! ♔xh7

If the sacrifice is refused, the win is easier: 1...♔h8 2 ♘g5!, followed by 3 ♕h5 or 3 ♕g4.

2 ♘g5+ ♔g8

If 2...♔h6?, 3 ♘xe6+ wins the queen, while 2...♔g6 is met by 3 h4, followed by 4 h5+.

3 ♕h5 ♖e8 4 ♕xf7+ ♔h8 5 ♕h5+ ♔g8 6 ♕h7+ ♔f8 7 ♕h8+ ♔e7 8 ♕xg7#

Important note: when starting a combination of this kind, it is necessary to ensure that the defender cannot protect the h7-square, for instance with a bishop on f5, which would refute the whole combination.

Let's look at a variation on this theme. Even when Black can capture the knight on g5, White may be able to win if there is a pawn on h4 with a rook lying in wait behind it. In the following example Black has a similar position to the previous one, except that the c6-knight is substituted by an e7-bishop.

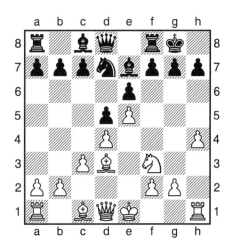

As for White, the only difference is that the h-pawn is on h4. The winning method is even easier here:

1 ♗xh7+! ♔xh7 2 ♘g5+ ♗xg5 3 hxg5+

This pawn is now the key: the opening of the h-file is decisive.

3...♔g8 4 ♕h5 f6 5 g6!

The black king will be mated.

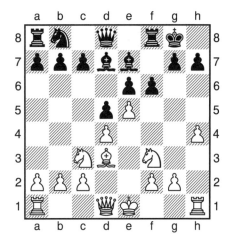

Schlechter – H. Wolf
Vienna 1894

Here we have a variation on the same theme. The f6-pawn seems to prevent the sacrifice on h7, but matters are more complicated than that.

1 ♘g5!?

1 ♗xh7+?! ♔xh7 2 ♘g5+ is a different attempt to make the same basic idea work; then

2...fxg5?? transposes to the game. However, after 2...♔g6! White has no clear way to continue his attack.

1...fxg5??

Now White has a forced mate. Instead 1...f5?! prevents the sacrifice, though 2 g4 gives White dangerous kingside play. 1...h6!? is more challenging, and leaves the game rather unclear.

2 ♗xh7+! ♔xh7 3 hxg5+ ♔g8 4 ♖h8+! ♔f7

The key line is 4...♔xh8 5 ♕h5+ ♔g8 6 g6, with mate to follow by 7 ♕h7+ and 8 ♕h8#.

5 ♕h5+ g6 6 ♕h7+ ♔e8 7 ♕xg6# (1-0)

Double Bishop Sacrifice

When one side has a very active position, with both bishops pointing to the opponent's castled position, there are sometimes possibilities of sacrificing the two bishops. We shall study the most typical cases.

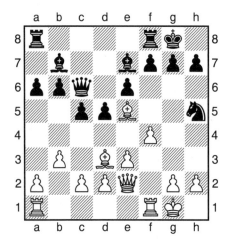

Em. Lasker – Bauer
Amsterdam 1889

Black has just taken a white knight on h5 and, naturally, expected 1 ♕xh5 in reply. However, White conceived a masterful combination, based on the sacrifice of both bishops.

1 ♗xh7+!

1 ♕xh5 is met by 1...f5!.

1...♔xh7 2 ♕xh5+ ♔g8 3 ♗xg7!

Completing the destruction of the pawn-barrier.

3...♔xg7

3...f6 is met by 4 ♖f3! ♕e8 5 ♕h8+ ♔f7 6 ♕h7, mating, and 3...f5 by 4 ♗e5! (4 ♖f3 is also winning but messier; why not keep the powerful bishop?) 4...♖f6 (otherwise White mates more quickly) 5 ♖f3 followed by 6 ♖g3(+), forcing mate in a few moves.

4 ♕g4+ ♔h7

4...♔f6? allows 5 ♕g5#.

5 ♖f3!

The rook enters the attack with decisive effect.

5...e5 6 ♖h3+ ♕h6 7 ♖xh6+ ♔xh6 8 ♕d7

Black is lost since he cannot avoid losing a bishop. Note that the double bishop sacrifice was only winning here due to the 'accidental' possibility of forking the black bishops. In positions where there is no additional tactic such as this, the double bishop sacrifice may only provide a draw by perpetual check unless extra forces can be brought into the attack.

In the next example we shall see a repetition of the above theme:

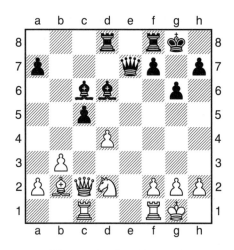

Nimzowitsch – Tarrasch
St Petersburg 1914

1...♗xh2+!

The white king is defended only by its pawns, so Black rips them away.

It's worth mentioning that Black could also have won with a 'Single Bishop Sacrifice': 1...♗xg2! is strong, based on 2 ♔xg2 ♕g5+ 3 ♔h1 (3 ♔f3 ♖fe8) 3...♕f4.

2 ♔xh2 ♕h4+ 3 ♔g1 ♗xg2! 4 f3

4 ♔xg2 is met by 4...♕g4+ followed by 5...♖d5.

4...♖fe8!

Not 4...♕g3?? 5 ♘e4!.

5 ♘e4 ♕h1+ 6 ♔f2 ♗xf1

Black is winning, since 7 ♖xf1 ♕h2+ costs White his queen.

As the game Lasker-Bauer was played 25 years before this one, we may suppose that the master with the black pieces knew that he had all the elements needed to put Lasker's lesson in attacking technique into practice. The key, in both cases, is the possibility of immediately incorporating a rook into the attack.

Knowing the above two positions, the reader should have no great difficulties in seeing how White might launch an attack in the following position. However, analysing the critical lines to a finish is rather more complex.

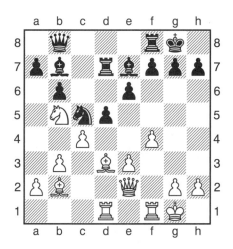

Junge – Kottnauer
Prague 1942

White won with the sacrifice already familiar to us:

1 ♗xh7+! ♔xh7 2 ♕h5+ ♔g8 3 ♗xg7! f5?!

This makes things easy for White.

If 3...♔xg7, there follows 4 ♕g4+ ♔h8?! (4...♔g5 is a better try, but 5 ♕xg5+ ♔h8 6 ♕h6+ ♔g8 7 ♖f3 f6 8 ♖g3+ ♔f7 9 b4! wins) 5 ♖f3 f5 6 ♖h3+ ♗h4 7 ♕xh4+ ♔g8 8 ♕h8+ ♔f7 9 ♖h7+ ♔e8 10 ♕xf8+!.

3...f6!? is more challenging, but one way to win is then 4 ♖f3 ♗d6 5 ♗h6 ♖ff7 6 ♘xd6 ♕xd6 7 ♖h3!? (threatening 8 ♕g6+ ♖g7 9 ♗xg7 ♖xg7 10 ♕e8+ ♕f8 11 ♖h8+) 7...♗c6 (defending e8) 8 ♖g3+ ♖g7 9 ♕e8+ ♕f8 10 ♖xg7+ ♖xg7 11 ♕xc6.

4 ♗e5!

Black is lost, as White is threatening mate (5 ♕g6#) as well as the queen.

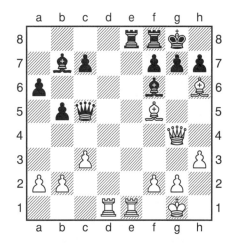

Vasiukov – Kholmov
USSR Team Ch, Moscow 1964

This position gives rise to a combination with different characteristics, although again both bishops are sacrificed. White ended the game brilliantly:

1 ♗xg7! 1-0

After 1...♗xg7 2 ♕h5! White threatens not only mate on h7, but also a discovered check, winning the black queen, and Black can't parry both threats: 2...h6 3 ♗h7+ ♔xh7 4 ♕xc5.

In the following diagram, White has four active pieces (queen, bishop, knight and the e1-rook), and it feels like he should have a clear-cut win. At the moment, sacrificing the bishop by 1 ♗xg6 fxg6 2 ♕xg6+ does not seem completely clear. After 2...♔h8 3 ♕h6+ ♔g8, White obviously has a draw by perpetual check, but it would be hard to establish at the board if he can try for more; in fact, 4 ♖e6! should be winning.

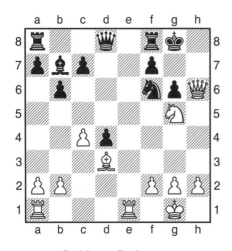

Dobias – Podgorny
Prague 1952

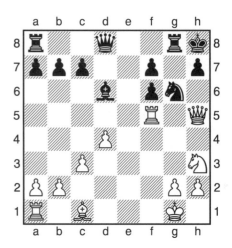

Santasiere – Adams
USA 1926

But instead we can play an excellent sacrifice that destroys the black defences:

1 ♖e6!

Threatening 2 ♖xf6, followed by mate on h7.

1...♖e8

After 1...fxe6 2 ♕xg6+ ♔h8 3 ♕h6+ ♔g8 there follows the familiar procedure with discovered check using the ♕+♗ tandem: 4 ♗h7+ ♔h8 5 ♗f5+ ♔g8 6 ♗xe6+ and mate next move.

2 ♗xg6! 1-0

Now this wins on the spot, since 2...fxg6 3 ♕xg6+ forces mate: 3...♔h8 4 ♘f7# or 3...♔f8 4 ♕f7#.

When the pawns protecting the castled position are doubled or isolated, many combinative possibilities arise, including queen sacrifices.

In the diagram at the top of the next column, White conceived a mating combination based precisely on a queen sacrifice:

1 ♕xh7+! ♔xh7 2 ♖h5+ ♔g7 3 ♗h6+ 1-0

Black must play 3...♔h7 or 3...♔h8, and in both cases a discovered check by the bishop (4 ♗f8#) is mate.

Sacrifices on g7

Piece sacrifices on the g7-square (or on g2 by Black) can be quite effective, as the g-pawn is the axis of the three that usually make up the king's pawn-cover after castling.

We shall look at some typical cases, categorizing them according to the piece sacrificed.

Rook Sacrifices

Let's look at some practical examples of the effectiveness of a rook sacrifice on g7, which generally means the destruction of the king's cover.

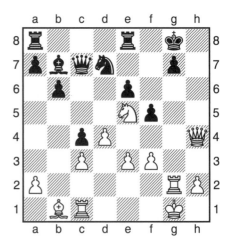

Foguelman – de Oliveira
Leipzig Olympiad 1960

The black king is practically left to its fate, as he lacks defenders and so, despite the limited attacking material available, White can fulfil his objectives.

1 ℤxg7+! ♔xg7 2 ♕g3+! 1-0

Black resigned in view of 2...♔f8 3 ♘g6+, winning the queen, and 2...♔h7 3 ♕g6+ ♔h8 4 ♘f7#.

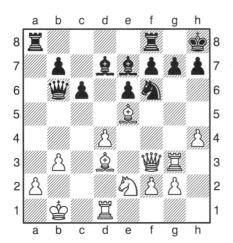

Radulov – Soderborg
Helsinki 1961

Both the white bishops and the g3-rook occupy threatening positions against Black's kingside, and with the help of the queen a quick finish is possible:

1 ℤxg7! ♔xg7 2 ♕g4+ 1-0

After 2...♔h8 3 ♕h5! White wins easily.

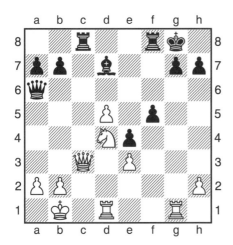

Padevsky – Tsinkov
Bulgaria 1955

In this position several combinative themes are mixed together, such as decoy, discovered attack and clearance. There is obviously a potential threat against g7 and that gives us a clear hint:

1 ℤxg7+! ♔h8

1...♔xg7 loses to 2 ♘e6++: 2...♔f7 3 ♕g7+ ♔e8 4 ♕xf8# or 2...♔g6 (or 2...♔h6) 3 ♕g7+ ♔h5 4 ♕g5#.

2 ♘c6! 1-0

The discovered check after moving the rook will be lethal: if 2...bxc6 or 2...♗xc6, 3 ℤf7+ mates.

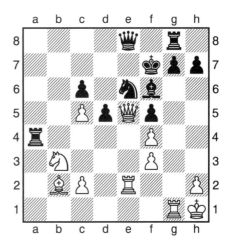

Levenfish – Yudovich
USSR Ch, Leningrad 1933

This is an untypical position, with a king partially 'uncastled'. The black fortress seems in order, but White detected a weak point:

1 ℤxg7+! ♗xg7

1...ℤxg7 loses to 2 ♕xf6+ ♔g8 3 ℤxe6.

2 ♕xf5+ ♔e7 3 ℤxe6+ ♔d8 4 ℤxe8+ 1-0

More Bishop Sacrifices

In the following diagram, Black is hoping to exploit his control of the long light-square diagonal, but the legendary Bobby Fischer has powerful threats against the black kingside. The c3-knight is attacked, but in such a dynamic position there are more important issues to address.

1 ♗xg7+?!

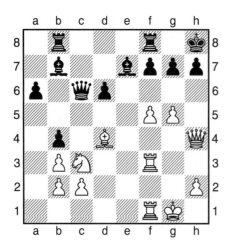

Fischer – Cardoso
Match (game 2), New York 1957

However, this natural attacking move turns out not to be very convincing. Stronger is 1 ♕h5!, with the point that 1...bxc3?? 2 g6 leads to mate. The forced 1...♔g8 is strongly met by 2 f6.

1...♔xg7 2 ♕h6+ ♔h8

2...♔g8? loses to 3 f6.

3 g6!

Mate on h7 is threatened.

3...♕c5+?

Curiously enough, a miraculous defence for Black was later discovered: 3...fxg6 4 fxg6 ♖f7!!, when the game should end in a draw in a line like 5 gxf7 ♖f8 6 ♕e6 ♕c5+ 7 ♖1f2 (7 ♖e3 ♗g5 8 ♘d1 ♗d5) 7...♗xf3 8 ♘e4 ♕d4 9 ♕xe7 ♕d1+ 10 ♖f1 ♕d4+, etc.

4 ♖1f2! fxg6 5 fxg6 ♕g5+

The only move to avoid the mate.

6 ♕xg5 ♗xg5 7 ♖xf8+ ♖xf8 8 ♖xf8+ ♔g7

Rook and knight are attacked but White's next move solves all the problems:

9 gxh7! 1-0

The finish from the following diagram is somewhat more difficult, but it is not surprising that there is a forced win, as the white pieces all stand in optimal positions. The finish was:

1 ♗xg7!! ♔xg7 2 ♘h5+ ♔h8

Or: 2...♔h6 3 ♘f6 ♕c8 4 ♕h5+ ♔g7 5 ♕xh7+ ♔xf6 6 ♕h6#; 2...♔g8 3 ♕g3+ ♗g4 4 ♖xe7!, winning.

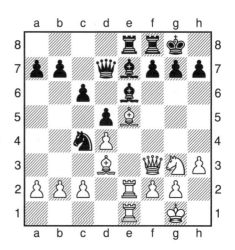

B. Thipsay – Abhayankar
Indian Ch 1991

3 ♘f6! ♗xf6 4 ♕h5! 1-0

Thanks to the self-blocking caused by 3 ♘f6, the threat against h7 is now decisive.

Knight Sacrifices

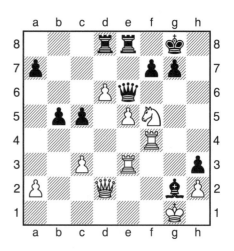

Spassky – Smyslov
Bucharest 1953

Both white rooks are ready to participate in the assault on the black king and this, in connection with the strong advanced pawns and the f5-knight, gives him an obvious advantage. This led a future world champion to believe that there should be a winning sequence. And he was right:

1 ♘xg7! ♖xd6

Or 1...♔xg7 2 ♖g3+ ♔f8 3 ♖xf7+! and now 3...♔xf7 4 ♕f4+ or 3...♕xf7 4 ♕h6+, followed by mate.

2 ♘xe6! 1-0

The three remaining white pieces are more than enough to terminate the game: 2...♖xd2 3 ♖g3+ and now 3...♔h7 and 3...♔h8 are both met by 4 ♖h4#.

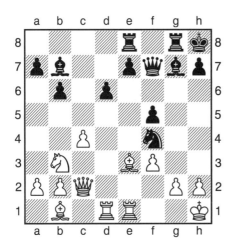

Tringov – Hurme
Malta Olympiad 1980

Here Black knew how to exploit the greater activity of his pieces and the lack of defensive resources around the white king:

1...♘xg2! 2 ♕xg2 (D)

2 ♔xg2 loses to 2...♕h5 3 ♘d2 (3 ♕xf5 ♗xf3+ 4 ♕xf3 ♗h6+) 3...♗h6+ 4 ♔f1 ♕xh2.

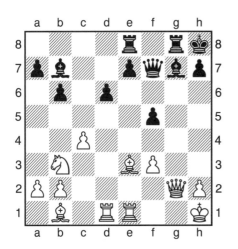

2...♕h5 3 ♖f1 ♗e5 4 ♕e2 ♗xh2! 0-1

5 ♕xh2 fails to 5...♗xf3+.

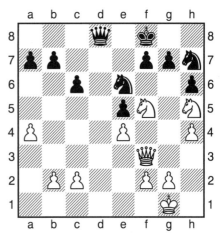

Faibisovich – Bukhman
Spartakiad, Leningrad 1967

Black is about to consolidate with ...c5, but White gave him no respite.

1 ♘hxg7! ♕d2

The knight is taboo: 1...♘xg7 2 ♕a3+ ♔e8 (or 2...♔g8 3 ♘xh6+ ♔h8 4 ♘xf7+) 3 ♘xg7+ ♔d7 4 ♕d3+ ♔c7 5 ♕xd8+ ♔xd8 6 ♘f5 h5 7 ♘d6.

2 ♘xe6+ fxe6 3 ♕a3+ ♔g8 4 ♕g3+ 1-0

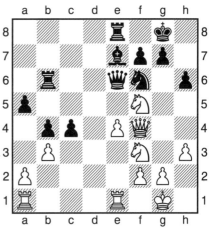

Nezhmetdinov – Estrin
Baku 1951

The f5-knight is very strong, but although Black's pieces are not well coordinated (the e8-rook and the bishop interfere with each other), he does not seem to have anything to fear, especially after his ...c4 advance. White, however, played the unexpected...

1 ♘xg7! ♔xg7 2 ♘d4! ♕c8

Now the black queen is too far away to help the king.

3 ♘f5+ ♔g8 4 ♕g3+

Black is lost.

4...♘g4 5 ♕xg4+ 1-0

Illustrative Games

In the following game White exploits his great advantage in development and space to launch a typical attack against Black's castled position.

B. Stein – Langeweg
European Team Ch, Plovdiv 1983
Giuoco Piano

1 e4 e5 2 ♘f3 ♘c6 3 ♗c4 ♗c5 4 c3 ♘f6 5 d4 exd4 6 0-0 ♘xe4 7 cxd4 ♗e7?!

With this move Black falls into an inferior position. 7...d5 is correct, and is at least OK for Black. In the Open Games as a whole, ...d5 is a move that very often solves Black's problems in the centre.

8 d5! ♘b8 9 ♖e1 ♘d6 10 ♗d3 0-0

At the moment all Black's queenside is hemmed in, including the four pawns.

11 ♘c3 ♘e8? *(D)*

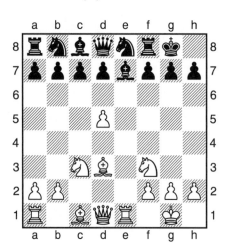

After this understandable (to free the d-pawn) but erroneous move, Black has all his pieces and pawns on the last two ranks.

12 d6!

An excellent advance and a prelude to the combination that follows.

12...cxd6

12...♘xd6 is not good either, in view of 13 ♖xe7! ♕xe7 14 ♘d5 ♕d8 15 ♗xh7+!, while after 12...♗xd6 White would play 13 ♘d5, threatening 14 ♗xh7+.

13 ♗xh7+! ♔xh7 14 ♖xe7!

The perfect follow-up, eliminating Black's control of g5 and decoying the queen to gain a decisive tempo for the attack.

14...♕xe7 15 ♘d5 1-0

White's attack is unstoppable after 15...♕d8 16 ♘g5+ ♔g6 17 ♕g4.

In the miniature that follows, White undertakes an energetic attack, in which practically all his pieces collaborate in breaking down Black's kingside defences.

Geller – Vatnikov
Kiev 1950
Sicilian Defence

1 e4 c5 2 ♘f3 ♘c6 3 d4 cxd4 4 ♘xd4 ♘f6 5 ♘c3 d6 6 ♗c4

At that time this move was not well known and started to become popular in the 1950s.

6...e6 7 0-0 ♗e7 8 ♗e3 0-0 9 ♗b3 ♘a5?! 10 f4 b6

In these structures it is usually better to advance with ...a6 and ...b5, equally so that the queen's bishop can be developed on b7, but also with active play on the queenside.

11 e5! ♘e8

11...dxe5 12 fxe5 ♘d5 (not 12...♘d7?, losing to 13 ♖xf7! ♖xf7 14 ♘xe6) 13 ♘xd5 exd5 14 ♕f3 may be the lesser evil for Black.

12 f5! dxe5 13 fxe6 f6?

Later games investigated 13...fxe6, 13...exd4 and 13...♘xb3.

14 ♘f5! ♘xb3

Finally, Black is able to eliminate the dangerous white bishop, but... too late!

15 ♘d5! ♘d4

If 15...♘xa1, 16 ♘dxe7+, winning the enemy queen.

16 ♘dxe7+ ♔h8 *(D)*

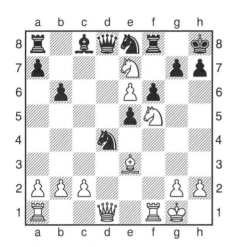

17 ♘g6+! 1-0

Black resigned since 17...hxg6 is met by 18 e7. A spectacular attacking game.

The following battle features opposite-side castling, which usually gives rise to mutual attacks, a theme that we shall not study in this book. But in this particular case, White executed an impressive direct attack on the black king, which explains its inclusion in this chapter.

Malishauskas – Sorokin
Norilsk 1987
Petroff Defence

1 e4 e5 2 ♘f3 ♘f6 3 ♘xe5 d6

It is dubious to take the e4-pawn immediately. After 3...♘xe4?! 4 ♕e2, if the knight retreats (e.g. 4...♘f6??), Black loses his queen after the discovered check 5 ♘c6+, so he should play 4...♕e7 5 ♕xe4 d6 6 d4, when White wins a pawn, but Black may obtain compensation.

4 ♘f3 ♘xe4 5 c4

A rarely played move. The idea is to hinder the advance ...d5, with which Black usually protects his e4-knight.

5...♗e7 6 d4 0-0 7 ♗d3 ♘g5

7...♘f6 is more natural.

8 ♗e3 ♘c6 9 ♘bd2 ♗g4 10 ♕b3 *(D)*

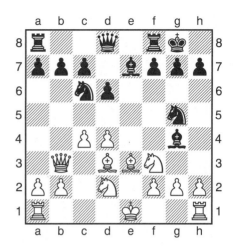

A double-edged idea. White unpins the f3-knight, while also attacking b7. It remains to be seen whether the doubling of White's pawns on the f-file constitutes a serious weakening of his structure or if this will be outweighed by the attacking chances offered by the half-open g-file.

10...♗xf3?!

An unforced and risky exchange. Both 10...f5 and 10...♘xf3+ may be preferable.

11 gxf3! *(D)*

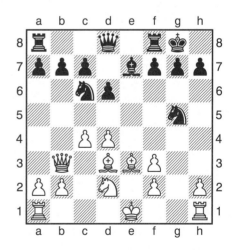

Further piece exchanges are of no interest to the side with attacking intentions.

11...d5

A clever central reaction.

12 cxd5 *(D)*

12 ♕xb7?? is not possible on account of 12...♘b4, attacking the d3-bishop and threatening 13...♖b8, which would win the white queen.

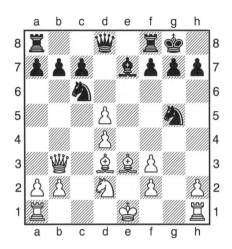

12...♘a5 13 ♕c2 ♗b4?!

It is far from clear that this improves the bishop's position. The immediate 13...♕xd5 is preferable.

14 0-0-0 ♕xd5

Black has recovered the pawn and his position seems the more active. His queen is attacking the a2-pawn.

15 ♔b1 h6?!

This weakening of the pawn-cover aggravates Black's problems and his opponent immediately takes the offensive.

16 ♖hg1!

Now Black is tempted by an illusory win of the **exchange** (reminder: this term refers to the difference in value between a rook and a minor piece), but he was already short of defensive resources.

16...♗xd2 17 ♗xd2 ♘xf3 *(D)*

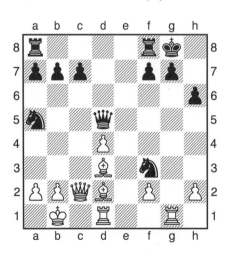

18 ♗xh6!

White pieces are too active and now sack Black's castle.

18...♘xg1 19 ♖xg1 ♖fe8

There was nothing better. If 19...g6, 20 ♗xg6 fxg6 21 ♕xg6+ mates.

20 ♗h7+ 1-0

Black resigned since 20...♔h8 allows 21 ♗xg7#, while 20...♔f8 is met by 21 ♗xg7+ ♔e7 22 ♕xc7+ ♕d7 23 ♖e1#.

Attacks against the King in the Centre

Every weakness can give rise to combinative ideas. So it should be kept very much in mind that a **king in the centre** can constitute a serious weakness.

If our king is still in the centre, we must be aware that it could be exposed to attack. When it is our opponent's king that has lingered too long in the centre, then we should be on the lookout for combinations. We have to question the position and force it to reveal its *secrets*.

A king in the centre is generally vulnerable since it is exposed to the opponent's pieces that were developed during the opening, precisely towards the centre of the board. Among other things, a king that is still on its initial square in the middlegame impedes the connection between the rooks.

The more advanced the king, the more exposed it is. In other words, a king on its first rank (e1 or d1 for White; e8 or d8 for Black) is less vulnerable than one on its second or third rank. Be well aware of the fact that your opponent will spare no sacrifice of his material to get at your king.

The following game is an extreme example of the dangers that can beset a king in the centre, the more so if some of the diagonals leading to its initial square have been weakened.

Aronin – Kantorovich
USSR Team Ch, Moscow 1960
Sicilian Defence

1 e4 c5 2 ♘f3 g6

It seems that Black intends to play a form of the Accelerated Dragon.

3 c3 b6?!

Now we are in almost unknown territory. This is an irregular variation.

4 d4 ♗b7 5 ♗c4 d5?

A blunder. Black creates a weakness on the a4-e8 diagonal. Before that he had also weakened the long light diagonal.

6 exd5 ♗xd5?

Black should not have taken this pawn, although he was already in serious difficulties.

7 ♕a4+! ♗c6

An apparently natural move in answer to the *stupid* check by the white queen, but...

8 ♘e5! *(D)*

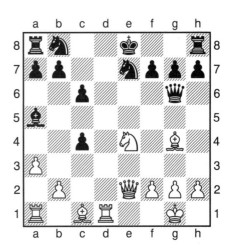

Petroff – Szymanski
Warsaw 1847

1 ♗f5! ♘xf5

1...♕xf5 is met by 2 ♘d6+ followed by 3 ♘xf5.

2 ♘f6++ 1-0

This double check is instantly lethal: 2...♔f8 3 ♕e8#.

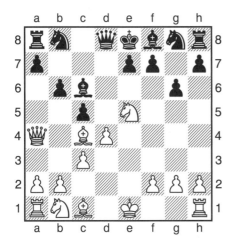

1-0

Double attack, on c6 and f7 (mate)!

The next two examples are related to the Arabian mate (♖+♘, or ♕+♘, do you remember?).

In the following diagram, Black has two extra pawns, but in winning them he has lost time and his king is still in the centre. However, it's clear that if given just one tempo, Black would castle and his main problems would be solved. Thus, White has to proceed forcefully. Any player can see that 1 ♘d6+ and 1 ♖d6 are the main options. In fact, 1 ♖d6! seems very strong, winning the queen, since 1...f6 is not possible because of 2 ♗h5, pinning it. However, there is an even stronger move:

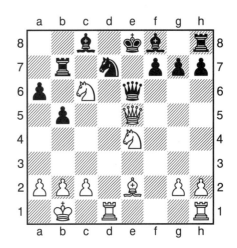

Zimmermann – W. Hübner
Bundesliga 1975/6

Here you have to concentrate a bit harder to discover the key to the position. Don't you hear something telling you that *something has to be there*? Indeed, there is something. White won brilliantly:

1 ♘f6+! 1-0

Black's resignation was a pity, since it avoided a pretty mate: 1...♘xf6 2 ♖d8# (Arabian mate) or 1...gxf6 2 ♕xe6+! fxe6 3 ♗h5# (♗+♘ mating pattern).

Now we are going to see some fireworks. If we examine this position carefully, we shall soon understand that a quick finish should not be a surprise. The five white pieces are hyperactive, whereas the black king remains in the centre and one of the white bishops has the e7- and d8-squares under control. The finish is very spectacular:

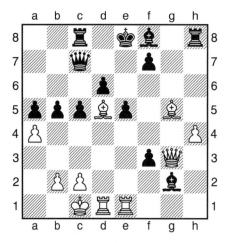

Mackenzie – NN
London 1891

1 ♖xe5+!

Forcefully demolishing the black king's pawn-cover.

1...dxe5 2 ♕xe5+!!

Almost an insult! The queen is sacrificed to deflect its black counterpart.

2...♕xe5 3 ♗c6+!

A third consecutive sacrifice, this time to deflect the rook from its defence of the back rank.

3...♖xc6

Does White still have any pieces left? Yes, just enough:

4 ♖d8#

A mate which should be familiar to us by now.

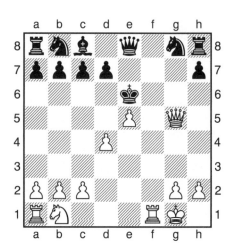

When, as here, the king is not only in the middle but also close to the board's geometrical centre (i.e. he has gone for a walk in the open air), its position is doubly exposed. In such cases a *king-hunt* takes place that usually ends in mate.

This position results from a variation of Lolli Gambit in the King's Gambit (1 e4 e5 2 f4 exf4 3 ♘f3 g5 4 ♗c4 g4 5 ♗xf7+ ♔xf7, etc.). White has sacrificed two pieces but has been rewarded with a position where he now has a mate in all lines. Let's look at the most logical one, which was analysed by Greco:

1 ♖f6+!

White makes a fresh sacrifice, this time of the exchange.

1...♘xf6 2 ♕xf6+ ♔d5

The king is now in the *true* centre.

3 ♘c3+ ♔xd4 4 ♕f4+ ♔c5 5 b4+ ♔c6 6 ♕c4+ ♔b6 7 ♘a4#

Sometimes, king-hunts on an open board are longer, requiring a greater number of moves, but although the attacker's calculations also have to be longer, these are helped by the conviction that, sooner or later, the monarch will be trapped amid the jungle of enemy pieces.

In the following diagram from the modern era, we shall appreciate the vulnerability of a king in the centre. Black has development problems, as only his queen and knight are mobilized, which means that his extra pawn will cost him dearly.

1 ♘d5!

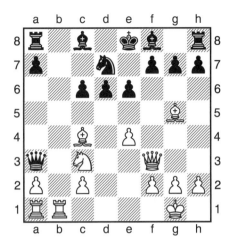

Rogoff – Bertok
Sarajevo (blitz) 1971

With a double threat: mate on c7 and an attack on the queen.

1...♕a5

The only move to defend against both threats, but now the c7-square (and, consequently, the black king) hangs by a thread.

2 ♕a3!!

A stunning deflection, exploiting the situation of the black king. The white queen cannot be taken, which means that Black loses his queen or... he should resign, which is what he did!

1-0

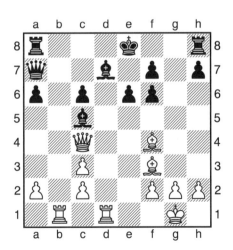

F. Olafsson – Quinteros
Las Palmas 1974

Here GM Fridrik Olafsson emphasized the bad position of the black king, finishing off the game with:

1 ♖xd7! ♔xd7

Obviously not 1...♕xd7, as the c5-bishop would be left defenceless.

2 ♗xc6+!

This move is more difficult to see but it is very logical: if the king refuses the sacrifice, then simply ♗xa8, winning material.

2...♔xc6 3 ♕a4+ 1-0

The black king is forced out into open country, where he will soon be trapped: 3...♔d5 4 ♖d1+.

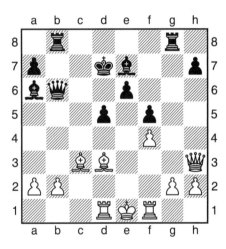

Reggio – Mieses
Monte Carlo 1903

The white king is boxed in by its rooks, but does not seem to be in any immediate danger, as the invasion point of the black queen (e3) is covered by the white queen. But then... haven't you heard of the magician's hat? Black finds a powerful sequence!

1...♖g3!!

A combination based on interference.

2 ♕xg3

2 hxg3?? allows 2...♕e3+ 3 ♗e2 ♕xe2#.

2...♗h4!!

This pin deflects the white queen from the e3-point. Black is better since 3 ♕xh4?? allows 3...♕e3+, mating, so White must give up his queen.

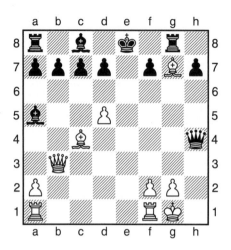

Fischer – Fine
New York (blitz game) 1963

This position was reached in a casual game, included by Bobby Fischer in his book *My 60 Memorable Games*. Black is two pawns up, but his pieces on the queenside are still undeveloped and, last but not least, his king is exposed in the centre. Fischer showed the relevance of these factors with a masterly simple (or simply masterly) combination:

1 ♖fe1+ ♔d8

1...♗xe1 2 ♖xe1+ changes nothing.

2 ♕g3!! 1-0

The queen cannot be taken due to 2...♕xg3 3 ♗f6#, nor can the f6-square be protected any more. For instance, 2...♕d4 3 ♗f6+! ♕xf6 4 ♕xg8#.

Illustrative Games

In the next game, Paul Morphy, without doubt the best player of his time, is playing against an amateur, to whom he has given odds of a rook. Black commits several mistakes, but the game shows the kind of attack to which a king in the centre is exposed.

Morphy – NN
New Orleans (simul.) 1858

This was an odds game: White played without the a1-rook.

1 e4 e5 2 ♘f3 ♘c6 3 ♗c4 ♘f6 4 ♘g5

The immediate threat to f7, characteristic of this opening.

4...d5 5 exd5 ♘xd5?!

This move is considered very dubious. The usual move (with a white rook on a1, naturally) is 5...♘a5 (giving rise to several variations), while there are some other possible moves such as 5...b5 (Ulvestad Variation).

6 ♘xf7!?

The *Fried Liver Attack*, known since time immemorial.

6...♔xf7 7 ♕f3+ ♔e6

This is the key to White's attack. The black king must advance in order to protect the d5-knight.

8 ♘c3 ♘d4?

Here both 8...♘e7 and 8...♘b4 are possible. In the latter case, a possible continuation is 9 ♕e4 c6 10 a3 ♘a6 11 d4, etc.

9 ♗xd5+ ♔d6 10 ♕f7! (D)

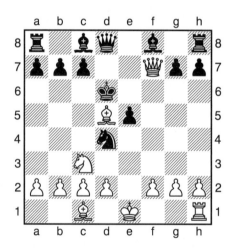

Threatening 11 ♘e4#.

10...♗e6? 11 ♗xe6 ♘xe6

Black forced the exchange of bishops, according to the general principle that the defender side should exchange the opponent's pieces. The problem is that the resulting position is already lost.

12 ♘e4+ ♔d5 13 c4+! ♔xe4 14 ♕xe6 ♕d4 15 ♕g4+ ♔d3 16 ♕e2+ ♔c2 17 d3+ ♔xc1

The black king has reached the first rank, but... it's not a pawn! Thus, he will pay for his audacity with mate.

18 0-0# (1-0) (D)

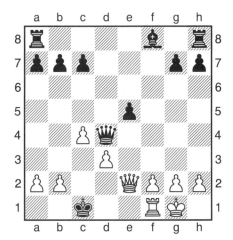

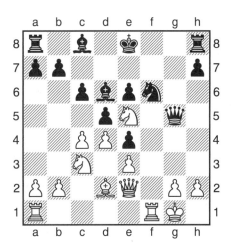

In the following game we shall see how a badly conceived counterattack (13...g5?) allows White to start a direct attack against the opponent's king in the centre.

Heinicke – Reinhardt
Bad Saarow 1935
Queen's Gambit Declined

1 ♘f3 ♘f6 2 c4 e6 3 d4 d5

The game started as a Réti Opening. Then, with 2 c4, it transposed into an English Opening and, finally, it's a Queen's Gambit Declined.

4 ♘c3 c6 5 e3 ♘e4 6 ♗d3 f5

The structure of central pawns with d5+e6+f5 (or d4+e3+f4 by White) is known as a *Stonewall*.

7 ♘e5 ♕h4

An early outing of the queen, difficult to justify.

8 0-0 ♘d7 9 f4 ♗d6 10 ♗xe4 fxe4 11 ♕g4?!

11 ♕b3 is more ambitious.

11...♕h6?

Black is starting to go off-course. He should have swapped queens with 11...♕xg4 12 ♘xg4, followed by 12...0-0, with a satisfactory position.

12 ♗d2 ♘f6 13 ♕e2 g5?

An error of judgement. This advance is suicidal.

14 fxg5 ♕xg5 (D)

15 ♖xf6!

This exchange sacrifice gives rise to a typical attack in this kind of position, allowing the penetration by the white queen and, afterwards, the other rook via f1.

15...♕xf6 16 ♕h5+ ♔e7

16...♔d8 loses to 17 ♘f7+ ♔c7 18 ♖f1 ♕g7 19 ♘xd6! ♔xd6 20 ♖f7.

17 ♖f1 ♗xe5

It's clear that the queen has no good retreat. If 17...♕g7?, 18 ♖f7+. Consequently, Black gives back some material.

18 ♖xf6 ♗xf6 (D)

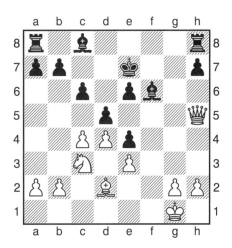

Black considers that his position is defendable and, in fact, it's not easy to see how White can continue his attack. The key idea is to introduce the bishop into the attack.

19 ♘xe4! dxe4 20 ♗b4+

This is the way! White is relying on the underdevelopment of the black pieces on the queenside. This move is very strong.

20...♔d8

Only move.

21 ♕h6! *(D)*

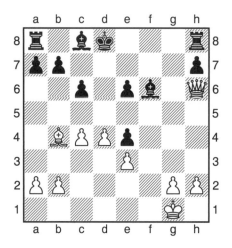

The key move! The f6-bishop is attacked and there is no defence. If 21...♗e7, 22 ♗xe7+ ♔xe7 23 ♕g7+.

21...♗xd4 22 exd4 ♗d7

Black consoles himself by concluding that the material is equal (queen and bishop vs two rooks and bishop), so he 'completes his development'. However, he is unable to avoid material loss without getting mated, as we shall soon see. It is a similar story after 22...♖e8 23 ♕f6+ ♔c7 24 ♕e5+ ♔d8 25 ♗e1!.

23 ♕f6+ 1-0

Black resigned since 23...♔c7 (the only way that the rooks remain connected) allows 24 ♕e5+ ♔b6 25 ♕a5#.

Tal – Benko

Amsterdam Interzonal 1964
Caro-Kann Defence

1 e4 c6 2 d4 d5 3 ♘c3 dxe4 4 ♘xe4 ♘d7 5 ♗c4 ♘gf6 6 ♘g5 e6 7 ♕e2 ♘b6 8 ♗b3 h6

Not 8...♕xd4? in view of 9 ♘1f3 and 10 ♘e5, winning the f7-pawn.

9 ♘5f3 ♗e7 10 ♘h3

A strange move. Better is 10 ♗d2.

10...c5?!

10...g5!? is an interesting response to White's odd knight development.

11 ♗e3 ♘bd5 12 0-0-0 ♘xe3 13 fxe3 ♕c7 14 ♘e5 a6 15 g4! ♗d6 16 g5 hxg5?! 17 ♘xg5 ♗xe5 18 dxe5 ♕xe5? *(D)*

This capture is a serious mistake. 18...♘d7 avoids instant loss.

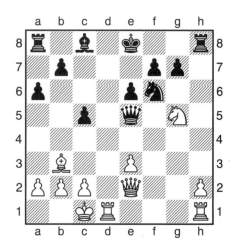

19 ♖d8+!

Decoying the king into a knight fork...

19...♔e7

If 19...♔xd8, 20 ♘xf7+ and 21 ♘xe5.

20 ♖xh8 ♕xg5 21 ♕d2 1-0

To avoid the mate on d8 Black has to adopt a hopelessly passive position (with 21...♘d7), or try 21...♘d5. Then Tal would have probably have answered 22 c4!, winning more material.

Exchange Sacrifices

Several times, throughout the book, the term **exchange** has appeared, in the sense of the difference between a rook and a minor piece. Consequently, an **exchange sacrifice** means sacrificing a rook for a bishop or knight.

Against the King in the Centre

Exchange sacrifices against the king in the centre are not too common, as it is not easy for the rook to establish an early contact with the opponent's minor pieces. But still there are cases in which sacrificing a rook for a key defensive piece is an important weapon to tip the balance. Let's look at some examples.

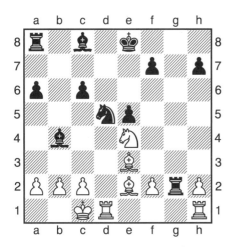

Averbakh – Osnos
USSR Ch, Kiev 1964/5

White's pieces are well-coordinated and he has no weaknesses, whereas Black has three active pieces (the g2-rook, b4-bishop and d5-knight), but two that are not yet developed and his king remains in the centre. The great endgame expert Yuri Averbakh found the way to exploit White's advantages:

1 ♖xd5!

Eliminating Black's most active piece.

1...cxd5 2 ♘f6+ ♔f8

2...♔d8 3 ♗b6+ ♔e7 4 ♘xd5+.

3 ♗h6+ ♔e7

3...♔g7 4 ♖g1.

4 ♘xd5+ ♔d8 5 ♘xb4

White has a decisive advantage.

In the following diagram, Black has an extra (doubled) pawn. But if we evaluate the positional factors, Black fails the examination: all his pieces, except the queen, are still undeveloped. However, it is not easy to see a winning method for White. Bobby Fischer found it though:

1 ♖xf8+! ♕xf8 2 ♕a4+! 1-0

The only possible reply 2...b5 (any move by the king to the d-file would allow the white rook to enter decisively into the attack) allows a clear winning line: 3 ♕xe4 ♖d8 4 ♕c6+ ♖d7 5

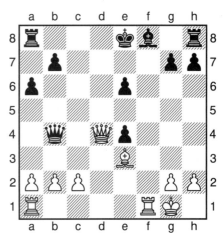

Fischer – Dely
Skopje 1967

♖d1 (or 5 ♗c5 ♕f5 6 ♖e1) 5...♕e7 and now 6 ♖d3! threatens the decisive 7 ♗g5 (the immediate 6 ♗g5? 0-0! allows Black some hope).

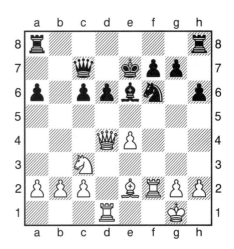

Nezhmetdinov – Sergievsky
RSFSR Ch, Saratov 1966

Here the black king on e7 attracts our immediate attention. Then, we start evaluating other factors, such as piece placement and material. White's pieces are all more active and better coordinated, whereas the black rooks remain on their initial squares. White, a renowned attacking player, found the decisive sequence:

1 e5! dxe5

Or 1...♘e8 2 exd6+, when 2...♛xd6 loses to 3 ♛b6!, while 2...♘xd6 3 ♛xg7 gives White a great advantage.

2 ♛c5+ ♚e8 3 ♖xf6! 1-0

3...gxf6 is met by 4 ♘e4!, with the threat of 5 ♘xf6#, against which there is no viable defence.

In this example, the exchange sacrifice was the culmination of and the key to White's combinative manoeuvre.

Against the Castled King

The exchange sacrifice against the castled king usually takes place on f6 (or f3), with devastating consequences, because it breaks up the king's pawn-cover and opens the g-file. If the rest of the pieces are reasonably well placed, this kind of sacrifice is frequently lethal.

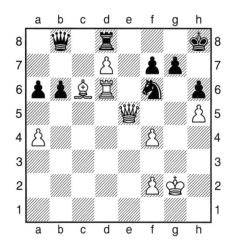

F. Olafsson – Unzicker
Lugano 1970

1 ♖xf6!

This is not so much with an attack in mind as to exploit the strong passed d-pawn.

1...gxf6

1...♛xe5 2 fxe5 gxf6 3 exf6 gives White a decisive endgame advantage as Black's king is imprisoned.

2 ♛xf6+ ♚g8 3 ♛xh6 ♛c7 4 ♛f6! 1-0

Black resigned in view of the decisive threat of 5 h6.

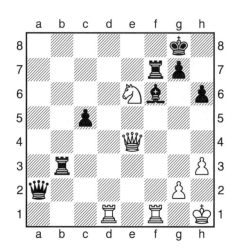

Levy – J. Feller
Praia da Rocha Zonal 1970

In this example, White's exchange sacrifice doesn't create damage to the pawn-structure, but brings about a decisive clearance of lines:

1 ♖xf6! ♖xf6

1...gxf6 loses to 2 ♛g6+.

2 ♖d8+ ♚f7

Now comes a concluding clearance sacrifice.

3 ♘g5+! hxg5 4 ♛e8# (1-0)

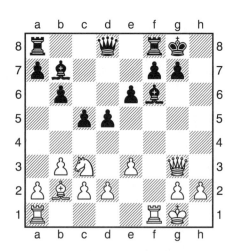

Mildenhall – Ardin
Coventry 1978

Black's kingside is missing the h-pawn. We shall soon see why this is important.

1 ♖xf6! ♕xf6 2 ♘xd5!

Discovered attack by the b2-bishop on the queen; the bishop cannot be taken, because 2...♕xb2 is met by 3 ♘e7+ ♔h7 4 ♕h4#.

2...♕h6

But now follows a new and devastating sacrifice.

3 ♗xg7! 1-0

3...♕g6 4 ♘e7+ costs Black his queen, while 3...♕xg7 is met by 4 ♘f6+ ♔h8 5 ♕h3+.

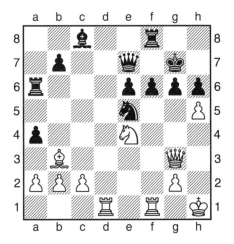

Tal – Bilek
Miskolc 1963

An exchange sacrifice on f6 would be an obvious option, were it not for the fact that the b3-bishop is attacked. Nevertheless, the ex-world champion Mikhail Tal still played...

1 ♖xf6! ♖xf6 2 ♕xe5 axb3 3 axb3!

Totally calm. The key threat is now ♖f1, increasing the pressure on the pinned rook, but now Black has a tempo to organize his defences.

3...b6

Is there a defence? Definitely not; for example, 3...♔f7 4 ♘xf6 ♕xf6 5 ♕c7+ or 3...gxh5 4 b4!!, followed by 5 ♖f1.

4 b4!! 1-0

The 5 ♖f1 threat cannot be parried. The immediate 4 ♖f1 is inferior, owing to 4...♖a5, when the black rook comes into play.

Questions

106) What is the ideal position for the black pawns in front of a king castled on the king-side?

107) What is the ideal position for the white pawns in front of a king castled on the queen-side?

108) With the black king on g8, a black rook on f8 and a black pawn on g7, on which square does the white queen mate, with the help of a pawn on g6?

109) What is meant by *the exchange*?

110) What is meant by a *fianchetto*?

111) What is meant by a *pawn-storm*?

112) What is the first requirement to start an attack?

113) What is an *escape-square*?

114) Which are the most dangerous open files in an attack on a king castled on the king-side?

115) What kind of pieces are, in general, the most dangerous in the attack on a castled king?

116) What is the key to the sacrifice of both bishops against a castled king?

117) Why is a king in the centre often subject to attack?

118) Which pieces are least often involved in an attack on the king in the centre?

119) Where is a king more exposed in the centre: on its first rank or on its second rank?

120) On which squares do exchange sacrifices against the castled king most often take place?

Exercises

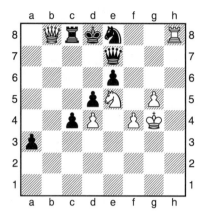

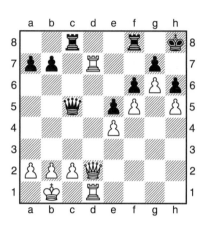

141) The absolute domination of the white pieces leaves no doubt about the outcome. How would you win?

143) White (to move) controls the whole board and has an extra pawn. Relevant factors, such as the d-file, rook on the seventh and the g6-pawn suggest prompt action. What do you think?

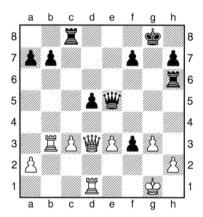

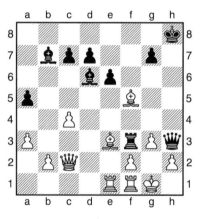

142) This is a fight between heavy pieces. White has pressure against d5, but Black (to move) has a strong pawn on f3. What would you do?

144) White has just captured on f5, with the hope of reorganizing his defences after 1...℞xf5. But Black has something much better. Think about clearance and discovered checks.

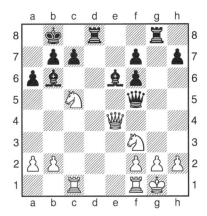

145) The position is sharp. White is proposing a queen exchange, fearing that his opponent has greater possibilities of attack against his king. How would you justify White's fears? Black to move.

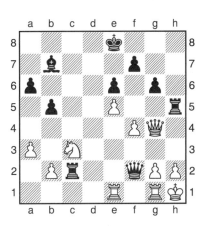

147) Just observe the four black pieces all directed against the white king. The game should be won, but the question is how?

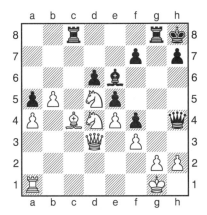

146) Despite appearances, the black position is so strong that he doesn't even have to recapture on d4. How would you win for Black here? Think, once again, about open lines.

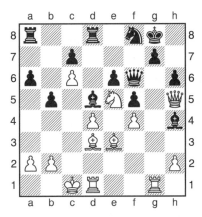

148) Here too the position suggests a quick finish, but this time in White's favour. Can you see the winning line?

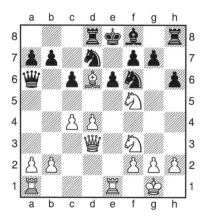

149) The black king is stuck in the centre, with White to move. Active pieces: d6-bishop, f5-knight and e1-rook. Potentially active: the queen. With these elements, analyse, evaluate and win.

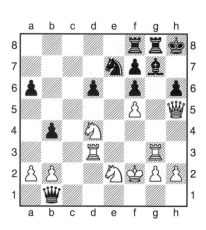

151) Black has problems protecting his king, especially because the queen is far away and cannot easily join in the defence. How would you continue with White?

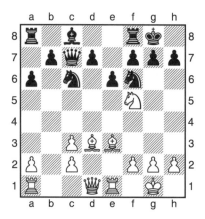

150) Black's queenside is not yet developed. White has a knight on f5, a pair of active bishops and the e1-rook can easily be activated. Is that enough to launch a direct attack?

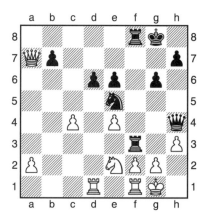

152) The strong pressure of the rooks along the f-file and the active position of both queen and knight allow Black to launch a brilliant direct attack. Indicate the winning line.

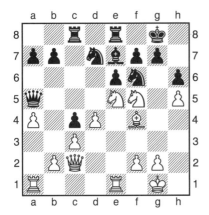

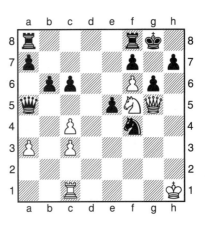

153) Here the white pieces are assailing Black's castled position: knights, queen, bishop and e1-rook, everything suggests a dynamic sequence of play should be possible. What can you see?

155) This is a composed position which is a good illustration of the problems of a weakened castled position. How can White highlight these problems?

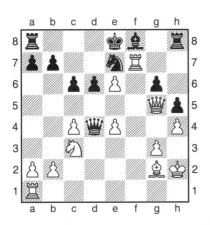

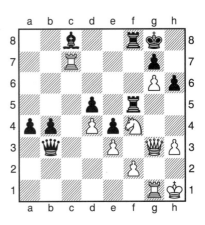

154) A former child prodigy conducted the white pieces here and, given the exposed situation of the black king and White's strong f7-rook and e6-pawn, it's not surprising that he was on the lookout for something decisive. What do you think happened now?

156) Black's passed pawns would decide the battle if White did not have an immediate attack. Can you see the way?

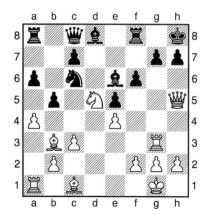

157) White's major pieces are threatening the black king and also the bishops exert latent pressure. Meanwhile the strong white knight has many possible jumps. Find a typical combination, involving a neat finesse.

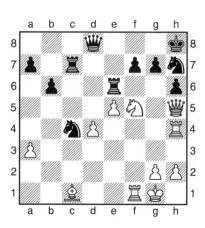

159) There is a lot of heavy artillery fire concentrated against Black's kingside, but it's not clear how White can break the opponent's resistance. What do you suggest?

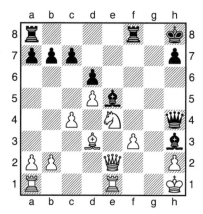

158) All the black pieces except the a8-rook are directed against the white king, although it seems that the white queen and knight can hold the position. However, the f3-pawn is a glaring weakness. What would you play for Black here?

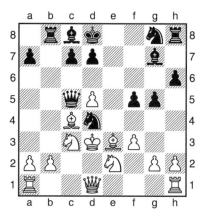

160) In this complicated position, with both kings in the centre, White's is clearly the more exposed. Notice, however, that Black still has two pieces undeveloped. Another factor is that the d4-knight is attacked. Which factor is of most relevance? It's Black to move. Show the whole variation.

Further Tips

Study typical attacks on the castled king with major pieces, trying to memorize in particular the typical queen mates on h7.

Practise the double bishop sacrifice using positions of your own invention, introducing small variations. Discover which factors can refute the intended combination, so that you become familiar with all the characteristic details.

Practise attacks on the king in the centre in blitz games, sacrificing pieces. Reach conclusions and write them in a notebook.

Look for master games featuring brilliant attacks on the king.

Investigate the exchange sacrifice on f3 (or f6 by Black) with the aim of eventually posting a knight on f5 or h5. Include cases in which such a sacrifice is dubious.

Don't miss the chance to analyse for yourself any and all attacking games you may come across, for instance on chess news websites or in chess magazines or perhaps a spectacular game shown to you by a more experienced player.

9 Your First Opening Repertoire

• **The Principal Openings** • **Strategic Opening Fundamentals**
• **How to Build an Opening Repertoire** • **Further Tips** •

The Principal Openings

Taking into account that the opening is the first stage of the game, and the one most studied, let's mention the most important openings, with the moves that characterize them, as a starting point for examining the general strategic foundations and building a personal repertoire of openings.

Open Games

Ruy Lopez: 1 e4 e5 2 ♘f3 ♘c6 3 ♗b5
Giuoco Piano: 1 e4 e5 2 ♘f3 ♘c6 3 ♗c4 ♗c5
King's Gambit: 1 e4 e5 2 f4
Scotch Game: 1 e4 e5 2 ♘f3 ♘c6 3 d4
Centre Game: 1 e4 e5 2 d4
Vienna Game: 1 e4 e5 2 ♘c3
Bishop's Opening: 1 e4 e5 2 ♗c4
Four Knights Game: 1 e4 e5 2 ♘f3 ♘c6 3 ♘c3 ♘f6
Ponziani Opening: 1 e4 e5 2 ♘f3 ♘c6 3 c3
Petroff Defence: 1 e4 e5 2 ♘f3 ♘f6
Philidor Defence: 1 e4 e5 2 ♘f3 d6
Two Knights Defence: 1 e4 e5 2 ♘f3 ♘c6 3 ♗c4 ♘f6
Hungarian Defence: 1 e4 e5 2 ♘f3 ♘c6 3 ♗c4 ♗e7
Latvian Gambit: 1 e4 e5 2 ♘f3 f5

Semi-Open Games

French Defence: 1 e4 e6
Sicilian Defence: 1 e4 c5
Caro-Kann Defence: 1 e4 c6
Alekhine Defence: 1 e4 ♘f6
Scandinavian Defence: 1 e4 d5
Pirc Defence: 1 e4 d6
Modern Defence: 1 e4 g6
Nimzowitsch Defence: 1 e4 ♘c6
Owen Defence: 1 e4 b6

Closed Games

Queen's Gambit Accepted: 1 d4 d5 2 c4 dxc4
Queen's Gambit Declined: 1 d4 d5 2 c4 e6
Slav Defence: 1 d4 d5 2 c4 c6
Catalan Opening: 1 d4 d5 2 c4 e6 3 g3
Nimzo-Indian Defence: 1 d4 ♘f6 2 c4 e6 3 ♘c3 ♗b4
Queen's Indian Defence: 1 d4 ♘f6 2 c4 e6 3 ♘f3 b6
Bogo-Indian Defence: 1 d4 ♘f6 2 c4 e6 3 ♘f3 ♗b4+
King's Indian Defence: 1 d4 ♘f6 2 c4 g6 3 ♘c3 ♗g7
Grünfeld Defence: 1 d4 ♘f6 2 c4 g6 3 ♘c3 d5
Modern Benoni: 1 d4 ♘f6 2 c4 c5 3 d5 e6
Benko Gambit: 1 d4 ♘f6 2 c4 c5 3 d5 b5
Torre Attack: 1 d4 ♘f6 2 ♘f3 e6 3 ♗g5
Trompowsky Attack: 1 d4 ♘f6 2 ♗g5
London System: 1 d4 ♘f6 2 ♘f3 e6 3 ♗f4
Dutch Defence: 1 d4 f5
Réti Opening: 1 ♘f3
English Opening: 1 c4
Bird Opening: 1 f4
Nimzowitsch-Larsen Attack: 1 b3
Sokolsky Opening: 1 b4

Strategic Opening Fundamentals

In Chapter 3, when talking about the classic openings, we considered some principles that, with some nuances, are still the same for all kinds of openings: **fight for the centre, development** and **optimal use of the move (tempo)**, always paying attention to **king safety**.

In fact, when choosing a given opening, a player is already opting for some plan of action in the very first stage of the game. We shall look a little bit more at these concepts.

Open Games

In the Open Games, i.e. all that start with 1 e4 e5, White immediately occupies a central square and, since that square is on the same file as the king, the advance is slightly risky. Black answers with a symmetrical move (1...e5) preventing the further advance of the opponent's pawn by placing his own pawn in front of it. It's as if he says 'I shall not hand over an inch of ground'. Black's attitude is similar to White's, thus starting a strategic struggle to the death.

Immediate aggression against the black centre is characteristic of the King's Gambit (2 f4) and the Centre Game (2 d4).

In other openings where White proceeds to a fast break in the centre, that break is usually prepared by the development of one or more pieces, as in the Scotch Game (2 ♘f3 ♘c6 3 d4), or in the Vienna Gambit (2 ♘c3 ♘c6 3 f4), a variation of the Vienna Game.

There are other opening systems, such as the Italian (2 ♘f3 ♘c6 3 ♗c4), the Ruy Lopez (2 ♘f3 ♘c6 3 ♗b5) or the Four Knights (2 ♘f3 ♘c6 3 ♘c3 ♘f6), where White gives priority to a methodical development before making any sharp pawn advances in the centre.

Black also has some choice. He may opt for flexible but initially defensive systems (after 2 ♘f3 ♘c6), or the Philidor Defence (2 ♘f3 d6), trying to hold the centre. The alternatives are *counterattacking* systems, such as the Petroff Defence (2 ♘f3 ♘f6), or even more aggressive ones, such as the Latvian Gambit (2 ♘f3 f5) or the so-called Elephant Gambit (2 ♘f3 d5).

Thus, the opening choice is, from the very beginning, mainly a matter of taste. But the taste should be directly related to the player's preparation, i.e. his knowledge of the opening he wants to play.

Logical as it is, you should take into account that the greater the aggression, the riskier it is. If you want to protect yourself against big surprises, then you should opt for the openings resulting from 1 e4 e5 2 ♘f3 ♘c6. If, on the contrary, you want more excitement, then you could try the King's Gambit.

When studying in depth the construction of an opening repertoire, we shall examine the factors you should consider, from the specific point of view of your taste and preparation.

Semi-Open Games

Usually the education of a chess-player goes in parallel to the evolution of chess history. First we play gambits and hazardous openings. Who cares about risk when you are young? Attacks, open lines, violent attacks on the king attract all of us initially. Later, when he has suffered some heavy defeats, a player tries to find set-ups that suit his style and, at the same time, protect him, i.e. trying to act in line with the principle of covering one's back. Thus, he may find a defence against 1 e4 that, without depriving him of chances, avoids to some extent the violent clashes of the Open Games. And here comes on stage a relevant term to understanding some keys to the game: control. A good player should always try to keep control of the game. In this sense, you will recall that the elite sport teams, be it soccer, basketball or handball, start their attacks from the basis of a good defence. But you should not be misled: I am not recommending you to look for defensive structures or defensive openings. Far from it. I am simply explaining what tends to happen.

Closed Games

When the players of old were tired of seeing the board continually full of threats to both kings, they started to try out on the first move the advance of the queen's pawn: 1 d4. At first, with this advance the king's file remains closed, and the move opens the way for both queen and queen's bishop. The symmetrical answer, 1...d5, was the best answer they found for Black, and this move remains very popular nowadays.

Most games then go down the path of the Queen's Gambit (2 c4). From the last decade of the 19th century to the 1940s, there was a period where players developed a series of new ways for Black to respond. The path immediately splits: either 2...dxc4 (Queen's Gambit Accepted) or various forms of the Queen's Gambit Declined, such as the Orthodox Defence, the Tarrasch, the Slav or the Semi-Slav (in roughly the order in which they first became topical). These systems all contain a considerable dose of poison, though they also feature a number of relatively dull variations.

It should be mentioned that the classification as Open and Closed Games is only by convention – view them as labels rather than descriptions. Many systems within the Queen's Gambit (especially the Semi-Slav) feature more open battles than you find in the Ruy Lopez or some other Open and Semi-Open Games.

But as some variations of the Queen's Gambit became heavily explored and led to rather dry positions, some innovative masters started to introduce the **Indian Defences** against the Queen's Pawn Opening, deriving from 1 d4 ♘f6. Black decides to control the e4-point with a piece, instead of a pawn. These defences, together with the Dutch Defence (1 d4 f5) came onto the stage from the 1920s to the 1940s. The play in these openings is more complex, as Black tends to keep his head down, waiting for the opportunity to deploy his pawns in the fight for the centre. That is the main spirit of the Nimzo-Indian, Queen's Indian, King's Indian, Grünfeld and Modern Benoni.

The basic principles concerning open lines and weaknesses in the position are still valid in all these openings; they have their fair share of opening traps, and there is plenty of scope for the unwary to lose games in the opening and early middlegame.

The game that follows, for instance, is a famous miniature, in which Black harshly punishes the opponent's blunder.

Gibaud – Lazard
Paris 1924
Queen's Pawn Opening

1 d4 ♘f6 2 ♘d2

A strange and artificial move. Normal are 2 c4 and 2 ♘f3.

2...e5 3 dxe5 ♘g4 4 h3??

A serious mistake. The black knight only wanted to recover the pawn, but with the text-move White fatally weakens the e1-h4 diagonal.

4...♘e3! *(D)*

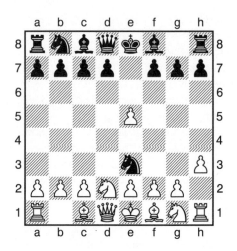

0-1

White cannot prevent the loss of his queen. If 5 fxe3, then 5...♕h4+ 6 g3 ♕xg3#.

It should be noted that this wasn't a tournament game, and many details are far from certain (including the identity of the player with White). One version runs instead 1 d4 d5 2 b3 ♘f6 3 ♘d2 e5 4 dxe5 ♘g4 5 h3?? ♘e3! 0-1 NN-Lazard, Paris c. 1922.

To help you understand that the Closed Openings can perfectly well lead to open lines and sharp play, perhaps there is no better example than the following one, played during the so-called *Match of the Century*, between the USSR and a Rest-of-the-World team. The game was played on the top board (the match was played over ten boards), and is considered one of the most spectacular of all time.

Larsen – Spassky
Belgrade 1970
Nimzowitsch-Larsen Attack

1 b3 e5 2 ♗b2 ♘c6 3 c4 ♘f6 4 ♘f3 e4 5 ♘d4 ♗c5 6 ♘xc6 dxc6 7 e3 ♗f5 8 ♕c2 ♕e7 9 ♗e2?! 0-0-0 10 f4?

If White's previous move was dubious, this one is clearly bad. Preferable was 10 a3 or 10

♘c3. White is delaying his development and his king is still in the centre.

10...♘g4! 11 g3 h5!

Trying to exploit the 'hook' created by the advance g3.

12 h3 h4! *(D)*

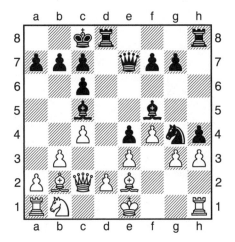

13 hxg4 hxg3!

Spassky exploits the important trump of his passed pawn.

14 ♖g1

14 ♖xh8 ♖xh8 15 gxf5 ♖h1+ 16 ♗f1 g2 is winning for Black.

14...♖h1!! *(D)*

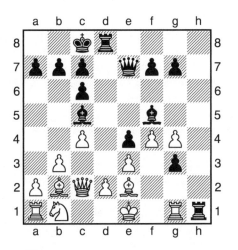

15 ♖xh1

After 15 ♔f1 ♖xg1+ 16 ♔xg1 ♕h4! the queen and pawn create a mating attack.

15...g2 16 ♖f1

White is also lost after 16 ♖g1 ♕h4+ 17 ♔d1 ♕h1.

16...♕h4+ 17 ♔d1 gxf1♕+ 0-1

White resigned in view of 18 ♗xf1 ♗xg4+ 19 ♔c1 ♕e1+, mating.

A miniature played at the chess summit, which should be treasured as a work of chess art.

In the next game you can also see how a typical Closed Game can, through the contacts between pieces, become an open one. In this case, one of the players is forced to resign in only eleven moves!

Spassov – Adorjan
Sochi 1977
Benoni

1 d4 ♘f6 2 c4 c5 3 d5 d6 4 ♘f3 g6 5 g3 ♗g7

Both sides fianchetto on the kingside.

6 ♗g2

6 ♘c3 keeps more control.

6...b5!?

A sharp and audacious pawn sacrifice, which 6 ♗g2 permitted.

7 cxb5 a6 8 bxa6 *(D)*

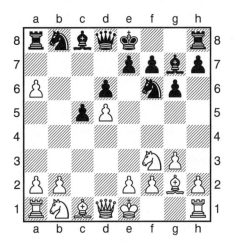

White is harvesting pawns, ignoring Black's actions. In chess, ignoring the opponent's plans is rather like going on a picnic on a stormy day.

8...♕a5+ 9 ♘c3?

This is a mistake. White should choose 9 ♘fd2 or 9 ♗d2, although neither move is ideal in this structure.

9...♘e4 10 ♕c2??

This loses on the spot. The lesser evil was 10 ♗d2, after which Black would play 10...♘xc3 11 bxc3 ♗xc3, recovering the pawn with advantage.

10...♘xc3 11 ♗d2 *(D)*

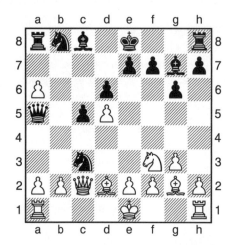

This was the move on which White had placed his hopes, expecting to recover the piece, but...

11...♕a4! 0-1

...this **unpinning** of the knight not only neutralizes the previous move, but is so strong that it forces immediate resignation, since 12 ♕xa4+ ♘xa4 leaves White a piece down, while after 12 b3 ♕e4! there is no defence. GM Adorjan declared that this game was "the shortest one of my career".

How to Build an Opening Repertoire

By this stage, you will already have played hundreds of friendly games, and it's possible that you have begun to play in competitions.

Studying openings is fundamental and you don't have to take this on faith: very likely you know this already from the many beatings you have received, right in the opening (don't be offended: it's happened to everyone, and not just once but many times). At such a moment, faced with a somewhat superior opponent, you will have been left with an odd feeling, as if something has happened that doesn't seem quite 'normal'. This strange sensation might have been, for example, one of 'sliding' out of control into an unknown opening variation... unknown to you, but not to your opponent!

Faced with the huge range of possibilities you will have already met over the board, no matter how little you have played, together with the numerous references you come across at every turn in books and magazines, on the Internet or in things your friends say, I am sure that you feel confused about openings. What's more, that is how you *should* feel. It's not that I want to discourage you. It's just that, quite simply, chess openings are one of the closest things there is to a jungle; to survive there you need to know how to find your way around and to have the right weapons with you.

I shall try here to help you find your way, and between us we'll find those weapons. The rest will come automatically.

How to Prepare for a Game with White

Open, Semi-Open and Closed Openings. Defences, gambits and counter-gambits. White and Black. There is a lot of ground to cover, all of it inhabited by hostile beings. But we shall manage to reach our destination. Have no doubt about it.

Before we do anything else, we are going to sketch a map of the terrain. What is on offer to us? Let's consult the range of openings. Faced with a series of equally good first moves, which one should you choose? And why not all of them?

Let us imagine that you tend to open the game with 1 e4. How have things gone for you with that move? Do you have a clear idea of the results you have achieved with White playing 1 e4? Have you felt comfortable in the opening positions that have been produced in those games?

Let us suppose that your answers to these questions have, on the whole, been positive. Let's go into it a little more deeply: have you often been surprised by your opponent's reply? Do you have an idea, even an approximate one, of the possible defences you could be faced with? Even though I am not a mind reader, I could almost bet that your reply to the last question (be honest) is that you don't have the least idea.

We're going to do a little planning exercise. Tomorrow you are going to be White in your club championship, and although you know your opponent personally, you have no idea of his chess-playing preferences and you cannot even imagine how he will respond. You decide, therefore, to play your usual move, 1 e4. Now let us consider, ruling out wildly extravagant possible moves, your opponent's most logical and most solid responses. They are:

1...e5 – The complex of Open Games
1...e6 – French Defence
1...c6 – Caro-Kann Defence
1...c5 – Sicilian Defence

Let's stop here. As you can see, we are discounting some quite important openings such as the Alekhine, Pirc and Scandinavian Defences. My aim here is to explain how you should set about your preparation, rather than to cover every possible variation.

If your opponent answers with 1...e6, 1...c6 or 1...c5, you should have prepared in advance at least one variation against each of these defences. It is not possible for a chess-player to sit down at the board and be surprised by a French or Sicilian Defence: they are routine, everyday matters. The variation you choose to study in each of these cases should be one that gives you confidence, where you like the kind of play that it produces and where you feel able to control the play up to at least the sixth or seventh move. I expect you to obtain a couple of books on openings and that, by following their suggestions, you will skip the variations which at first sight you don't like and you will take a look at the ones which attract your interest, for whatever reason.

Well now, what we don't yet know is whether you will be able to *impose* your ideas on the opening.

Let's think about the French Defence. It's quite easy to imagine that the moves 1 e4 e6 2 d4 d5 will show up on the board. Therefore, you

(White) still do not have the least problem since it's for you to decide whether you want to play 3 exd5 (Exchange Variation), 3 e5 (Advance Variation), 3 ♘d2 (Tarrasch Variation) or 3 ♘c3, which gives rise to several variations. The important thing, for now, is for you to carry on being in command. Don't forget that what matters is to keep things going our way, making our opponent follow our lead. That won't be enough to win the game, but it will be enough to make us feel comfortable and safe, and also to keep us on familiar territory. You have to foresee all this, because if you don't know what might be waiting for you after, say, 3 ♘c3, it's better to decide on a scheme of play that you know quite well and in which the opponent cannot surprise you, for example 3 ♘d2, after which Black has a smaller set of playable responses and which therefore are foreseeable.

When you come to decide on a variation, I advise you to try particularly to choose one with a manageable amount of 'theory', and not one of those that branch out into a forest of subvariations, where it would take you years to find your way.

In a similar way, you need to do a preliminary study of the Caro-Kann and the Sicilian and prepare a variation against each one. Against the Caro-Kann (1 e4 c6) it's relatively easy, because there are scarcely three variations worthy of consideration, and also, after 2 d4 d5 you can choose a *controlling* variation, like 3 e5 (Advance Variation), or 3 exd5 cxd5 4 c4 (Panov-Botvinnik Attack), playing it safe, therefore. However, in the case of the Sicilian (1 e4 c5), you have a tougher task because, unless you plan to go for one of the Anti-Sicilian variations (such as 2 c3, 2 ♘c3 or 2 f4), the normal continuation, 2 ♘f3 (in order to follow with d4, the Open Sicilian), gives rise to a real tangle of possibilities, among which it is Black who chooses which way to go. He could continue, for example, with 2...e6, 2...d6, 2...♘c6, 2...g6 or even with 2...♘f6, to mention only the most common possibilities. This means that nothing can spare you from preparing at least one variation against each of these responses.

We have not finished yet. There is still the difficult matter of 1...e5. Well, here we are deep in the territory of Open Games and you decide to play seriously, which means you choose 2 ♘f3, because you intend to play the Ruy Lopez. But, lo and behold, your devious opponent can opt for 2...d6 (Philidor Defence), 2...♘f6 (Petroff Defence) or even 2...f5 (Latvian Gambit), spoiling your fun, because you don't have the slightest idea about any of these defences. But your fears turn out to be groundless, because Black decides to answer 2...♘c6, so that you pounce on your king's bishop and place it on the longed-for square, 3 ♗b5. We now have the Ruy Lopez on the board, and I trust you have examined some standard lines of this opening. However, there is a further worry: have you prepared something against each of the possible defences to the Ruy Lopez? Did you think Black was obliged to play 3...a6? Black has numerous other possibilities and almost all are playable. Let's review them:

3...f5 – Schliemann Defence (or Jaenisch Gambit)
    3...♘d4 – Bird Defence
    3...♘f6 – Berlin Defence
    3...♗c5 – Classical Defence
    3...d6 – Steinitz Defence
    3...g6 – Fianchetto or Smyslov Defence
    3...♘ge7 – Cozio Defence

But, however it may seem, it was not my intention to overwhelm you. Take a deep breath. I didn't list these moves to make you feel weighed down by them. I only did it to warn you that you need to prepare at least one line of play against each of them and, if you don't do so, you should know that you run the risk of coming up against a strong variation that is unknown to you.

"That's all right", you will tell me, "I've already found the solution: let's give up the Ruy Lopez. I'll restrict the play, from the start, to a King's Gambit." Correct. No one can prevent you, after 1 e4 e5, from playing 2 f4, choosing the time and the place. But it's not that simple, because in this case Black also has a lot of choice. For example, in addition to 2...exf4 (when both 3 ♘f3 and 3 ♗c4 have many ramifications), you need to consider 2...♗c5 (Classical Defence), 2...♘f6 and 2...d5 (Falkbeer Counter-Gambit), for instance. So, if you decide to

play the daring King's Gambit, you will have to be prepared against all these possibilities, leading to a game that is hard to keep under control, given the characteristics of such a sharp opening.

We have now taken a first look at this topic. Now it's time for the essential part: starting to study, something that no one can do for you. Furthermore, you need to do it critically, without taking for granted everything they say in articles and manuals about openings, no matter how good they are. One of the great things that ex-world champion Garry Kasparov has given to chess-players is this advice about studying his books: "Trust it, but check it".

In this way we have shown you the first step of the way to follow, but the full journey, on the other hand, you will have to work out for yourself.

These considerations make up a part of *how to prepare for a game*, rather than *how to prepare a repertoire*, but it's a way of telling you that in order to prepare for any game or series of games, you have to begin with a theoretical basis, in line with your tastes, your knowledge and your style. Oh, excuse me, you don't yet have a **style**. You will have one when you have found out what you want, when you have learnt to know yourself in chess, having discovered your strengths and accepting (but, careful, only for the time being) your weaknesses.

How to Prepare for a Game as Black

In your club championship you will also have to play with the black pieces. Let's work out a small repertoire of defences.

We have at least to prepare one defence to 1 e4 and another against 1 d4. For the moment, we shall give ourselves permission not to prepare defensive systems against the English, the Catalan or the Réti, perfectly playable openings and much played in top competitive play. The only excuse is that we don't have much time and, for now, your opponents do not know this.

If you face 1 e4, you have to think with your mind the other way round from how you thought as White. But now nobody can stop you from deciding your first move. You already know that if you play 1...e5 there are numerous options. With 1...c5 you will need to have very clear ideas from the start, because the Sicilian is a very dangerous opening and you have to be able to do more than just keep control of the possibilities – you need to be in *command* of them. So, if you decide to adopt the Sicilian, you will need sufficient ammunition to face the anti-Sicilian variations we have already talked about, as well as your own personal, well-analysed variation of the Open Sicilian.

But let us suppose that your tastes are relatively modest and that, with Black, you aim to maintain a balanced game, with the possibility of a draw always in sight. In that case, I recommend the Caro-Kann, where after 1 e4 c6 2 d4 d5, you don't have too many lines to prepare.

Now you must also think about a defence to 1 d4. The most natural response is 1...d5, and after 2 c4, opting for one of the solid variations of the Queen's Gambit Declined. You should not necessarily rule out the Queen's Gambit Accepted (with 2...dxc4), but you should be aware that this defence offers White many active possibilities. If you had all the time in the world (or a team of analysts, like the world champions), then you could review all the variations and come to some personal conclusions. But let's suppose that we shall narrow the choice to Black's various ways of declining the gambit. The main options are:

- Orthodox Defence: 2...e6 3 ♘c3 ♘f6 4 ♗g5 ♗e7. Very solid, but with few active prospects for Black, who normally seeks minor-piece exchanges in order to reach an equal middlegame.
- Tarrasch Defence: 2...e6 3 ♘c3 c5. More dynamic and recommended to those who don't want the sort of passive game typical of the Orthodox, but who at the same time want a rather classical struggle with healthy development.
- Slav Defence: 2...c6. This is the most solid defence against the Queen's Gambit. Black wants to develop his queen's bishop on f5 or g4, outside the pawn-chain. It has a high percentage of draws.

- Semi-Slav Defence: 2...e6 3 ♘c3 c6 4 ♘f3 ♘f6 (or one of the many other sequences that reach this position). The most complicated system in the Queen's Gambit. It gives rise to explosive struggles and the theoretical analyses are deep and with lots of forced variations. This means that not only should you have a taste for these types of position but also the time necessary to study the theory and play them with sufficient confidence.

You also need to be ready for other options such as the Catalan (e.g., 1 d4 d5 2 c4 e6 3 ♘f3 ♘f6 4 g3) and lines after 1 d4 d5 2 ♘f3 where White is in no hurry to play c4.

But let us suppose that the structures of the Queen's Gambit are not to your liking and that you prefer more unpredictable adventures, or a more devious type of game. In that case, you may base your defence against 1 d4 on the *Indian Systems*, in other words those that stem from 1...♘f6 (like the Nimzo-Indian Defence, the Queen's Indian, the King's Indian, the Grünfeld and the Benoni). Deciding which of these suits you best will depend on your style of play, your inclinations. In the Indian Defences, which are by definition asymmetrical, there is more emphasis than in any other openings on the idea of compensation; that is to say that Black is looking not so much for an absolute balance of material and position as on getting certain advantages in exchange for certain concessions. For example, in the Nimzo-Indian (1 d4 ♘f6 2 c4 e6 3 ♘c3 ♗b4), White often allows doubled c-pawns, after the exchange of bishop for knight, but in compensation he will have the pair of bishops at his disposal in a position that he plans to open up. Black is satisfied with having damaged the white pawn-structure and he will try to attack the c4-pawn, while keeping the position semi-closed, so that White cannot exploit his pair of bishops.

In other Indian Defences Black accepts from the start that until well into the middlegame he must operate within a restricted space, but in exchange he can count on a very solid and flexible position, which will allow him, when the time comes, to have various counterplay possibilities at his disposal.

A Tailor-Made Repertoire

Once you have played twenty or thirty competitive games you will understand that you need a *tailor-made* repertoire; in other words, you will realize that you need to know a certain number of openings, in order to be able to feel relatively secure in the initial stage of the game when you sit down at the board to play.

How will you manage to decide which are the openings and defences you need? Logically, when you have been faced with certain difficult problems or when you have found yourself outplayed in a certain opening, your first reaction, when you got home, will have been to take a look at the game to try to see at what point you went wrong and what you would play in that position or that line if it came up again. There is no substitute for this process of self-criticism and you must *never* stop doing it, for as long as you continue to play chess (which may be your whole life).

As a result of this exercise you will come to know yourself as a chess-player and, as we have said before, your strengths and weaknesses will be clearly revealed to you. But so will your preferences, which are not necessarily either strengths or weaknesses. In this precise way your *style* will begin to be formed.

So, in order to establish your repertoire needs, you must establish your preferences, your style. Nobody can do it for you. But we can help you bring to light what you know about yourself as a chess-player. Answer these questions honestly:

- Which do you like best: attacking or defending? (*Everyone prefers attacking to defending but what the question is really asking is whether you attack at the first opportunity, or if you have to pluck up your courage again and again to do it.*)
- What kind of positions do you prefer: simple or complicated?
- In the opening, do you prefer quiet or dynamic play?
- How do you react to enemy attacks: by looking for logical and solid defensive moves, or by trying to find a way to counterattack?
- Do you prefer to play in symmetrical positions, within reach of a draw, or to play complicated positions where anything at all can happen?
- Do you seek out ways to simplify through piece exchanges, or would you rather avoid them?
- Where do you feel most at ease: in the middlegame or in the endgame?

Of course, your answer to any of these questions could vary over time and you could also ask yourself many others. The design of your repertoire will come from your own answers. We are going to imagine two consistent types of answers, which correspond to two different types of player and in both cases we shall suggest a repertoire.

Player A prefers clear, logical positions, feels more at ease in the endgame than in the middlegame and responds to enemy attacks with the most solid defensive moves he can find. When he sits down at the chessboard he feels apprehensive about the initial position, because of the jungle of possibilities opening up before him. He also prefers to strengthen his own position, rather than trying to exploit his enemy's weaknesses.

I would advise this player, with White, to play the English Opening or the Queen's Gambit, choosing logical and manageable variations. With Black, I suggest the Caro-Kann Defence against 1 e4 and the Nimzo-Indian and Queen's Indian against 1 d4.

Player B prefers sharp positions, he likes to go on the attack whenever the slightest opportunity arises, he feels more at home in the middlegame than the endgame and he loves investigating opening positions that offer combinative possibilities. If he is attacked, he feels uncomfortable and seeks salvation in a counterattack.

I would advise this player to open with 1 e4, and to soak up information on the sharpest variations against the various Open Games and Semi-Open systems that the game can lead to. With Black, the Sicilian Defence against 1 e4, and against 1 d4 the King's Indian Defence or the Modern Benoni.

These first repertoire proposals are somewhat limited, but the player is taking his first tournament steps and cannot aspire to a much wider repertoire. Depending on his potential, the time he has available and his level of interest, he will broaden it (or he should broaden it) and also modify it, according to his experience and his results.

Further Tips

Get hold of a good openings book, not so much to study it from cover to cover as to consult it whenever you have a problem. If your chess club is well organized, it will have a library. Use it!

Trying to memorize opening variations like a parrot is useless, because the territory is so vast that neither you nor anyone else can manage it. The important thing is to absorb the ideas well: the importance of squares and lines, the reasoning behind a gambit, etc. That way you will also have a better chance of remembering the most important variations.

Begin by creating a small repertoire for yourself and try to master it. How do you do that? By thinking about its variations and its main lines, collecting everything that you encounter along the way and putting it through your analytical filter. I remember that the Spanish GM Juan Bellon used to say, years ago, that whenever he came across something relevant to the lines he played he used to file it in a personal notebook. Now that book is probably a computer.

Don't deny yourself the chance to borrow other people's ideas: we all learn from everyone else.

10 Competitive Chess

Competitive Chess

No other method of becoming a chess-player has been discovered except to play and play and play. If you have followed my advice, you will have dedicated at least twice as much time to playing as to studying. Do you remember my 2x1 formula?

If I am right, that means that by now you must have played quite a lot of games. Don't worry; you still have thousands more games to play.

You already know a lot of things about chess. You know how to win an endgame with queen against pawn on the seventh, you know what an Arabian Mate is and what the Sicilian Defence is. You are also familiar with the basic rules *(if you touch a piece, you must move it; one move per turn; draw by perpetual check; and don't speak to your opponent!)*. Together we have considered the matter of starting an openings repertoire and you know how to exploit numerous combinative possibilities. However... you still don't feel sure of yourself, each time you sit down at the board!

There is nothing more natural, believe me. Chess-players want to play well. Even more, they aspire to play like gods, that is if the gods play chess.

But at some time you have probably seen chess books on the shelves in big stores: books about openings, about endgames, about strategy, about tactics, collections of games, attacking the king, about combinations. There are all kinds of books about chess. But nobody knows them all. Neither is it necessary to read them all to play chess well. It's enough to have some technical knowledge, well understood, and to keep trying to improve your own play.

Although at the end of this chapter I shall permit myself to give you some final pieces of advice, I shall also permit myself now to give you the most important advice of all: **don't become obsessive, don't fall into the temptation of theoretical overload**. The most important thing, I say again, is to **play, play and play**. Think about your games, try to correct your mistakes, to maximize your strengths and to minimize your weaknesses. Criticize yourself, be hard on yourself. This is a long, slow job that must be done without haste, but without stopping either. The British have a saying, which can be helpful to all of us, so long as we learn from it: *How do you eat an elephant? One bite at a time.* And believe me, once again, chess is a large Indian elephant.

Before the Tournament

Congratulations! The moment has come when you need to concern yourself with the scoresheet, the rate of play, the clock, and your opponents' opening repertoires. How I envy you! You are going to experience magnificent new sensations. Marvellous sensations, which can change your life.

You have now left those little local competitions behind you, which does not have to mean that you won't play games against your friends and neighbours again. Do so, if it amuses you. But you have decided to take a step up into more serious competitions. Let us suppose that you have been going to a club for a while, but that the chance to take part in a tournament has not yet arisen. And now that chance has arrived. In a week's time a championship will start, with ten players, and you are going to take part in it. You know some of your opponents, you have even played the odd friendly game with them, but it would be hard to say that you have come to an opinion about *how* they play.

It's going to be played on an all-play-all system; you all play each other once. You already know the draw and you have to play five games with White and four with Black. How will you focus your preparation with scarcely seven days to go?

In the first place, your excitement and enthusiasm should more than overcome your fear. No panic. Consider that your opponents also have just seven days to prepare themselves, even though some of them are more experienced players than you.

How will you plan the games? To begin with, you have to convince yourself to play the way you know, not to change your manner of playing, nor your openings.

For your white games, try to study a bit more the theory of the openings you know, even if you only know them a little. Reach definite conclusions and establish which variations you will play, if your opponent should respond with Defence A, B or C. If you are afraid that your opponent might know your variation better than you do, don't discard it for that reason. It's better to play a variation that you know, rather than to try to 'confuse' your opponent with another one that he might not know, but that you don't know either. What you need to do in that case is study the theory a bit more and try to find some detail that you like and which seems to you to be effective and disconcerting to your opponent.

For your black games, carefully prepare your usual defences (one against 1 e4 and another against 1 d4). Do a preparation exercise for each of the four games, although you will be able to introduce modifications as you go along. We will talk about that later.

Before the Game

The big day has arrived. You are about to launch your career as a competitive player, no matter how modest the tournament. It's important for you and that is how it should be. How will you approach this first game? With enthusiasm, but with your head as cool as it can be. Try to feel at ease all day. Don't do anything you would not normally do and try not to think about other problems when you leave your routine activities (work, studies, other occupations) in order to go to the club. Switch off and 'change your chip'.

If you have a few hours left before the game begins, a good exercise would be to revise the variations you have prepared, in a relaxed way, without tiring your brain. In any case, it's a good idea to stop thinking about chess an hour or two before the game. You can check through what you've decided to play, just in case, to make sure all the loose ends are tied up. Tell yourself that you want to play well, that you want to win, that if you rush your games the much feared zero will appear on the results board. And that would be horrible, but not the end of the world.

At the Board

Time has flown by. You are already seated at the board. *Your fate is decided!* But remember that in chess there is no such thing as fate, or that it only exists in 1% of cases. Now all you have to do is concentrate and **believe** that the world does not exist or, rather, that all that remains of the world is contained **on your chessboard**. Because that is how you must see it: **the chessboard belongs to you**. You are going to dominate it. You have it all: the necessary basics, the fighting spirit and the will to win. Only three things are missing, and you will be displaying them as the game progresses: control of the opening, evaluation of positions and specific calculation of the moves. In other words: **playing**.

You have made an opening plan which, just as in real life, may well not go quite as you foresaw it. Nonetheless, you must try to make your ideas in this respect assert themselves; you must try not to be taken by surprise in the opening. If you don't manage it, by no means must you allow defeatist ideas such as *what am I going to do now?* go through your head. Such an idea can be valid, but only from a constructive point of view. What am I going to do now? Well, reconsider all your plans. The problem is not serious. Your opponent does not know he has surprised you and your features should give nothing away. You: poker face. You are neither happy nor unhappy. Take stock of the position, draw on your knowledge and act accordingly. Precisely that very chess knowledge that you have acquired both from this book and from your own practice of the game will be dictating to you the analysis (**your** analysis) of the positions that arise. Mistakenly or not (and you will try to make your thinking be as correct as possible), you will be judging, evaluating again and again, asking yourself: who is better and why?, who has the advantage and why? Be brutally honest with yourself in your reply and act accordingly. If you think that you are better but that your advantage is small, try to increase it, gradually improving the position of your pieces. If you consider that you have a clear advantage, try to carry out an effective attack in the appropriate sector. If you think you are worse, try to improve your position and strengthen your weak points. If you see your opponent preparing to launch an attack, take appropriate steps to oppose it. And, in every case, **calculate all the variations**. Once you have done all the calculations, **go over the key variations again**. Which are the key variations? The ones that contain the crux of the position, the ones you have decided to play and any forced diversion from them.

Once the first round is done, some players will have 1 point, others a half point, and others 0. Let's hope you are not among the last group. In any case, yours was not the only game. Others have also been played, which you might have observed at some point, or you might even have been present at the *post-mortem* analysis or, better yet, managed to get hold of the scoresheet of one of the other games. This is important. Everything is important in a tournament. Looking at what is happening on the boards and observing the players: nerves, gestures of surprise, of happiness, of fear, tensions, players who walk about and players who never get up from their table... **Everything is important, because it is all valuable information**. Why are poker players such good observers and why is it important for them to be so? Because with

their ability to observe and interpret, and with their shrewdness, they can gain specific advantages.

If you have managed to watch your adversaries' games, you will get to know them better, you can see what openings they play, which they don't handle well and which they are dangerous in. You will have seen 'things'. All this will be of help to you in modifying (or confirming) your theoretical planning for the tournament. Adapting Archimedes' saying "*give me a place to stand and with a lever I will move the whole world*", we could declare "*tell me how your opponent plays and I shall tell you how to defeat him*". Information will be your basic lever here for raising your play to a higher level.

The Psychological Factor

We have spoken about your opponents' reactions, but not about your own gestures and reactions. I said earlier that you should keep a poker face. Call it '*sang froid*', 'bottling it up inside', or whatever you like. But pay attention to what I say.

Not only must you not show anxiety or joy. The most important thing is that you must not feel *euphoria* nor, most of all, *get depressed*. Chess is hard. All chess competitions are hard. You have to harden yourself to the tournaments. Bobby Fischer (World Champion 1972-5) used to say: "There are tough players and nice guys, and I'm a tough player."

Let's suppose you had a good position. Let's suppose you have let the advantage slip away and now you are in a difficult position. Are you in a desperate situation, with no way out? Well then, resign and think about the next game, not about how unfortunate you are. The position is not desperate? Then forget about what you have let slip away. That was the past. Nobody reads yesterday's papers, nor should you cry over spilt milk. Think, and fight to find a good solution so you can draw. If you can't find a good solution, accept that it's precarious, but keep looking and fight for the best possible outcome. If, after all that, you don't manage it, what can it do to you? Tomorrow you play again.

On another occasion, you might find yourself in the reverse situation. After you have been playing for a long time in a practically lost position, your opponent has made a mistake and now the game has taken a different direction, which allows you to hope for salvation. In such situations, the great pressure you've been under makes itself felt in the game, and now that it seems the worst is over, it could be that you might relax and, as a result, your concentration will be affected. What would you say, then, if you lost at the moment when you were closest to a draw? (Don't tell me...).

You can lose a game, of course. You can lose lots. Like everyone. If you insist, even like the great champions. But I shall tell you what you can never lose: **tension, concentration, fighting spirit**. We could even sum it up in just one word: **concentration**. What would you do if you lost a piece on the fourth move in a game that's important to you? Do you think that can't happen to **you**? It can happen to anyone... through lack of concentration of course! In the Folkestone Olympiad (1933) the following game was played: 1 e4 c5 2 d4 cxd4 3 ♘f3 e5 4 ♘xe5?? ♛a5+, and White had to resign, because he was losing the e5-knight. For your records, the players were Combe (Scotland) and Hasenfuss (Latvia). Why did that happen? Solely because of lack of concentration.

The Time Factor

We have spoken about the pure chess struggle and the psychological aspects but we still have to deal with the **time** factor.

The whole competitive struggle of chess is controlled by time, without which we would not be able to reach clear conclusions. In other eras they did not use clocks to control the game and this led to some players even falling asleep at the board! On the other hand, in a time like ours, where everything is measured and codified, you and I will surely agree that if, in order to come up with the same move in a certain position, one player needs two minutes and another needs ten, the former is five times better than the latter. If that was repeated ad nauseam, one player would have used an hour and the other five hours! Naturally, this is not fair, just as it would not be fair in a cyclists' time trial for one rider to be allowed to spend five times as long as his opponent on the same distance!

The time must be controlled and in modern tournament chess there are various rates of play, ranging from the classical or international rate all the way down to *blitz* chess (5 or 3 minutes per player per game), through rapidplay games of 15 or 30 minutes. Depending on the time-limit stipulated, especially if it is based on a fixed number of moves (with controls), the player can divide up the time on his scoresheet. For example: if the time-limit is 40 moves in 2 hours, he can indicate with red lines moves 10, 20 and 30, which will remind him that he should have used up at the most half an hour for each of these groups of moves.

There can be other methods, because in the opening you usually spend less time thinking, but in any case what matters is for the player to set a standard for himself: a time-limit set according to his own criteria.

Training Techniques

A player who wants to make progress absolutely must set up a training regime for himself. Some people do this by going regularly to their club and playing rapidplay games. Others study theory and play through games by professional players, depending on the time they have available. Others, again, adopt a mixed formula: they play one day of the week, two or three tournaments a year and consult chess books and publications from time to time.

It's hard to specify what suits each person, because there is an infinite variety of chessplayers: from the amateur, who only wants to play a tournament now and again, to the professional who, of course, does not need advice from anyone. Between these two extremes, there is a huge range of players who, depending on their level, their professional and personal circumstances, and where they live, may all carry out their chess-playing in very different ways.

We are therefore going to define three types into which we will try to group (even though it might be in a rather artificial fashion) all the kinds of players who are just beginning, or who are returning to chess, and therefore have chosen to study this book.

Player X

A child, between eight and fourteen years old. As part of his school's extracurricular activities (with or without his parents' influence) he has become interested in chess and is beginning to come across school or youth competitions.

Player Y

He's a beginner. He's young, a student (in secondary school or beyond) between fifteen and twenty-two years old. He has just come into contact with chess and is beginning to play in his spare time. He wants to play in tournaments and he wants to make progress. He is hopeful, although he doesn't know how far he wants to go in chess. But he is very interested and has the ability to absorb new theoretical knowledge.

Player Z

Middle-aged. After a number of years establishing himself professionally and/or setting up a family, etc., he has decided to return to chess and take part in occasional tournaments and team matches. He is not terribly keen on theory and knows that he needs to acquire some technical knowledge. As a youngster he played at a basic level and wants to enjoy himself. (Sometimes it turns out that his son has also started to play.)

Training Plan for Player X

For such children, I recommend very little theoretical training (which they possibly get already at school) and a lot of practical play, as long as this does not get in the way of their studies and as long as they prefer it to other activities in their free time. It will be enough for them to learn fully the basic techniques contained in this book. From the age of ten they could get used to a certain level of training, consisting basically of analysing their own games and games by chess masters which are at their level of understanding; plus tactical positions, following the guidance in this book, technical mating

procedures, and basic strategic planning. Openings, concentrating on ideas rather than specific lines. Ideally they should have lessons with a chess teacher or trainer.

Recommended time per week:
Study: 2 hours
Play: 4 hours

Training Plan for Player Y

This type of player, who is at the ideal age for becoming a really strong chess-player, can be advised to opt for a quite demanding level of training, the intensity of which he can determine for himself or, if he has a trainer, leave the planning of the training to him. Naturally, we would have to separate out the different levels of interest (a youngster who likes to enjoy a good game of chess from time to time is not the same as one who has set his sights on the world junior championship). His reaction to his first tournament experiences will be crucial for determining his level of interest. We will recommend here a kind of weekly training that is somewhere in the middle.
- Analysis of his own tournament games (written)
- Creation of a demanding opening repertoire for himself
- Theoretical work on openings with other players of a similar level
- Endgame technique
- Middlegame plans
- Strategy and tactics
- Playing through master games (15-20)
- Solving tactics puzzles (4-6 a day)
  Study: 4-5 hours
  Playing: 8-10 hours

Training Plan for Player Z

In this case as well, logically enough, his training will depend on his level of interest. If he is an adult player, he will be better able than the other two types of player to decide what are his needs and how much of his free time he wants to devote to chess.

As he might well find it difficult to concentrate and he might grow tired because of the length of tournament games (four hours is a long time to spend thinking), I would advise specific training in this respect, in other words, practising combinative sequences and analysing, even if not too deeply, his own games. A good openings book would help him to design a repertoire to suit himself. As it is quite reasonable to suppose that this player no longer aspires to be world champion, it will be enough for him to get up to date in opening theory and to practise tactical positions in order to overtake his friends and colleagues.

I recommend the following weekly plan:
- Five- or ten-minute games to sharpen reflexes
- Studying openings he likes, trying to incorporate some modern system or other
- Studying his own games critically
- Playing through master games
- Post-mortem analysis of team games, since it is something 'live' that he can do with his team mates and so learn in a pleasant social setting

Study: 3 hours
Playing: 6 hours.

Final Tips

The cards are on the table: the reader must have an idea by now of what he can expect from chess and to what extent he is really interested. The author is not a psychoanalyst, but he is certainly a kind of invisible instructor, who hopes to have set the reader's steps onto the right path.

My final tips will err on the side of repetition. I'm sorry, but it is inevitable. I believe that if you want to become a real chess-player (and not someone who frantically 'pushes wood'), you must make yourself get down to serious work on a personal level. If this personal work, in other words, *studying chess*, can be properly guided and controlled by an instructor, then you are lucky, and it is possible that in that case these tips are superfluous, because it is more than likely that your instructor can give you accurate advice, in line with your abilities and needs.

If that is not the case, and you have studied this book on your own, some final tips will do you no harm (I won't call it advice because nobody follows that):
- Follow chess news on the Internet. If you subscribe to a specialist magazine, so much the better.
- Play through modern games. Looking at a game from a century ago is not the same as looking at one that Carlsen or Caruana has just won yesterday, or watching it live: **chess is a living thing and you need to feel the excitement**.
- Consult opening theory (encyclopaedias, books, magazines, Internet sites) about the variations which give you problems, even if these problems arise in the most insignificant of friendly games (for instance, when you lose again and again, with the same opening, against one of the club veterans).
- Be self-critical about each and every one of the games you play.
- I take it as read that you have access to ChessBase (if you don't, I highly recommend it to you). Set up a database of all the positions that you find interesting, from your own and other people's games.
- Create another database of all the opening ideas that occur to you, together with any analysis you have done, in spite of the fact that one day you might have to update them. ChessBase codifies the games according to the Informator system, which will make classification of opening material easier for you.
- Study some openings more deeply and include in the above-mentioned database any games with those openings that you find interesting. Keep up to date. You don't have to follow developments in the whole range of openings, just the ones in your repertoire.
- As regards your repertoire, put off playing the Indian Defences for a couple of years. They are excellent, but it would be hard for you to develop within their cramped positions. The professionals do it, but you are not (yet) a professional.

- Study endgames and strategy. Look for a list of recommended books about these topics from a source you trust.
- Set yourself short-term and long-term objectives.
- Take advantage of ChessBase Mega Database and huge databases available free on the Internet. Use these to search for particular openings and players and copy any games that you consider useful.
- Get a copy of the Laws of Chess from the FIDE website (fide.com).

Answers to Questions

Chapter 1

1) Light.

2) The initial square of the white king (e1) is dark. The one of the black king (e8) is light.

3) Checkmating the opponent's king.

4) 16.

5) A horizontal row of eight squares.

6) A vertical line of eight squares.

7) The four ranks in Black's half of the chessboard, i.e. ranks 5-8.

8) The e-, f-, g- and h-files.

9) Eight.

10) Thirteen.

11) Fourteen in both cases.

12) In a corner: two. In the centre: eight.

13) ...d6 and ...d5.

14) No.

15) Checkmate.

Chapter 2

16) No.

17) No. The king cannot move to a square next to the enemy king, as he would then be in check himself. (That is not to say that a king move can't give check, as we shall see when we examine *discovered check* later in the book.)

18) b6.

19) d8.

20) Yes: exd6.

21) No.

22) Yes, as the rook does not attack a square over which the king moves.

23) In checkmate the king is attacked; in stalemate it isn't. In a stalemate, none of the other pieces have any legal moves.

24) Two knights and a pawn: 3+3+1=7. The side gaining a rook and a bishop scores 5+3=8 and so benefits more.

25) It's better to have the bishops, because they can force checkmate, whereas two knights cannot.

26) Not always. Sometimes, it's better to promote to rook or bishop to avoid stalemate (though this is very rare in practice), or to a knight, in order to give check (or double check, or to fork two pieces, or to avoid a fork by an enemy knight).

27) Yes.

28) Either one bishop, one knight, or two knights.

29) Kingside castling: 0-0. Queenside castling: 0-0-0.

30) No. A king loses the right to castle once it has moved, and kingside castling constitutes a move.

Chapter 3

31) For its mobility. From a central position the bishop can move to 13 squares on an open board, whereas the knight can only move to 8.

32) d4, d5, e5 and e4.

33) A sacrifice of a pawn (or pawns) in the opening, generally to speed up development.

34) One move by one side.

35) The mobilization of all the pieces.

36) 1 e4 e5.

37) When the opening is defined by a move, or several moves, by Black.

38) The safety of the king.

39) On one of the edges of the board (first and eighth ranks, a- and h-files), near one of the corners.

40) Major (or heavy) pieces.

41) 'Touch-move'.

42) e- and d-pawns.

43) On the edge the knights have less mobility, and less influence over the centre, than they do on more central squares.

44) By stating the number of the rank on which the rook that moves stands, e.g. ♖1c3.

45) On one of the edges of the board (first and eighth ranks, a- and h-files).

Chapter 4

46) 1 e4 e5 2 ♘f3 ♘c6 3 ♗b5.

47) 1 e4 e5 2 ♘f3 ♘c6 3 ♗c4 ♗c5.

48) 1 e4 e5 2 f4.

49) It depends. If you can set a trap with a move that is good and useful even if the opponent doesn't fall into the trap, then it is OK. But setting a trap with a move that has strategic drawbacks is not a good idea.

50) Opening, middlegame and endgame.

51) The 'square' rule.

52) Yes.

53) No.

54) Opposition.

55) No.

56) It is a draw by stalemate.

57) In any corner.

58) No.

59) Black could interpose a friendly piece between the queen and the enemy rook. Also, it might be possible to capture the rook or pin the rook.

60) White, the side capturing knight and three pawns, comes off best: 3+3=6 vs 5 points for the rook.

Chapter 5

61) Strategy defines what's to be done.

62) A plan is a series of moves with a set aim.

63) No. There can also be positional or strategic attacks.

64) A counterattack is an energetic plan of counteraction, not merely defensive.

65) The safety of the king.

66) The concrete interplay between the pieces.

67) A consistent and concrete sequence of moves.

68) A pawn whose advance is not impeded by enemy pawns, either on the same file or on either of the two adjacent ones.

69) A structure consisting of connected pawns, generally arranged diagonally.

70) A square that cannot be protected by pawns.

71) Its base.

72) A pawn on the same file as another friendly pawn.

73) The knight.

74) A pair of pieces operating together.

75) In either of the two corners whose corner-square can be controlled by the bishop.

Chapter 6

76) Pawn on its seventh rank and the king on the pawn's potential promotion square.

77) When the pawn, supported by the king, is on one of these files: a-, h-, c- or f-.

78) To the square immediately in front of the pawn.

79) From behind.

80) Theoretically, the knight.

81) No.

82) Preserving them. In the endgame, pawn exchanges increase the drawing possibilities.

83) Here are some you could have chosen: Sicilian (1 e4 c5), French (1 e4 e6), Caro-Kann (1 e4 c6), Pirc (1 e4 d6), Alekhine (1 e4 ♘f6), Scandinavian (1 e4 d5).

84) With 6...♘c6. He can also play the more complex 6...♗g7!?, and meet 7 e5 with 7...♘h5.

85) It avoids a pin by 3...♗b4, and it allows the c-pawn to advance to c3 to defend the d4-pawn.

86) To avoid early piece exchanges and create more chances to play for a win.

87) No. He can also answer 2...♘f6.

88) 3...cxd4.

89) The c8-bishop is blocked in by the pawn-chain.

90) To provoke the advance of the e4-pawn.

Chapter 7

91) 1 e4 c5 2 ♘f3 d6 3 d4 cxd4 4 ♘xd4 ♘f6 5 ♘c3 g6.

92) 1 e4 c6 2 d4 d5 3 exd5 cxd5 4 c4.

93) Moves executed in a different order that reach the same position.

94) Yes, by transposition.

95) French Defence, Tarrasch Variation.

96) A sequence of forcing moves with a specific goal, involving tactical themes and normally a sacrifice.

97) An unforced offer of material.

98) a) A line of play within an opening; b) a line of play within a game or a combination.

99) A discovered attack is not executed by the piece that moves. A double attack is a direct threat to two pieces or two points.

100) There are also, e.g., combinations for reaching a draw from a theoretically inferior position. In general, combinations can have a wide variety of aims – essentially anything that the player feels (rightly or wrongly!) is in his interest.

101) You could have chosen some of the following: fork, double attack, pin, discovered attack, discovered check, double check, removing the guard, interference, deflection, X-ray, decoy, skewer, self-blocking, clearance.

102) The king.

103) With the rook: ♖f8+ (skewer). With the knight: ♘e4+ or ♘g4+ (fork). It is not possible with the bishop.

104) The bishop can be on any of the squares a8, b7, c6, d5 and e4, and the rook must be on the diagonal between the bishop and the king. With a bishop on b7 and a rook on c6, for example, any rook move gives discovered check to the white king.

105) Two of the same colour at least, plus an enemy piece interposed.

Chapter 8

106) f7, g7 and h7.

107) a2, b2 and c2.

108) On h7.

109) The difference between a rook and a minor piece.

110) The development of a bishop on the flank by means of advancing the knight's pawn. For example, White might play g3 in order to develop the f1-bishop on g2.

111) A method of attack in which pawns are advanced against the enemy's king position in order to break open lines.

112) It is a prerequisite to have some kind of advantage in the area to be attacked.

113) A square that allows the king to escape from an attack.

114) The g- and h-files.

115) The major (or heavy) pieces.

116) The possibility of bringing a rook into the attack without delay.

117) In the centre, the king is often subject to attack because that is usually where there are more open lines and more pieces concentrated.

118) The rooks.

119) On its second rank.

120) On f6 and f3 (also c3 in the Open Sicilian).

Solutions to the Exercises

Chapter 1

1) All three black pieces.

2) Besides giving check, the bishop is attacking the rook.

3) The black queen is attacking all six white pieces. At the same time, it is attacked by the b5-rook and the b8-bishop.

4) The rook could be placed, for instance, on b6, b5 (and also on d8) and the bishop on d6.

5) A black knight may check the white king from f5, f7 or g8.

6) The b- and d-pawns (b3+, d3+).

7) Yes, *en passant*, ...fxg3.

8) Both bishop and knight can move to g7, protecting the king from check.

9) The two pieces (♖d3, ♗d3 or ♗f3) and also the pawn (c3).

10) No. The king and the queen are on the wrong squares. The king should be placed on e8 and the queen on d8.

11) The rook may take the f3-pawn (...♖xf3), but could then be captured by the other pawn (gxf3).

12) Yes. With ...♖c8#.

13) Yes. With ♖f8#.

14) Yes. With b3# or b4#.

15) No. One king can never move to a square attacked by the other king, as he would be captured and the game over.

16) Yes; ...♘d7 and ...♘f6; ...♗e8 and ...♗b5.

17) ♖a4 and ♖h4; ♘f3 (or ♘e2) and ♘d4.

18) b2, c3, d4, e5, f6, g7 and h8.

19) b1, g1, b8 and g8.

20) A rook on a8 can reach f5 in two moves: ♖a5-f5 or ♖f8-f5.

Chapter 2

21) Calculation of material. White: one rook (5) + two bishops (6) + four pawns (4) = 15.

Black: one rook (5) + one knight (3) + six pawns (6) = 14. So White has a material advantage.

22) Calculation of material. White: one queen (9) + one rook (5) + three pawns (3) = 17. Black: two bishops (6) + one knight (3) + two pawns (2) = 11. So White has a material advantage.

23) 1 ♕a8+ ♔c7 2 ♕a7+ ♔c8 3 ♕a8+, etc.

24) No. After 1...♖a1+ 2 ♔e2 ♖a2+ 3 ♔d1 ♖a1+ 4 ♔c2 ♖a2+ 5 ♔b3, the king escapes the checks.

25) Yes, with 1...0-0-0#.

26) Yes, with 1 0-0#.

27) There are many possibilities. See the text.

28) There are many possibilities. See the text.

29) There are many possibilities. See the text.

30) Yes, with 1 ♕a4#.

31) Yes, with 1...♖h4#, 1...♖g1#, 1...♕h4#, 1...♕g2# or 1...♕g1#.

32) No, since one of the rules of chess is that castling cannot take place if the king is in check.

33) No. The knight attacks the f8-square, which the king would have to cross.

34) No. The bishop attacks the f8-square, which the king would have to cross.

35) Yes. The black bishop does not attack any of the squares to be crossed by the king.

36) A knight. With 1...f1♘# the white king is mated.

37) Knight or bishop. Not queen or rook, as then the black king would be stalemated. Of course, it would be more practical to delay promotion by one move; e.g., 1 ♗c5+ ♔a8 2 c8♕#.

38) 1 e8♘+ with a fork, winning the queen.

39) White. After 1...a1♕ 2 h8♕+, the black king must move, and then his queen is lost. This is known as a skewer, a tactical theme we shall examine in more detail later.

40) Twelve! There are two possible captures (bxa8 and bxc8), and with each of these the pawn can be promoted into four different pieces. The pawn can also advance to b8, with four more different promotion possibilities. Thus, 4+4+4=12.

Chapter 3

41) Yes, with ♕a8# or ♕h8#.

42) Yes, with ...♕d2#.

43) Yes, with ♖a8#.

44) Four: ♕c7#, ♕f8#, ♕g8# and ♕h8#.

45) The bishops, as they cover 24 squares (13+11), whereas the knights only cover 12 (6+6).

46) 4 ♘xd4 is better, since 4 ♕xd4?! allows Black to gain a tempo with 4...♘c6.

47) Yes, since it attacks the central squares d5 and e4.

48) 1 ♖c3 followed by 2 ♖b2(+) and 3 ♖a3#.

49) 1 ♔b6 followed by 2 ♕e8#.

50) First the king moves in: 1 ♔c6. Then when the black king tries to flee by 1...♔d8, the rook cuts off its escape by 2 ♖e5, and the king must reverse course with 2...♔c8. This allows 3 ♖e8#. If instead Black tries 1...♔b8, the white rook makes a waiting move on the a-file (such as 2 ♖a1), and then follows 2...♔c8 3 ♖a8#.

51) 1 ♘xe5!. Then 1...♗xd1? allows 2 ♗xf7+ ♔e7 3 ♘d5# (Legall's Mate), while after 1...dxe5 2 ♕xg4 White wins a pawn.

52) Both moves are good for White, but 1 ♕d5 is stronger, since White wins a piece, whereas after 1 ♗xf7+ ♔xf7 2 ♕d5+, although the black king loses the right to castle, White wins only a pawn.

53) 1 ♘g4!. Black is lost, because after 1...♕e7+ 2 ♗e2 the threats against f6 are decisive.

54) No. Instead, 4...exd4 would have been much better. Now (after 4...♘xd4?) White can play 5 ♗xf7+ ♔xf7 6 ♘xe5+ followed by 7 ♕xd4, winning a pawn, with the black king uncastled in the centre.

55) 1 ♘e6! wins the black queen, because 1...fxe6 allows 2 ♕h5+ g6 3 ♕xg6#.

56) Black wins by 9...♘xd4! 10 ♘xd4 ♕h4, with the point 11 ♘f3 ♕xf2+ 12 ♔h1 ♕g1+! 13 ♖xg1 ♘f2#.

57) **Bronstein – NN**
Sochi (simul.) 1950
1 ♖d8+! ♔xd8 2 ♕xe4 1-0

58) With 1 ♖c1!, and if 1...♕xa4, then 2 ♖xc8#.

59) **Springe – Gebhard**
Munich 1927
1 ♕xe6+! fxe6 2 ♗g6# (1-0)

60) **O. Bernstein – Smyslov**
Groningen 1946
Yes, White salvaged a draw from what had been a hopeless situation by taking the pawn:
1 ♖xb2!
Black had counted on an indirect defence of the pawn: 1...♖h2+ followed by 2...♖xb2 wins the rook. But after 1...♖h2+ 2 ♔f3! ♖xb2 it's stalemate.

Chapter 4

61) White should win in both cases, thanks to the opposition. If it's his move, 1 ♔f6 (or 1 ♔d6 ♔d8 2 e6, etc.) 1...♔f8 2 e6 (gaining the opposition) 2...♔e8 3 e7 ♔d7 4 ♔f7, and the pawn queens. If it's Black to move, White already has the opposition, and after 1...♔f8 2 ♔d7 or 1...♔d8 2 ♔f7, White controls the queening square and will promote his pawn.

62) The endgame should be a draw in both cases. If it's White to move, after 1 ♔d6 ♔d8 Black gains the opposition. With Black to move, 1...♔c7 draws.

63) No, as it's a rook's pawn and the white king controls the promotion square (h1) and cannot be ejected from g1-h1.

64) Yes: 1...c3!. Now, if 2 dxc3, 2...b3! 3 cxb3 d3 and this pawn promotes. And after 2 bxc3 d3! 3 cxd3 the b-pawn has a free run.

65) Yes, as otherwise he will lose the d1-rook for nothing. With the exchanging sequence 1 ♕xd5 ♖xd5 2 ♖xd5, giving up his queen for two enemy rooks, White gains a material advantage (10-9).

66) Yes, with 1 ♖xb8+! ♘xb8 2 ♖e8+ ♔f7 3 ♖xb8, White gains one point in material (6-5).

67) 1...♘e6 or 1...♘f5, and the attacked piece is now the attacking one.

68) 1 ♗e6 or 1 ♗h5 (the attacked piece is now the attacking one).

69) 1 ♘f5, attacking both rooks.

70) 1...♗c5, pinning the pawn, since the king is on the same file.

71) Yes, with 1...♖d1+, followed by capturing the a2-bishop with the queen.

72) Yes, 1 ♗c3, blocking the attacking line.

73) The knight is much better than the bishop in such a position. The knight occupies a dominant square in the centre of the board, whereas the bishop is hindered by its own pawns (fixed on dark squares) and it's very difficult for Black to bring the bishop into play.

74) The f3-knight is very strong and allows the creation of threats against the white king. 1...♘xe1 would be a poor move, especially as Black has a very strong alternative in 1...♖h8!, when White cannot prevent the threatened mate (2...♕xh2+! 3 ♖xh2 ♖xh2#).

75) Yes. The d4-bishop dominates the long diagonal and, in connection with the queen, can create serious threats against the black king. 1...♘xd4 is a practically forced exchange.

76) **Fleischmann – NN**
Bamberg 1930
The pawn can queen with mate by means of a combination:
1 ♖f8+! ♖xf8 2 ♕h8+!! ♔xh8 3 exf8♕#

77) **Haider – Kamler**
Vienna 1959
1 ♖xh6+! ♔xh6 2 ♕xg7+!!
So that the knight cannot block the following check on h5.
2...♖xg7 3 ♖h3+
and mate next move.

78) **Farwig – Lundin**
Stockholm (team event) 1963
1...♘d2+! 2 ♖xd2 ♖xe1+ 3 ♔xe1 ♖g1#
(0-1)

The knight check had a triple purpose: to block the escape-square (d2) of the white king; to rule out ♖xd1 as a reply to ...♖xe1+; and to open the e-file.

79) **Alekhine – Reshevsky**
Kemeri 1937
1 ♖xb8+! ♔xb8 2 ♕xe5+! 1-0
2...fxe5 3 ♖f8+ and mate in two. Black can interpose his major pieces, but only to postpone the outcome. If you found the solution, you played like a world champion!

80) **Lutikov – Tal**
USSR Ch, Kiev 1964/5
White wins by means of two stunning sacrifices:
1 ♕xd8!?
There are several other ways to win, such as 1 ♕e7, but your task was to win by promoting the f-pawn!
1...♖xd8 2 ♖xd7+! ♖xd7 3 f8♕
Black resigned a few moves later.

Chapter 5

81) White, because of his well-advanced 'outside' pawn-majority, i.e. on the wing furthest away from the kings.

82) White has weak points on a4 and e2 (the two bases of the pawn-chain). Black on c7 and g7.

83) On b7.

84) On f3, h3, f2 or h2.

85) **Marache – Morphy**
New Orleans (blindfold simul.) 1857
1...♘g3!! 0-1
2 ♕xg6 ♘de2#.

86) **Speyer – Couvée**
Amsterdam 1902
1 ♕xh7+! ♖xh7 2 ♘g6#

87) **Sköld – Lundin**
Gothenburg 1943
1...♕xf2+! 0-1
2 ♖xf2 ♖b1+ 3 ♖f1 ♖bxf1# (or 3...♖fxf1#).

88)   Bareev – Izeta
Erevan Olympiad 1996
1 ♕xf7+! 1-0
After 1...♘xf7 2 ♘e6+ White wins the exchange.

89)   Duras – Olland
Karlsbad 1907
White has many ways to win; in the game he chose a rather prosaic method, but he could have mated as follows:
1 ♗f8+! ♗h5 2 ♕xh5+! gxh5 3 ♖h6#

90)   Tryandafylidis – Vlahos
Greece 1980
1...♕xh3+! 2 gxh3 ♖f1+ 3 ♔h2 ♖8f2#

91)   Winter – Friede
1978
1 ♕f8+! ♔xf8 2 ♖xf7+ ♔e8
2...♔g8 3 ♖f8#.
3 ♖f8+ ♔d7
3...♔e7 is met in the same way.
4 ♖2f7#

92)   Yakovich – Azmaiparashvili
New York 1994
1...♖xc2+! 2 ♔xc2 ♖a2+ 0-1
3 ♔c1 ♘b3#.

93)   Field – Tenner
New York 1923
1...♕h3!! 0-1
2 gxh3 ♘xh3# or 2 gxf3 ♕g2#.

94)   E. Torre – Timman
Hamburg 1982
1...♘f3+! 2 ♔g2
2 exf3 ♕xf1+! 3 ♔xf1 ♗h3+ 4 ♔g1 ♖e1#.
2...♕xf1+! 0-1
3 ♔xf1 ♗h3#.

95)   O. Rodriguez – F. Olafsson
Las Palmas 1978
1...♕g2+! 0-1
2 ♖xg2 ♘f3+ 3 ♔h1 ♖d1+ and mate.

96)   Podzerov – Kunstowicz
Poland 1970

1 ♕g8+!! ♔xg8
1...♖xg8 2 ♘f7#.
2 ♘e7++ ♔f8
2...♔h8 3 ♘f7#.
3 ♘7g6+ hxg6 4 ♘xg6#

97)   Horowitz – Duncan
Philadelphia 1952
1...♘d4+! 2 ♔xd1 ♘e3+ 3 ♔c1 ♘e2#

98)   Alekhine – Fletcher
London (simul.) 1928
1 ♕xe4!! fxe4
1...♗xf1 2 ♖xf1.
2 ♗xe4+ ♔h8 3 ♘g6+ ♔h7 4 ♘xf8++
It's necessary to eliminate this rook in order to have the f7-square available.
**4...♔h8 5 ♘g6+ ♔h7 6 ♘e5+ ♔h8 7 ♘f7#
(1-0)**

99)   Andersson – Mestel
London 1982
Black played 1...♖d5? and lost. He could have won by **1...♖d2!! 2 ♖xd2 ♕xe1+ 3 ♔h2 ♗e5+ 4 g3 ♕xd2+**.

100)   Larsen – Najdorf
Lugano Olympiad 1968
1...♕h5!
Black has several other ways to win, but this is the neatest.
2 ♕xd5+ ♔h7 3 ♕xa2 ♖xh3+! 4 gxh3 ♕xh3+ 5 ♕h2
The last hope.
5...♘f2# (0-1)

Chapter 6

101) No, after 1...♔g8 the black king can never be dislodged from the g8-h8 squares.

102) The knight is superior. The bishop is blocked by its own pawns and has little prospect of entering the game.

103) In this endgame the bishop is superior, as there are many open lines and good diagonals to play freely for the whole board.

104) Bad, because 5...♕a5+ wins the e5-pawn.

105) No. After 2...d5 3 exd5, Black has to recapture with the queen, 3...♕xd5, allowing White to gain a development tempo with 4 ♘c3.

106) No. After 3 e5? Black can play 3...dxe5 4 dxe5 ♕xd1+ 5 ♔xd1 ♘g4!, when the knight is threatening a fork on f2 as well as the e5-pawn, which Black will therefore win.

107) No. 3...cxd4 is better. The basic point of the Sicilian Defence is to prevent White from setting up a d4-e4 pawn-centre by being ready to exchange the pawn as soon as it advances to d4.

108) It arises from the Alekhine Defence, after 1 e4 ♘f6 2 e5 ♘d5 and now 3 c4 ♘b6 4 d4 d6 or 3 d4 d6 4 c4 ♘b6.

109) It arises from the Sicilian Defence, after 1 e4 c5 2 ♘f3 d6 3 ♗b5+ ♗d7.

110) Draw, since the white king can hide on a8 when the black queen moves to b6 and ...♕xc7 will then be stalemate.

111) Black can win. A possible winning line is 1...♕d5+ 2 ♔c8 ♕e6+ 3 ♔d8 ♕d6+ 4 ♔e8 ♔e5 5 ♔f7 ♕f6+ 6 ♔e8 ♔d6, etc.

112) 1 ♗e3+, winning the queen, because 1...♕xe3 is met by 2 ♘d5+ and 3 ♘xe3.

113)   Perenyi – Eperjesi
Hungary 1974

1 ♘c6 ♕c7

1...♕b6 is answered in the same manner.

2 ♕xe6+! fxe6 3 ♗g6#

114)   Bronstein – Keres
Budapest Candidates 1950

1 ♕h6!! 1-0

After 1...♕xb1+ 2 ♔h2 ♖g8, White has 3 ♕xh7+! ♔xh7 4 ♖h4#.

115) After 1...♕xd4 White plays 2 ♘1f3 followed by 3 ♘e5, when Black can't avoid the loss of the important f7-pawn. 2...♗b4+ is met by 3 c3! ♗xc3+ 4 ♔f1!, when Black loses material as both queen and bishop are attacked.

116)   Kotenko – Balendo
1977

1...♖xe3! 2 ♖xe3

If 2 fxe3, then 2...♕h2+ 3 ♔f1 ♗g3 wins.

2...♗h2+ 3 ♔h1 ♗g3+ 4 ♔g1 ♕h2+ 5 ♔f1 ♕xf2#

117)   Četković – Molerović
Belgrade 1951

1 ♗h7!!

This discovers an attack to the queen and, at the same time, threatens mate on h6. There is no defence against both threats.

118) After 1 ♖c8+!! ♖xc8 2 ♕a7+! ♔xa7 3 bxc8♘+!, Black loses the queen and the game.

119)   Zeipel – Arnegaard
Correspondence 1902

1 ♕e7+!! ♖xe7 2 d7!!

The rook is now pinned and the pawn will promote.

120)   G. Lolli
Osservazioni teorico-pratiche sopra
il giuoco degli scacchi, 1763

1 ♖f8+ ♔a7 2 ♖a8+!

2 ♕c5+! is an alternative solution, the point being 2...♕xc5 3 ♖a8+ ♔b6 4 ♖xa6+ with stalemate whichever way Black captures the rook.

2...♔xa8 3 ♕f8+ ♔a7 4 ♕c5+

White draws, since 4...♕xc5 is stalemate, while 4...b6 allows perpetual check, starting with 5 ♕xc7+ (but not 5 ♕xg5?? ♖a1+).

Chapter 7

121)   Rosenblatt – Wolk
Biel 1977

1 ♖b8! and White wins.

122)   Sveshnikov – Scherbakov
USSR Ch, Moscow 1991

1 ♕g7+! 1-0

The double check proves deadly: 1...♔xg7 2 ♘f5++ ♔g8 3 ♘h6#.

123)   Beliavsky – Timman
Manila Olympiad 1992

1...♘g4!

To open the long light-squared diagonal so that the black queen can invade.

2 fxg4

2 ♖e2 ♕c5+ 3 ♔g2 ♖h6.

2...♕h1+ 0-1
3 ♔f2 ♕h2+ 4 ♔e1 ♖xe3+, etc.

124) Tal – Timman
Reykjavik 1988
1 ♖c1! 1-0
1...♕xa3 2 ♖xc8+ ♔d7 3 ♖c7+ followed by 4 bxa3.

125) Benko – C. Hartman
Gausdal 1984
1...♕xg2+! 0-1
2 ♔xg2 ♗f3+ 3 ♔g1 ♘h3#.

126) Marciano – Prié
French Ch, Narbonne 1997
1 ♕xc6+! 1-0
In view of 1...♖xc6 2 ♖d8#.

127) Mecking – Tan
Petropolis Interzonal 1973
1 ♗xf7+! ♔xf7 2 ♖xc7+! ♕xc7 3 ♕h7+
White wins the queen.

128) Korchnoi – Karpov
World Ch (game 17), Baguio City 1978
1...♘f3+! 0-1
2 gxf3 ♖g6+ 3 ♔h1 ♘f2# or 2 ♔h1 ♘f2#.

129) Andruet – Spassky
Bundesliga 1987/8
1...♕f3! 0-1
2 gxf3 ♘exf3+ 3 ♔h1 ♗h3! with mate on g2 to follow.

130) Erbis – Kempf
Stuttgart 1954
1 ♗c6! 1-0
In view of 1...♕xc6 2 ♕e7# and 1...♗xc6 2 ♕d8+ ♖xd8 3 ♖xd8#.

131) Troianescu – Dumitrescu
Bucharest 1970
1 ♗a6!! ♕xa6 2 ♕g4
and mate is unavoidable.

132) C. Horvath – Szabolcsi
Hungarian Ch, Budapest 1995
1 ♗d6! 1-0

In view of: 1...♖xd6 2 ♕h8+ ♕g8 3 ♕xg8#;
1...♕xd6 2 ♕h8#; 1...♔e8 2 ♕h8+ ♔d7 3 ♖c7+
♔xd6 4 ♕xd8+.

133) D. Garcia – Shirov
Villarrobledo (rapid) 1997
1...♖xh4+!! 2 gxh4 ♕g4+! 0-1
3 ♕xg4 fxg4#.

134) Fischer – Durão
Havana Olympiad 1966
1 ♘xa5!
White wins a pawn and smashes apart Black's queenside defences. The main point is 1...bxa5 2 ♘f6+ ♔e7 3 ♖b7+, mating.

135) Z. Nilsson – Geller
Sweden vs USSR match, Stockholm 1954
1...♖xc2! 2 ♕xc2
2 ♖xc2 ♕b1+.
2...♕xc1+! 0-1

136) Liu Wenzhe – Donner
Buenos Aires Olympiad 1978
The Chinese player forced the black king into the precarious situation we see here.
1 ♕xg6+!!
Decoy.
1...♔xg6 2 ♗h5+ ♔h7 3 ♗f7+
Discovered check.
3...♗h6 4 g6+!
Clearance for the c1-bishop.
4...♔g7
4...♔h8 5 ♖xh6+ ♔g7 6 ♖h7#.
5 ♗xh6+ 1-0
5...♔h8 6 ♗xf8+, mating.

137) Hort – Portisch
Madrid 1973
1 ♖g4+! fxg4 2 ♕g5+! ♔h8 3 ♕h6!
The key to the tactical manoeuvre: mate on h7 is threatened as well as the f8-rook.
1-0

138) Honfi – Barczay
Kecskemet 1977
1...♖xc4!! 2 ♕xc4 ♕xb2+! 3 ♖xb2 ♘a3+ 4 ♔a1 ♗xb2+ 5 ♔xb2 ♘xc4+ 6 ♔c3 ♖xe4
Black has won two pawns.

139)   Alexander – Marshall
Cambridge 1928
1 ♘a4!!
Why this leap in the dark? We shall soon understand it.
1...bxa4 2 ♖f4!! exf4 3 gxf4
The g-file has been opened and there is no defence to the threat of 4 ♖g1+ followed by mate.
Why not immediately 1 ♖f4? Because then simply 1...exf4 2 gxf4? dxc3 and the black bishop and queen control the g1-square!

140)   Larsen – Spassky
Linares 1981
1...g4+! 0-1
White resigned in view of 2 ♔xg4 ♗h5+! 3 ♔xh5 ♕g5#.

Chapter 8

141)   Campora – Eslon
Coria del Rio 1996
1 ♖xe8+!
There are many other ways to win, such as the simple 1 ♘c6+ ♔d7 2 ♕xc8+ ♔xc8 3 ♘xe7+.
1...♔xe8
1...♕xe8 2 ♕d6+ ♕d7 3 ♕xd7#.
2 ♕xc8+ ♕d8 3 ♕xe6+ 1-0

142)   Przepiorka – W. Cohn
Berlin 1907
1...♖xh2! 2 ♔xh2 ♖c6! 0-1

143)   Rozentalis – G. Meier
Liechtenstein 1996
1 ♖xg7! 1-0
Black resigned due to 1...♕xc2+ 2 ♕xc2 ♖xc2 3 ♖h7+ ♔g8 4 ♔xc2 and 1...♔xg7 2 ♕d7+ ♔g8 3 ♕h7#.

144)   Schmidt – Helms
Germany 1925
1...♕g2+! 2 ♔xg2 ♖xg3#

145)   Koskinen – Sköld
Finland 1957
1...♖xg2+! 2 ♔h1

2 ♔xg2 ♕h3+ 3 ♔h1 ♗d5.
2...♖xh2+! 0-1
3 ♔xh2 ♕h3+ 4 ♔g1 ♖g8+! or 3 ♘xh2 ♗d5!.

146)   Ivanović – Velimirović
Yugoslav Ch, Subotica 1984
1...♖xg2+! 2 ♔xg2 ♗h3+ 3 ♔h1 ♕f2! 4 ♘xf4 exf4 5 ♖g1 ♖g8 0-1

147)   Lame – E. Rubinstein
Cracow 1934
1...♗xg2+! 2 ♕xg2 ♖xh2+! 3 ♔xh2 ♕h4#

148)   J. Polgar – Bareev
Hastings 1992/3
1 ♖xg7+! ♔xg7
1...♔xg7 2 ♖g1.
2 ♖g1+ ♔h8
2...♔h7 3 ♘g4! ♕g7 4 ♘xh6.
3 ♘f7+ ♔h7 4 ♘xh6! 1-0
4...♕xh6 5 ♕f7+ ♔h8 6 ♖g8#.

149)   Klitsch – Gratschal
East Germany 1948
1 ♘xg7+! ♗xg7 2 ♖xe6+! fxe6 3 ♕g6#

150)   Voskanian – Khodos
USSR 1964
1 ♘xg7! ♔xg7 2 ♗h6+! ♔xh6
2...♔g8 3 ♕f3!.
3 ♕d2+ ♔h5
After 3...♔g7 4 ♕g5+ ♔h8 5 ♕xf6+ ♔g8, the neatest mate is 6 ♕g5+! ♔h8 7 ♕h6!, mating on h7 or f8.
4 ♖e3! 1-0

151)   Cruz Lima – Fedorowicz
Havana 1984
1 ♖xg7! ♖xg7
1...♔xg7 2 ♖g3+ ♔h7 3 ♖h3.
2 ♕xh6+ ♔g8 3 ♖h3 ♘g6 4 fxg6 fxg6 5 ♘e6 ♕f5+ 6 ♘2f4 1-0
6...♕c2+ 7 ♔g3.

152)   Robatsch – Hug
Biel 1977
1...♖xh3! 2 gxh3 ♘f3+ 3 ♔g2 ♕xe4! 4 ♔h1 ♘e1+ 5 f3 ♖xf3! 6 ♔g1 ♖g3+ 0-1

153) Gaprindashvili – Nikolac
Wijk aan Zee 1979

1 Nxg7! Kxg7 2 Bxh6+! Kxh6

Or 2...Kg8 3 Re3, threatening 4 Rg3+.

3 Nxf7+ Kxh5 4 g4+! Kh4

Or: 4...Nxg4 5 Qh7+; 4...Kxg4 5 Qg6+ Kh4 6 Kg2!.

5 f3 Nxg4

5...Qc7 6 Re5!, threatening 7 Qh2#.

6 Re4 1-0

154) Schwartzmann – Asanov
Metz 1994

1 Nb5! 1-0

White wins after 1...cxb5 2 Qxb5+ Nc6 3 Qxb7 or 1...Qxb2 2 Nxd6+ Kd8 3 Rd1.

155) 1 Qh6 Nh5

If 1...Ne6 then 2 Rc2! threatens not only the simple 3 Rh2 with mate on h7 but also 3 Ne7+! Kh8 4 Qxh7+!! Kxh7 5 Rh2#, against which there is no good defence.

2 Qxh5!! gxh5 3 Rg1+ Kh8 4 Nh6

There is no defence against mate with 5 Rg8+! Rxg8 6 Nxf7#.

156) Blackburne – Lipschütz
New York 1889

1 Rxg7+!

1 Nh5!, based on the same idea, also wins.

1...Kxg7 2 Nh5+!

Clearing the way for the queen.

2...Rxh5

Or: 2...Kh8 3 g7+; 2...Kg8 3 Qc7!.

3 Qc7+ Kf6 4 Qd6+ 1-0

White mates after 4...Kg7 5 Qe7+.

157) Dely – Brzozka
Miskolc 1963

1 Rxg7! Kxg7 2 Bh6+ Kg8

2...Kh8 3 Bxf8.

3 Nb6!

The key idea, pinning the e6-bishop and thus allowing the queen check on g4.

3...cxb6 4 Qg4+ Kf7 5 Qg7+ Ke8 6 Qxf8+ Kd7 7 Rd1+

and White won.

158) Donner – Gligorić
Match (game 6), Eersel 1968

1...Rxf3! 2 Qxf3

2 Rg1 Raf8.

2...Bg4! 3 Qf2 Bf3+! 4 Kg1

4 Qxf3 Qxh2#.

4...Bxh2+! 0-1

5 Qxh2 Rg8+ or 5 Kf1 Qh3+.

159) Kotov – Unzicker
Saltsjöbaden Interzonal 1952

1 Nxg7! Kxg7 2 Bxh6+ Kg8

2...Kh8 3 Bg7+ Kxg7 4 Qxh7+ Kf8 5 Qh8+ Ke7 6 Rxf7+.

3 Rg4+ Rg6 4 e6! 1-0

4...Nd6 5 exf7+ Rxf7 6 Rxg6+ Kh8 7 Rxf7 Nxf7 8 Bg7+.

160) Seirawan – Browne
Lone Pine 1979

1...Qxc4+!! 2 Kxc4 Ba6+ 3 Nb5

The only move, because 3 Kc5 is met by 3...d6#.

3...Nxb5! 0-1

In view of:

a) 4 Qa4 Na3++ 5 Kc5 d6+ 6 Kc6 and now 6...Ne7# or 6...Bb7#.

b) 4 Nd4 Nxd4+ 5 Kc3 Ne2++ 6 Kd2 Rxb2+ 7 Ke1 Bc3+ 8 Kf2 Nf4+ 9 Kg1 Rxg2#.

Index of Players

Numbers refer to pages. A **bold** number indicates that the named player had White.

Did you know...?

You can read nearly 100 Gambit books on your tablet or phone!

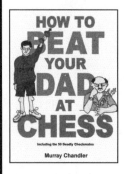

And you don't need a set or board – you can see all the positions and play all the moves just by tapping on the screen. It's like a chess book that has magically come to life.

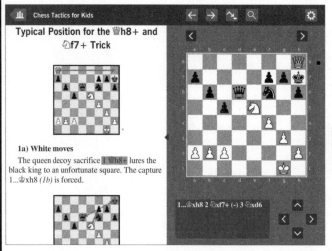